A C
Introduction
to Testimony

BLOOMSBURY CRITICAL INTRODUCTIONS TO CONTEMPORARY EPISTEMOLOGY

Series Editor:

Stephen Hetherington, Professor of Philosophy, The University of New South Wales, Australia

Editorial Board:

Anthony Brueckner, University of California, Santa Barbara, USA; Richard Fumerton, The University of Iowa, USA; John Greco, Saint Louis University, USA; Jonathan Kvanvig, Baylor University, USA; Ram Neta, University of North Carolina, Chapel Hill, USA; Duncan Pritchard, The University of Edinburgh, UK

Bloomsbury Critical Introductions to Contemporary Epistemology introduces and advances the central topics within one of the most dynamic areas of contemporary philosophy.

Each critical introduction provides a comprehensive survey to an important epistemic subject, covering the historical, methodological, and practical contexts and exploring the major approaches, theories, and debates. By clearly illustrating the changes to the ways human knowledge is being studied, each volume places an emphasis on the historical background and makes important connections between contemporary issues and the wider history of modern philosophy.

Designed for use in contemporary epistemology courses, the introductions are defined by a clarity of argument and equipped with easy-to-follow chapter summaries, annotated guides to reading, and glossaries to facilitate and encourage further study. This series is ideal for upper-level undergraduates and postgraduates wishing to stay informed of the thinkers, issues, and arguments shaping twenty-first-century epistemology.

New titles in the series include:

A Critical Introduction to the Epistemology of Perception, Ali Hasan
A Critical Introduction to Formal Epistemology, Darren Bradley
A Critical Introduction to Knowledge-How, J. Adam Carter and Ted Poston
A Critical Introduction to Skepticism, Allan Hazlett

BLOOMSBURY CRITICAL INTRODUCTIONS TO CONTEMPORARY EPISTEMOLOGY

A Critical Introduction to Testimony

AXEL GELFERT

BLOOMSBURY
LONDON • NEW DELHI • NEW YORK • SYDNEY

Bloomsbury Academic
An imprint of Bloomsbury Publishing Plc

50 Bedford Square	1385 Broadway
London	New York
WC1B 3DP	NY 10018
UK	USA

www.bloomsbury.com

Bloomsbury is a registered trade mark of Bloomsbury Publishing Plc

First published 2014

© Axel Gelfert, 2014

Axel Gelfert has asserted his right under the Copyright, Designs and Patents Act, 1988, to be identified as the Author of this work.

All rights reserved. No part of this publication may be reproduced or transmitted in any form or by any means, electronic or mechanical, including photocopying, recording, or any information storage or retrieval system, without prior permission in writing from the publishers.

No responsibility for loss caused to any individual or organization acting on or refraining from action as a result of the material in this publication can be accepted by Bloomsbury or the author.

British Library Cataloguing-in-Publication Data
A catalogue record for this book is available from the British Library.

ISBN: HB: 978-1-4411-8636-2
PB: 978-1-4411-9350-6
ePDF: 978-1-4725-6998-1
ePub: 978-1-4725-6999-8

Library of Congress Cataloging-in-Publication Data
A catalog record for this book is available from the Library of Congress.

Typeset by Newgen Knowledge Works (P) Ltd., Chennai, India
Printed and bound in India

Contents

Series editor's preface, *Stephen Hetherington* vi

Introduction 1

  1 What is testimony? 7

  2 The testimonial conundrum 39

  3 Testimony, perception, memory and inference 55

  4 Testimony and evidence 77

  5 Reductionism and anti-reductionism 95

  6 Hybrid theories of testimony 125

  7 Testimonial knowledge: Transmission and generation 145

  8 Trust and assurance 163

  9 Expert testimony 179

  10 Pathologies of testimony 193

  11 Testimony and the value of knowledge 215

Glossary 227
Bibliography 235
Index 247

Series editor's preface

It would be an exaggeration to say that philosophy is nothing without epistemology. But this much is true: philosophy *has* long been greatly enriched and empowered by epistemology. At times, epistemology has been the lungs of philosophy. It has never been far from philosophy's elusive heart. Epistemology discusses such apparent phenomena as knowledge, evidence, reason, perception, memory, probability, testimony, fallibility and more. It discusses methods of inquiry, too – including methods that might underlie all philosophical thought. Self-awareness, inference, intuition, hypothesizing, doubting and so on: methods as fundamental as these fall within the epistemological gaze.

This is where Bloomsbury's series, *Critical Introductions to Contemporary Epistemology*, enters the philosophical ferment. The series consists of accessible introductions to aspects of how epistemology proceeds – its past, its present, perhaps its future.

Each book in the series brings to the fore some key epistemological concepts and methods, along with a sense of their history. Each book will guide readers to and through a central piece of the expanding puzzle that is epistemology. Each book will engage critically both with older and with newer epistemological ideas.

The series as a whole is unique – a compact reference library devoted to this central part of philosophy. Advanced philosophy students, graduate students, professional philosophers, and others wishing to partake of epistemology's opportunities, challenges and skirmishes will welcome this series.

Stephen Hetherington
The University of New South Wales, Australia
Editor-in-Chief, *Bloomsbury Critical Introductions to Contemporary Epistemology*

Introduction

One of the most exciting developments in recent epistemology is the increasing attention that is being paid to knowledge based on what others tell us: that is, on their testimony. Testimony stands alongside perception, memory, reason and inference as one of our main sources of knowledge: think of the countless things that you have been told by others, or that you have read about, or that you have learned in school or from the media. Inquiring into the nature of such testimonial knowledge, and analysing when and how we can acquire knowledge from others by taking their word for it, lies at the heart of the epistemology of testimony.

As social creatures equipped with language, humans have, of course, always relied on each other for knowledge about their physical surroundings, the social world they are part of, the mental states of their fellow human beings and knowledge of the past. Philosophers throughout the ages have tried to make sense of how language allows us to represent the world, and how we can share such representations with others and communicate our thoughts to them. While this book is not primarily historical in orientation, at various points in the following chapters we will encounter many of the familiar historical figures in (Western) philosophy: John Locke, Thomas Reid, David Hume, Immanuel Kant, Bertrand Russell, Ludwig Wittgenstein and others, all of whom have had interesting and insightful things to say on the topics of language, communication and testimony. Yet, in spite of these historical continuities, the emergence of a distinct subdiscipline called 'epistemology of testimony' is a fairly recent development. Of course, subdisciplines in all academic fields have multiplied over the past decades. In part, this is an inevitable result of the very real growth of knowledge and the ever-increasing level of specialization it requires, especially in the sciences; but at least for the humanities, it also reflects the push towards professionalization in academia and the corresponding demand for neatly categorized 'areas of expertise'. (In fact, in Chapter 9, we will be looking at the rise of properly credentialed experts through the lens of *expert testimony*.)

In the case of the epistemology of testimony, its recent emergence as a recognizable subdiscipline within contemporary epistemology can be traced back to the publication, in 1992, of C. A. J. Coady's influential monograph *Testimony: A Philosophical Study*. In this richly textured book, Coady patched together historical precursors and analytical arguments concerning the status of knowledge acquired from others, and in doing so gave shape to a research programme that would bring into focus what was then at best a side issue within analytical epistemology: knowledge based on the say-so of others. As with most truly influential books in philosophy, perhaps the greatest significance of Coady's book lies in the responses and criticisms it provoked, as well as in the philosophical theories that it inspired others to develop. One debate it spawned – between reductionist and anti-reductionist theories of testimonial justification (to be discussed in Chapter 5) – may be considered the first truly professional 'stand-alone' debate within the epistemology of testimony. It certainly helped the standing of this new subdiscipline that, shortly afterwards, a collection of essays appeared, which assembled some of the best minds in the analytic tradition as well as some of the most astute interpreters of non-Western philosophical traditions (see Matilal and Chakrabarti 1994). In the almost quarter-century since, the epistemology of testimony has undergone rapid growth and diversification. However, while there have been numerous articles, special issues, monographs, and a number of edited volumes (see the section 'Further reading', p. 5), so far there has been no book-length survey of the different directions and approaches that the epistemology of testimony has taken over the past decades. The present book aims to fill this gap. In order to help the reader navigate the fascinating, if sometimes complex, terrain that is mapped out in the eleven chapters that follow, the next two sections give some guidance regarding the overall structure of the book and specific features that the reader may find useful when engaging with the debates, authors and primary texts covered in this book.

1. The goal and structure of this book

Although the chapters in this book are not formally grouped into distinct parts, it may be useful to think of Chapters 4 through 8 as the main part of the book, in that they cover the central questions and debates that have shaped the epistemology of testimony over the past 20-odd years: the question of whether testimony can be assimilated to other forms of evidence (Chapter 4), the debate between reductionists and anti-reductionists about the source of testimonial justification (Chapter 5), responses to this debate in the form of hybrid theories of testimony (Chapter 6), the controversy over whether testimony can generate, or only transmit, knowledge from one interlocutor to another (Chapter 7), and interpersonal theories which highlight the role of trust, and the legitimate expectation to be trusted, in testimonial exchanges (Chapter 8).

Chapters 1 through 3, by comparison, are of an introductory nature, yet are nonetheless important in setting the scene for much of the later discussion. Chapter 1 approaches the question 'What is testimony?' via a detailed characterization of various specific kinds of testimony and the different contexts in which we rely on one another for knowledge. Chapter 2 gives further depth to the phenomenon of epistemic dependence by considering the links between human sociality and our mundane practices of giving and receiving testimony. Chapter 3 contrasts testimony with the other main sources of knowledge – perception, memory and inference – and in doing so also offers some insight into the epistemological questions specific to those other sources.

The final three chapters apply the theoretical insights thus gained to several debates that have recently attracted attention: concerning the epistemic status of expert testimony and lay-persons' appeals to expert opinion (Chapter 9), the question of whether certain types of overtly informative speech merit moral and epistemic suspicion, for example because they inflict an injustice on another epistemic agent (Chapter 10), and finally the relation between our need for good informants and our concept of knowledge (Chapter 11). The final chapter ends on a – somewhat speculative – postscript on whether changes in our communicative practices may, over time, force us to reconsider some of our most treasured epistemological concepts, such as knowledge, justification and testimony.

The main goal of this book is two-fold: First, it aims to introduce the reader to the rich set of problems and puzzles raised by our extensive reliance on others for knowledge, which the epistemology of testimony seeks to analyse. Second, and perhaps more ambitiously, it also aims to lead the reader, *via* the topic of testimony, to a number of cutting-edge research questions in social epistemology more generally – in the hope that, perhaps, he or she will find sufficient stimulation in these pages to consider contributing to this increasingly diverse and exciting discipline.

2. How to use this book

While I have tried to keep technical jargon to a minimum, a certain amount of specialized vocabulary is inevitable, in epistemology as much as in any field of knowledge. This is why the book contains a glossary, which gives definitions (and in many cases short discussions) of terms of art that are used repeatedly in this book. While the glossary's emphasis is squarely on technical terms in relation to testimony, it also covers many general epistemological concepts.

Several concepts and debates are also discussed separately in the main text, in the form of text boxes in several of the earlier chapters. In conjunction with the fairly extensive index, this should make it easy for any reader who is in need of clarification to look up the relevant terms and resume his or her reading with a better understanding of the core concepts.

Throughout the book, I have tried to emphasize connections between the various theoretical positions that have been developed; wherever possible, I also indicate early precursors to positions that were later developed more fully. While, especially in the later chapters, I have not been shy about indicating where my philosophical sympathies lie, I have aimed for a balanced and comprehensive account of the many contributions that various philosophers and colleagues have made over the years. The bibliography at the back of the book conveys a sense of the range of relevant papers and books; while no doubt there are many gaps and omissions, it is my hope that those readers who wish to delve deep into the epistemology of testimony will also come across the occasional unexpected reference to an article they had previously overlooked. In a number of chapters and individual sections, I also draw on my own previous research; the discussion of testimonial pathologies in Chapter 10, especially, relates to themes I discuss more fully in several recent papers (Gelfert 2013a; 2013b; 2013c). At various points in the book, I also seem to be unable to hide my fascination with Kant's views on the epistemology of testimony, which have been discussed in (Gelfert 2006; 2010c; 2013b).

Each chapter is accompanied by study questions and suggestions for further reading. The purpose of the study questions is to stimulate further reflection on the issues and debates covered in the corresponding chapter; they may also serve as a way of encouraging classroom discussion if the book is used in a seminar setting. The recommendations for 'further reading' should be treated in a literal sense, as pointers to *additional* material not usually discussed in the main text of the chapter; by attending to the extensive citations in the body of each chapter, the reader should have no problem identifying which are the core texts that are central to each topic or debate. In the case of historical texts, for example from Locke, Hume and Kant, references are sometimes given to specific editions, where these are widely available, or follow established conventions – for example, by referring to book, part, section, and paragraph of Hume's *Treatise of Human Nature*, or, in the case of Kant's works, to the volume and page number of the Academy edition (AA).

Axel Gelfert
Singapore, December 2013

Further reading

Adler (2012) and Green (2008) are excellent general survey articles, which are freely available online via the *Stanford Encyclopedia of Philosophy* and the *Internet Encyclopedia of Philosophy*, respectively; Green's article is a little more introductory in character, while Adler's article is a sophisticated and detailed discussion of cutting-edge epistemology of testimony, including some of its history. Other useful survey articles include Lackey (2011), which helpfully groups various authors by their endorsement of competing philosophical theses, as well as Schiffer (2001) and Patterson (2012), both of which approach the topic from the angle of the philosophy of language and communication. In addition to Coady (1992), recent monographs exclusively devoted to the epistemology of testimony are Lackey (2008), Faulkner (2011) and McMyler (2011). The edited volume by Matilal and Chakrabarti (1994) contains a number of now-classic papers and several that have not received the attention they deserve (these include sophisticated discussions of the role of testimony within Indian philosophy); the collection by Lackey and Sosa (2006) presents a cross-section of recent work on testimony within the Western analytic tradition of philosophy.

1

What is testimony?

And since among men dwelling together one man should deal with another as with himself in what he is not self-sufficient, therefore it is needful that he be able to stand with as much certainty on what another knows but of which he himself is ignorant, as upon the truths which he himself knows.
AQUINAS (quoted after Coady 1992: 17)

No doubt, we all do pick up beliefs in that second-hand fashion, and I fear that we often suppose such scavengings yield knowledge. But that is only a sign of our colossal credulity: [it is] a rotten way of acquiring beliefs and it is no way at all of acquiring knowledge.
JONATHAN BARNES (Barnes 1980: 200)

[O]ne can often believe other people's testimony more than one can believe one's own experience.
IMMANUEL KANT (*Pölitz Logic*, AA, XXIV.2: 560)

Much of our knowledge depends on others. As social creatures, we take ourselves to know a great deal about our immediate social networks – who is friends with whom, who really calls the shots at our workplace, who owes whom a favour, etc. – and certainly all of this knowledge (if indeed it is knowledge!) is intrinsically social. It is, after all, knowledge about other people and their relations to one another. But our dependence on others for knowledge runs much deeper than this. A moment's reflection shows that knowledge of historical events before we were born, or of current events in geographically distant regions, could never have been acquired without a – hopefully reliable – chain of reporters connecting us to the original events. Some of our most commonplace beliefs – that the Earth is round, that the Second World War ended in 1945 or that humanity has (so far) not discovered extraterrestrial life – are in some way, shape or form the result of our relying on others for knowledge. I know that the Second World War ended in 1945 because, presumably, our history teacher in school told us so. Or perhaps I first inferred it from background knowledge (e.g. testimonial knowledge of when my mother was born), combined with my grandmother's vivid description of returning to the rubble of Berlin, with her 5-year-old daughter in tow, in the summer after the war. Either way, I know that this is the kind of knowledge claim I could not have acquired without, at some point, relying on the word of others as a source of knowledge. In short, much of our knowledge has a social component, not because it is about social facts, but because we rely on the social world – notably, our interlocutors – for its acquisition. As social animals endowed with language, we can turn to others for knowledge, and are often ourselves called upon as informants. It is this reliance on what others tell us which is at the heart of the epistemology of testimony. To a first approximation, the word 'testimony' in this connection is to be understood as an umbrella term covering the various ways in which the word of others can serve as a source of knowledge.

The above quotations, from three philosophers spanning some 750 years, give a first glimpse of how divergent philosophical opinion has been on the validity of testimony as a source of knowledge. Why is it that the topic of testimony elicits such strong – and, as in Barnes's case, occasionally impetuous – reactions among philosophers? (See also text box 'Locke on testimony', pp. 18–19.) The beginnings of an answer to this question lie in the dual characterization of human beings as social *as well as* rational animals. When is it rational to accept the testimony of others? Are we social beings first, accepting on trust what we are told, unless there are specific reasons not to do so; or are we rational beings first, demanding independent evidence of the speaker's reliability (or directly of the claim in question) 'up front', as it were, before accepting whatever additional information a given piece of testimony conveys? Many of the epistemological controversies surrounding the topic of testimony are driven by deep-rooted intuitions about the relative value of evidence and trust, sociality and autonomy, 'common sense' and 'healthy scepticism'. Before entering the fray about these and other philosophical questions in connection with testimony, however, it is worth exploring what exactly (or approximately) we mean when we describe certain acts of communication as 'testimony'.

1. Knowledge and epistemic dependence

Epistemology is the branch of philosophy that is concerned with the study of knowledge, and if – as I have suggested in the opening paragraphs – testimony is a major source of knowledge in our lives, this alone should merit detailed philosophical investigation. But before investigating *testimonial* knowledge in greater detail, are we even sure what *knowledge* is? The question 'What is knowledge?' is in many ways the ultimate question in epistemology, and it is – as one would expect from perennial philosophical questions – exceedingly difficult to answer. It is typically easier to say what knowledge is *not*, than to give a conclusive definition of the term. Knowledge is *not* merely a matter of opinion: we all know how volatile opinions are, and knowledge aspires to a higher degree of stability. If opinions are too fickle, perhaps it is the strength with which some convictions are held that turns them into knowledge? This too seems implausible. For one, opinions often do come with strong psychological attachments – think of political opinions or deep-rooted prejudices – and no matter how strongly someone feels about their convictions, if they fail to stand in the right sort of relation to the world, they could not be considered knowledge. It has even been argued that, whenever we encounter a debate in which the participants persistently disagree with each other on the points they regard as most fundamental, we may question whether any knowledge can be had at all in these matters. (Think of the persistent disputes over matters of religion, morality, politics, and, indeed, much of philosophy; for a discussion, see Feldman 2006.)

Rationalists believed they had found a solution to the problem of knowledge: nothing short of certainty could turn mere convictions into knowledge. If it was even so much as *conceivable* that one was mistaken about a particular claim, then this claim would have to be purged from one's (prospective) stock of knowledge. It is obvious that, simply by introspecting on the content and sources of our beliefs, we can come to see that many of these have at least some chance of being wrong – and hence would have to be ruled out as knowledge. As René Descartes (1596–1650) discovered, this methodological approach to sorting out true from (potentially) false beliefs, when taken to its extreme, risks degenerating into full-fledged scepticism. After all, even beliefs that we would not normally question – that 'there is an external world', that '2+2=4' – could conceivably be mistaken: what seems like an experience of the external world to me, *could* be merely an extremely vivid dream; and what seems to me the incontrovertible result of a simple addition *could* owe its subjective certainty to the machinations of an 'evil demon' fiddling with what is going on in my mind whenever I attempt to add two numbers. The only way of avoiding such debilitating scepticism, Descartes thought, was to posit a supremely perfect being – God – whose existence, Descartes claimed, was beyond doubt and who would not allow for such massive deception. But even if this avoids scepticism of the 'evil demon' type, as long as one insists on certainty and self-evidence as criteria of knowledge one will be faced with severe limitations on what one can take oneself to know. Given the obvious fallibility of our senses, no knowledge could ever be gained from experience, thus limiting all knowledge to a priori truths – those truths that, like logic and mathematics, could be learned without reliance on experience – and perhaps some 'innate' truths (truths that we could learn from introspecting into the workings of our mind).

While the demand for certainty embodies an important intuition about knowledge – namely, that to 'know' something means that one could not be wrong about it – it is far too restrictive. All else being equal, we may prefer to be more rather than less certain, but if the pursuit of certainty comes at the expense of usefulness and breadth of knowledge – for example by ruling out knowledge on the basis of sensory experience – this should count against certainty as the 'gold standard' of knowledge. Against the rationalists, empiricists argue that, rather than relying on reason and doubt as the key to truth, we should trust experience and attempt to build up knowledge on the basis of sense data. Even if we can never be sure that a particular sense datum corresponds to a particular aspect of the world, the fact that we navigate the world more or less successfully gives us some reason to believe that our sense organs are by and large reliable. And in any case, they are the only sources of information at our disposal when it comes to finding out first-hand about contingent matters of fact – that is, 'garden-variety' facts that, for all we know, could have been different (and therefore cannot be ascertained through armchair reflection alone). Given that empiricism credits our five senses – not just our capacity to reason and introspect – with being sources of knowledge, one can think of it as a significant broadening of our 'knowledge base', certainly as compared with rationalism.

And yet, empiricism – at least when construed 'individualistically', as the pursuit of an individual knower who relies on the evidence of his senses – has its own limitations. To be sure, there is a lot such an epistemic agent can learn by applying his senses to the study of his immediate physical environment, and first-hand experience will be indispensable to his orienting himself in the world. But there is an even greater number of things – including many perfectly ordinary knowledge claims – that such an agent could not hope to ever acquire by himself. If we could really only rely on what we know first-hand from our own experience, our knowledge would forever be confined to whatever happens inside the spatio-temporal 'bubble' that is constituted by the sensory experiences each of us has of their immediate physical environment. The empiricist approach, when taken to its extreme, again appears to result in a knowledge base that falls far short of what we usually take ourselves to know. Even if one were to bite the bullet on this and accept that all we can know are facts of which we have had direct experience, or which could be inferred on the basis of first-hand evidence, a further problem remains. For, even in interpreting our own experiences (and drawing inferences on their basis), we pervasively rely on classifications, known relationships of cause and effect, generalizations etc. that we did not ourselves establish. To the extent that such knowledge is presupposed in my observations, any knowledge I gain on their basis is no longer truly 'first-hand'.

The limitations on what we can know 'off our own bat', by either relying on reason alone or on our five senses (unaided by others), should by now be obvious. How, then, can we move beyond the narrow range of knowledge permissible by the standards of rationalism and (individualist) empiricism? A first hint of an answer lies in one of the quotations above from Immanuel Kant, who observes that 'one can often believe other people's testimony more than one can believe one's own experience'. What Kant hints at is that our first-hand experience is fallible, so that sometimes the best test of its veracity lies not in making additional first-hand observations, but in comparing our judgements against those of other people. This simple observation raises a more general question for empiricism: why, when it comes to matters of knowledge, should we privilege our own experiences over those of other people? To be sure, there is a sense in which my sensory experiences are mine alone, and yours are yours alone, and we cannot *actually* come to have another person's sensory experiences. (This is why sense data are sometimes called 'private mental items'.) But it is not at all clear that this difference is of central importance to epistemology (rather than, say, a mere matter of psychology). In particular, it is not clear why it should preclude my acquiring knowledge from your experiences, for example by accepting your testimony that you experienced such-and-such.

One of the guiding themes in the epistemology of testimony is that not only is it possible to partake in the knowledge of others in this way, but that this is indeed *the only way* we can acquire anything like the depth and breadth of knowledge we typically credit ourselves with – and which ranges from recent events in our neighbourhood to distant historical occurrences in faraway countries, from social trivia reported to us by friends and colleagues to specialist findings related to us by highly trained experts. This expansion of readily available knowledge – there for the taking, as it were, by accepting the testimony of others – comes at the price of an increased *epistemic dependence* on others. Nowhere is this more evident than in one of the most revered institutions of knowledge: science. The term 'epistemic dependence' itself is due to John Hardwig, who, in several influential papers, analysed the important role of trust in science. The kinds of claims we typically regard as scientific knowledge – that 'nothing can travel faster than the speed of light', that 'DNA encodes genetic information', etc. – are only the end product of a socially distributed process of inquiry and information-sharing: the 'tip of the iceberg', as it were. What warrants such claims are complex underlying processes of generating and testing hypotheses, accumulating scientific evidence and debating its implications. No individual knower could realistically hope to secure any significant portion of scientific knowledge all on his own. As a result, on an 'individualistic' conception of knowledge and evidence, it would seem that 'there can no longer be knowledge in many scientific disciplines because there is now too much available evidence' for any one individual to assess all on her own (Hardwig 1991: 699).

If we are to tap into the knowledge of others – including collective resources such as scientific knowledge – we must be prepared to accept various forms of epistemic dependence. 'Epistemic dependence' here is to be understood in a generic sense, as referring to any situation in which a subject's belief depends for its formation, sustainment, or reliability on the knowledge (or beliefs, or other cognitive states and processes) of other epistemic agents; to say of a subject H that he is epistemically dependent on S (where S may be, for example, an individual speaker testifying to a particular claim, or a community, such as a scientific institution) is simply to note this sort of dependence. Testimony, on this account, is a paradigmatic – and perhaps the most elementary – case of epistemic dependence. One natural (though, as we shall see, not unproblematic) interpretation of what goes on in the case of testimony is that, when I accept what another tells me, I am acquiring a belief that has already passed through another person's mind. (Let us assume, for the moment, that my interlocutor is indeed expressing his belief and is not, for example, dissimulating or merely uttering a sentence without conviction.) The other person's reasons for holding the belief in question need not, and typically will not, be readily available to me. Moreover, since we are not usually compelled to say whatever crosses our minds, we can reasonably take our interlocutor to have *made a decision* about what to tell us (and, of course, what *not* to tell us). Clearly, then, accepting what another tells us is an instance of epistemic dependence, given that our belief depends for its formation on the cognitive processes of our interlocutor.

Knowledge on the basis of testimony, thus, is a form of epistemic dependence, yet talk of 'dependence' should not obscure the important function of testimony as a source of knowledge for us. Recall that, without reliance on testimony, not only would our individual stock of knowledge be significantly poorer, but some of our most respected forms of knowledge – such as science or history – would be virtually impossible. Given the importance of testimony to how we think about the world, it will be useful to have a 'neutral' way of referring to those beliefs that we owe to the testimony of others. ('Neutral' here means that our characterization of such beliefs should not make too many substantive assumptions about what is the 'correct' theory of testimony.) Following a suggestion by Duncan Pritchard, let us use the phrase 'testimony-based belief' to refer to 'any belief which one reasonably and directly forms in response to what one reasonably takes to be testimony and which is essentially caused and sustained by testimony' (Pritchard 2004: 326). While this definition is suitably general, in that it allows for different understandings of the term 'testimony', it at the same time imposes some plausible constraints: for example, by requiring that a testimony-based belief be *sustained* by testimony, it rules out beliefs which we first acquired from testimony but have since verified first-hand, for example by visual inspection. (Beliefs of the latter kind should instead be regarded as perceptual beliefs.) With this characterization of epistemic dependence and testimony-based beliefs in hand, let us now turn to the various forms of testimony we encounter on a daily basis.

2. The formal origins of testimony

So far we have characterized testimony in general terms, as a source of knowledge that entails a specific form of epistemic dependence: when we acquire a testimony-based belief, we depend, at least in part, on the thought processes of our informant (as well as other features of our extended social environment). Thus understood, 'testimony' is a philosophical term of art, intended to capture a diverse array of sources and forms of communication: oral and written, individual and institutional, anonymous and attributable, and so forth. However, in ordinary parlance the term 'testimony' is seldom used in this generality. When the waiter tells us that the total bill comes to 25 dollars and 30 cents, or when the news anchor announces that the foreign minister of Russia has arrived in Tokyo for a state visit, it might seem pompous, perhaps even preposterous, to describe this as an instance of 'testimony' to an outside observer. 'Testimony', in ordinary usage, tends to be associated with legal, religious or otherwise formal contexts. Yet, for better or worse, the philosophical usage of the term as a catch-all for the communication of knowledge is here to stay – notwithstanding the fact that, even in philosophy, it has sometimes been used interchangeably with 'evidence', as in the dated expression 'the testimony of the senses'. (The relation between testimony and evidence will be discussed in more detail in Chapter 4.) But it would be hasty to think of this mismatch between philosophical and 'ordinary' usage as merely an unfortunate mismatch; as the remainder of this section will demonstrate, there is a lot to be learned from the formal origins of testimony as an epistemological problem.

2.1. Legal testimony

If there is one core area in public life where the term 'testimony' is frequently used, it would have to be the legal domain. The prototypical case here would be the testimony of a witness before a court of law. Such formal testimony is subject to strict demands for truthfulness, accuracy and relevance. The witness, in a well-worn phrase, is requested to 'tell the truth, the whole truth, and nothing but the truth', but not just any old truth: he is also expected to stick to the point. The guiding model is that of an eyewitness who is called upon by the court to report, as impartially as possible, 'the facts' as experienced first-hand. If the witness strays too far from the subject matter or violates the impartiality assumption (e.g. by freely passing judgement on the defendant's guilt or innocence), different legal systems have put various safeguards in place to police the boundary between admissible and inadmissible testimony. Thus, English law, the Federal Rules of Evidence in the United States, and many similar legal systems contain prohibitions against 'hearsay': a witness is not normally allowed to offer as testimonial evidence a statement made by a third party out of court. Such third-party testimony, so the rationale goes, could not be properly subjected to cross-examination, and allowing hearsay would therefore risk introducing evidence that was held to a lower standard of critical scrutiny than an eyewitness's first-hand account. (Exceptions to this rule exist – for example if the statement was made by the defendant himself, or one of his conspirators, in which case it may be held against him.)

The eyewitness model of testimony faces significant limitations, even within the legal domain itself. For one, empirical studies have shown that the testimony of eyewitnesses is not nearly as reliable as had long been thought. Various circumstantial factors – both during the witnessed events and subsequently – determine an eyewitness's actual reliability and his level of subjective certainty. Thus, the presence of a weapon is known to draw the attention of the witness away from faces, thus reducing the eyewitness's overall success rate in identifying the weapon holder. Similarly, whereas the majority of eyewitnesses are able to make a correct identification from a police line-up containing the actual culprit, the percentage of those claiming to have identified the culprit tends to go up – not down – when the line-up does not, in fact, contain the culprit. Finally, positive feedback from administrators – 'Good, you identified the suspect' – will boost an eyewitness's subjective level of certainty, reducing his willingness to entertain the possibility that he might have made a mistake. (See Wells and Bradfield 1998.) Perhaps because of the unreliability of single, non-corroborated eyewitness reports, some legal systems – such as Roman law – contain the rule '*testis unus, testis nullus*': 'one witness is no witness'. (Interestingly, the same rule was sometimes employed in England to dismiss a single dissenting voice in a jury of twelve – thereby going against the powerful intuition, promulgated for example in the 1957 movie *12 Angry Men*, that a single dissenter can sometimes protect a group from a premature consensus; see Pollock and Maitland 1898: 655.)

Other important limitations of the eyewitness model concern the subject matter of the testimony. For example, it is not uncommon in criminal proceedings to request testimony pertaining to the defendant's character and reputation, yet it is clear that such knowledge could not easily be acquired first-hand; indeed, where reputation among peers is concerned, such knowledge involves social facts and likely requires reliance on the testimony of said peers. With the increasing reliance on forensic science, such as DNA profiling as a means of identifying individuals on the basis of their genetic information, more and more legal testimony takes the form of expert testimony; the same holds for civil cases that depend on scientific or technical expert knowledge. Such testimony is not 'first-hand' in the way that eyewitness testimony is; instead, it is being solicited because of the unique standing of the testifier – the expert witness – as an epistemic authority. (See Chapter 9 for a discussion of expert testimony.) In both cases, the assumption of impartiality may be difficult to maintain, if the pool of witnesses is restricted. Perhaps this is why Aristotle suggests – alas, not very helpfully – that ancient (i.e. dead) witnesses should be deemed the most trustworthy, since they cannot be corrupted (1991: *Rhetoric*, 1376a).

The courtroom – with its many rules and conventions, and its clear division of social roles – provides a paradigmatic example of formal testimony. But it should be clear that there is a continuum of formal settings, each of which has its own set of explicit or implicit rules and standards for the management of testimony. Think of the continuity that exists between expert testimony in a court of law and in an expert panel advising the government, between decision-making among the 12 jurors in a criminal case and among the members of parliamentary committees, or between negotiations in the UN Security Council and in the local council. Clearly, then, formal testimony is not limited to the courtroom alone. Perhaps because (semi-)formal testimony is more widespread than we tend to acknowledge, it is sometimes claimed that our intuitions about formal testimony continue to influence how we think about more ordinary cases of acquiring knowledge from others. For example, we might think of testimony – in the broad epistemological sense – as being merely a way of *transmitting* information, since this is how 'ideal' eyewitness testimony would plausibly be construed in the legal context. (On the issue of transmission vs generation of knowledge, see also Chapter 7.) One might worry that this distorts our interpretation of the diverse ways of gaining knowledge on the basis of other people's say-so, since formal testimony is unduly restrictive. While there is some truth to this worry, it is also worth noting that formal contexts – such as the courtroom scenario – often provide us with valuable background information, which more 'generic' descriptions of testimonial encounters tend to lack. Indeed, Fred Kauffeld and John Fields (2003: 3) have argued that, since formal testimony 'makes explicit much that is assumed or goes unremarked upon in ordinary conversational settings', it 'can give us guidance as to where we should be looking in these less formal contexts' to find what we need in order to make sense of testimony as a source of knowledge.

2.2. Bearing witness

There is another sense in which the term 'testimony' is used in more formal contexts, which has its origins in religious usage, although it has since proliferated beyond the confines of religious practice. It has as its main function not the communication of empirical knowledge, but the assertion and reinforcement of fundamental (e.g. spiritual) beliefs. The key phrase in this connection is 'bearing witness', which indicates that the emphasis is more on the activity of the speaker, who testifies to the existence of a higher (transcendent) reality, and less on the hearer. For the religious believer, it may be of secondary importance whether he is addressing a (human) audience at all – or whether the audience is willing to give him any credence – as long as he professes his faith in a manner that is true to his fundamental beliefs. (This is not to say that the audience never matters in the giving of religious testimony – clearly it is of prime importance when it comes to, say, prayer meetings or missionary work.) Interestingly, the notion of religious testimony does not seem to be restricted to verbal testimony only: thus, the lives and deeds of prophets, martyrs and saints are sometimes thought to constitute testimony in their own right. The basic idea is this: just as testimony can be thought of as a form of evidence (as in the legal case), so the deeds of saints and the sacrifices of martyrs can be mustered as evidence for the sincerity and authenticity of their beliefs – which, in turn, may be seen as adding to whatever prior justification those beliefs had in the first place.

The kinds of knowledge claims involved in religion – concerning the existence of God, or the truth of certain religious doctrines – bring with them specific problems of their own. These tend to be discussed within the philosophy of religion rather than within analytic epistemology. However, as we shall see, there are important areas of overlap, especially where religious faith issues in specific empirical or moral claims. For example, religious traditions sometimes invoke testimony to miracles as evidence for the existence of God; or they claim that moral knowledge may be gained from the study of centuries-old scriptural texts. Biblical literalists have also been known to clash with science over the truth of such well-confirmed theories as the theory of evolution or continental drift theory. When religious texts are treated not as sources of inspiration or moral advice, standing in need of interpretation, but are seen as infallible sources of factual or moral knowledge, they must be held to the same epistemic standards as other (evidence-based) sources of knowledge. We will return to this point briefly in Chapter 5 ('Reductionism and anti-reductionism'), when we discuss David Hume's famous critique of miraculous testimony, which is often seen as a core historical source for the epistemology of testimony.

As noted at the beginning of this section, the notion of 'bearing witness' has moved beyond the religious realm and has entered, in modified form, other areas of human endeavour. While its newly gained independence from the religious context has imbued the phrase 'bearing witness' with considerable flexibility, it retains some of its original meaning. Rather than functioning merely as a conduit of knowledge, the figure of the witness – as well as the act of testifying – is credited with a special (typically moral) responsibility. While the testimony need no longer be about a transcendent reality (as in the religious case), it is often seen as aspiring to some degree of universality. Finally, although the act of bearing witness is usually an individual one, it contributes to what is sometimes called 'sensemaking' – the social activity of giving meaning to collective experiences. This is especially pertinent to cases of historical trauma and to the experiences of survivors of genocide, war and persecution. Thus, in the second half of the twentieth century, an important research programme at the intersection of oral history, education and psychoanalysis crystallized around the testimony of survivors of the Holocaust. As Dori Laub has argued, for many survivors of the Nazi concentration camps psychological survival – that is, an individual's ability to maintain a healthy mental life – was at least in part a matter of having an addressable other in the form of an 'inner witness'; all the more so since the Holocaust was a historical reality that aimed at extinguishing 'the very possibility of address, the possibility of appealing, or of turning to, another' (Laub 1995: 66).

Some of the most forceful cases of 'bearing witness' of historical trauma are surprisingly dispassionate. As Primo Levi, the author of *If This Is A Man* (1959), *The Truce* (1965) and *The Drowned and the Saved* (1989), wrote: 'I have deliberately assumed the calm sober language of the witness, neither the lamenting tones of the victim nor the irate voice of someone who seeks revenge' (1965: 210). Survivors of events such as the Holocaust, Levi argued, are 'witnesses in a trial of planetary and epochal dimensions' (1989: 149). As such, they testify not only to their first-hand experiences, but also to the enormity of the historical events and injustices they suffered. Empirical accuracy in such contexts takes second place to historical authenticity, and the quest for certainty in knowledge is secondary to the struggle for recognition.

As Kelly Oliver puts it, there is an inherent tension between the notions of 'witnessing in the sense of eye-witness to historical facts' and 'witnessing in the sense of bearing witness to a truth about humanity and suffering that transcends those facts' (2004: 81). Although, as Oliver notes, bearing witness retains both the juridical (legal) connotation of 'seeing with one's own eyes' and the religious connotation of 'testifying to that which cannot be seen' (ibid.), historical witnessing – in an interesting twist on both the legal and religious case – is often less about making information available to the hearer than about imparting responsibility for keeping the historical memory alive. As Laub puts it, based on his involvement in the creation of a video archive for Holocaust testimonies, 'the interviewer-listener takes on the responsibility for bearing witness that previously the narrator felt he bore alone, and therefore could not carry out' (Laub 1995: 69).

Locke on testimony

In a famous passage from *An Essay Concerning Human Understanding*, John Locke suggests that 'we should make greater progress in the discovery of rational and contemplative *Knowledge*' if we relied on our own thoughts, rather than on the authority of others:

> For, I think, we may as rationally hope to see with other Mens Eyes, as to know by other Mens Understandings. So much as we our selves consider and comprehend of Truth and Reason, so much we possess of real and true Knowledge. The floating of other Mens Opinions in our brains makes us not one jot the more knowing, though they happen to be true. What in them was Science, is in us but Opiniatrety [=obstinate adherence to opinion], whilst we give up our Assent only to reverend Names, and do not, as they did, employ our own Reason to *understand* those *Truths*, which gave them reputation. *Aristotle* was certainly a knowing Man, but no body ever thought him so, because he blindly embraced, and confidently vented the Opinions of another. And if the taking up of another's Principles, without examining them, made not him a Philosopher, I suppose it will hardly make any body else so. In the Sciences, every one has so much, as he really knows and comprehends: What he believes only, and takes upon trust, are but shreds; which however well in the whole piece, make no considerable addition to his stock, who gathers them. Such borrowed Wealth, like Fairy-money, though it were Gold in the hand from which he received it, will be but Leaves and Dust when it comes to use. (Book 1, chapter 4, section 23)

Locke here rejects the possibility of acquiring 'real and true Knowledge' on the basis of testimony. But it is worth keeping in mind that Locke's definition of Knowledge requires much higher standards of certainty than are typically demanded by contemporary epistemology. Scientific knowledge, which is the relevant contrast alluded to in the passage above, for Locke comprises only 'general, instructive, unquestionable Truths' – which means that in matters 'that fall under the Examination of our Senses', we 'are not capable of *scientifical Knowledge*' (book 4, chapter 3, section 26). If even perception and careful observation cannot generate Knowledge in Locke's sense, it is perhaps no surprise that he rejects the thought that such Knowledge could be communicated via testimony.

Elsewhere in the *Essay*, Locke is more lenient towards testimony as an epistemic source. In connection with the question of our knowledge of the past, Locke writes: 'A credible Man vouching his Knowledge of it, is a good proof' (book 1, chapter 16, section 10). Nor does Locke hide his own reliance on the testimony of others, as in this endearing bit of nature writing: 'I have been credibly informed that a bitch will nurse, play with, and be fond of young foxes, as much as and in place of her puppies, if you can but get them once to suck her so long that her milk may go through them' (book 2, chapter 2, section 7). Perhaps this attests to Locke's own gullibility, which the Earl of Shaftesbury, in a letter of 3 June 1709, laments when he scolds the 'credulous Mr. Locke, with his Indian, barbarian stories of wild nations' (Shaftesbury 1999: 154).

Further reading: For a discussion of Locke's views on testimony, see Shieber (2009).

3. Kinds of testimony: Some examples

The discussion so far already provides an inkling of the vast reach of testimony as a source of knowledge. Many of our basic social practices and institutions – from relying on others for simple information to the formal proceedings in a court of law – would be virtually unthinkable without it, and geographical, historical and scientific knowledge would likewise be out of reach in the absence of testimony. What is remarkable about testimony is that, in principle, *any* knowledge claim that can be stated in propositional form can be passed on via testimony. (Whether this 'passing on' of propositional content is always sufficient for the acquisition of knowledge is a question we will address later.) Whereas perceptual knowledge is limited to the appearance of material objects in our immediate vicinity (and requires at least the operation of reasoning and inference if it is to go beyond our immediate 'bubble' of experience), testimonial knowledge may include theoretical claims, abstract truths and facts well beyond what we could investigate first-hand. In this sense, testimony is a 'promiscuous' source of knowledge, which does not discriminate much between the kinds of content it conveys. It might seem futile, then, to attempt a full taxonomy of 'kinds of testimony', and indeed this is not the goal of this section. Instead, the following examples have been chosen as illustrations of the breadth and diversity of testimony and with an eye to bringing out some of the internal tensions which any theoretical account of testimony should try to resolve.

3.1. Types of content

In our everyday encounters with other people, we often learn a great deal from them about rather mundane matters. Our interlocutors tell us 'with a high degree of reliability though not with infallibility, who they are, what work they do, where they live, how old they are, details of their familiar environment, their spouses' and children's names, ages, occupations' and so forth (Coady 1992: 269). Not all such *mundane testimony* is based on first-hand experience. After all, some basic personal information – our birthday, our parents' names and backgrounds – is known to us on the basis of testimony, and yet we do not for this reason doubt such information when others volunteer it about themselves. What renders mundane testimony largely unproblematic is the fact that it concerns subject matters for which, as Elizabeth Fricker puts it, 'commonsense psychological knowledge licenses one to expect the speakers to be competent about them' (Fricker 1995: 405). It is the kind of knowledge that we can reasonably expect any interlocutor to be competent (and, by and large, sincere) about. Who, if not our interlocutor, would be in the best position to tell us their name, age, line of work or what they had for breakfast? Classifying such matters as 'mundane', of course, already presupposes an evaluation of some sort – if I suddenly took a heightened interest in my interlocutor's identity and background (perhaps because I had independent reason to suspect him of being a con man), I might no longer just take his word for it. But in the vast majority of cases, default acceptance of mundane testimony appears to be the norm.

However, in order to satisfy our informational demands, it will often not do to just ask anyone. Much of the factual information we are interested in – whether because of pressing practical needs or out of simple curiosity – presupposes some form of specific knowledge. This may require either some form of specialized knowledge on the part of our informant or some other form of epistemic advantage. Sometimes what is called for is what Bernard Williams has called a 'purely positional advantage' (2002: 42) – as in the case of the eyewitness who happened to be in the right place at the right (or wrong?) time. 'Specialized knowledge' in this context need not entail that only a small number of experts have access to it – most of us have an eclectic mix of specialized knowledge across such diverse subject matters as history, geography and science. All that is required is that the speaker have at his disposal knowledge that his interlocutor – perhaps because of his insufficient background knowledge in the subject area in question – could not easily acquire by himself. As an example, consider the following anecdote related by John Locke in *An Essay Concerning Human Understanding*:

> [THE KING OF SIAM.] As it happened to a Dutch ambassador, who entertaining the king of Siam with the particularities of Holland, which he was inquisitive after, amongst other things told him that the water in his country would sometimes, in cold weather, be so hard that men walked upon it, and that it would bear an elephant, if he were there. To which the king replied, Hitherto I have believed the strange things you have told me, because I look upon you as a sober fair man, but now I am sure you lie. (Book 4, chapter 15, section 5)

In an age when knowledge about the climate in other countries wasn't widely available, the Dutch ambassador clearly offered a piece of specialized *factual testimony*, even if, on this occasion, the information was deemed so implausible by the otherwise indulgent king that he could not bring himself to accept it. If the historical example sounds quaint, consider this example, given by C. A. J. Coady as an everyday case of requesting specific information that only a particular source could have:

> [PHONE BILL.] I ring up the telephone company on being unable to locate my bill and am told by an anonymous voice that it comes to $165 and is due on 15 June. No thought of determining the veracity and reliability of the witness occurs to me [. . .] given that the total is within tolerable limits[.] (Coady 1992: 143)

In the absence of prior conflicting beliefs, we tend to accept much of the factual testimony we receive from others – thereby implicitly acknowledging our indebtedness to them for much of what we take ourselves to know.

The cases discussed so far all concern empirical knowledge of contingent facts. It seems uncontroversial to say that if testimony can be a source of knowledge at all, then these would be the kinds of knowledge claims that it should be able to communicate. Yet there are also types of knowledge where we really do have to know things off our own bat, or so many people have argued. Although it may be possible to testify to such knowledge in a purely generic way, a hearer could not properly be said to acquire knowledge on the basis of such testimony. Three broad classes of examples are *mathematical*, *moral* and *aesthetic testimony*. Let us briefly discuss each in turn.

Imagine that you are a librarian cataloguing the collection of a renowned mathematician who died long ago and who made important contributions to a number of subfields in mathematics, often displaying considerable ingenuity in deriving complex mathematical theorems and rarely making a mistake. In a dusty tome on arithmetic you come across the following statement, neatly recorded in the great man's distinctive handwriting:

> [MATHEMATICAL TESTIMONY.] It is impossible to separate a cube into two cubes, or a fourth power into two fourth powers, or in general, any power higher than the second, into two like powers. I have discovered a truly marvellous proof of this, which this margin is too narrow to contain.

What this passage asserts is that, for $n > 2$, no natural numbers a, b and c exist such that $a^n+b^n=c^n$. (For $n = 2$, the formula becomes Pythagoras' theorem, which has many solutions, e.g. $a = 3$, $b = 4$ and $c = 5$.) Mathematically knowledgeable readers will recognize this as Fermat's Last Theorem, and the passage above quotes Fermat's own words (or rather, an English translation of the Latin original). Generations of mathematicians tried, unsuccessfully, to derive a proof of this deceptively simple mathematical relation, and it was not until the mid-1990s that a proof was found by the British mathematician Andrew Wiles. (At more than 100 pages in length, the proof indeed turned out to be too long for the margins of Fermat's tome; for a popular account of Wiles's proof, see Singh 1998.) Let us assume – implausibly, and only for the sake of argument – that Fermat did, in fact, possess a proof. As the librarian who comes across Fermat's (truthful) record of his achievement, would you acquire *mathematical knowledge* of the theorem by accepting his testimony? Many people feel strongly that this could not be the case. Thus, Williams argues that someone who believes a mathematical proposition, p, on the basis of someone else's authoritative testimony, but cannot mathematically demonstrate its truth, cannot be said to know it. On Williams's account, even a perfectly reliable informant could not succeed in communicating mathematical knowledge by mere say-so, since 'access to mathematical truth must necessarily lie through proof, and [. . .] therefore the notion of non-accidental true belief in mathematics essentially involves the notion of mathematical proof' (Williams 1972: 9). Williams is otherwise sympathetic towards testimony as a source of knowledge, and so it is plausible that his position is motivated by the assumption that mathematical knowledge has to meet higher standards than 'ordinary' knowledge, and in particular requires *understanding* of the proof rather than just of the content of the theorem.

Similar considerations apply to *moral testimony* and the problem of whether it is possible to acquire, in a phrase due to Karen Jones (1999), 'second-hand moral knowledge'. Robert Paul Wolff explicitly likens the case of morality to the case of mathematics:

> He [the responsible reasoner] may learn from others about his moral obligations, but only in the sense that a mathematician learns from other mathematicians – namely by hearing from them arguments whose validity he recognizes even though he did not think of them himself. He does not learn in the sense that one learns from an explorer, by accepting as true his accounts of things one cannot see for oneself. (Wolff 1970: 13)

As with mathematical knowledge, the intuition behind the rejection of moral testimony is that no one can be said to know a moral truth unless they know it *for the right reasons*. Perhaps one can *remind* someone of their moral obligations via testimony, but unless they themselves have the necessary understanding of the reasons and moral principles underlying these obligations they cannot truly be said to have moral knowledge. At the same time, it may sometimes be necessary to accept moral testimony at face value, in order to sharpen one's moral sensibilities. For example, even when interlocutors are in broad agreement on general moral principles – that 'racism is wrong', for example – they may differ in their judgements concerning what constitutes a case of racism. Deferring to the judgements of others, especially those who have suffered racist treatment (and whose experiences may have been excluded, precisely for this reason, from the majority view on what constitutes racism), may be a first step towards becoming better at identifying actual instances of morally blameworthy racism. (This point is developed in detail by Jones 1999.)

Aesthetic testimony, like moral and mathematical testimony, is often thought to be incapable of transmitting knowledge directly to its recipient. How could it, given that, in order for us to form an aesthetic response to a work of art, we must encounter it in experience? And yet, those of us who are consumers of film and book reviews often rely on the aesthetic judgements of others. Consider the following example of aesthetic testimony, from a review by the late film critic Roger Ebert, regarding the 1998 movie *Armageddon*:

> [MOVIE REVIEW.] The movie is an assault on the eyes, the ears, the brain, common sense, and the human desire to be entertained. No matter what

they're charging to get in, it's worth more to get out. (*Chicago Sun-Times*, 1 July 1998)

On the face of it, it would seem that by accepting Ebert's testimony I could come to know that *Armageddon* is an extraordinarily bad movie. And yet, many people would disagree with this analysis (not least those viewers who have given the movie a respectable 6.4/10 rating on the popular IMDb movie database). Perhaps aesthetic testimony is to be taken in the spirit of advice or as a mere expression of an opinion. But this would overlook the fact that aesthetic testimony is not always about matters of taste – that is, it is not always in the business of making predictions about whether or not the recipient would enjoy the movie, artwork, performance or novel in question. Much aesthetic testimony concerns the merit of a work, irrespective of personal taste. Thus, an art historian may be able to point out specific accomplishments and achievements of a painting – in terms of its style, technique, and composition, say – and a layperson may come to acquire aesthetic knowledge this way (without thereby necessarily coming to like the painting). Whether testimony can be a *reliable* source of aesthetic knowledge is open to debate, given that the usual markers of expertise – relevant skills, demonstrable competence and track record – seem to be especially difficult to judge in this case. (See Meskin 2004.)

Historically, testimony has been associated with the communication of knowledge based *on the experiences of others*, and the restrictions on moral and mathematical testimony may be seen as a remnant of this tradition. Morality and mathematics concern truths that can only be properly acquired through an exercise of one's own reason, or so the argument goes. (The case of aesthetic knowledge is different, insofar as it requires not an exercise of reason, but acquaintance with an aspect of one's own experience – how one is affected by a work of art – which cannot be acquired by relying on someone else's experience.) If testimony is understood as a source of empirical knowledge only, this would rule out certain kinds of testimonial content. Thus, Immanuel Kant, though broadly sympathetic to testimony as a source of empirical knowledge, categorically rules out purported *supernatural testimony*: 'The assent of a testimonial is always something empirical; and the person whom I am supposed to believe on the basis of his testimony must be an object of experience' (Kant 1993: 61). Not only must the content be empirical, but the source, too, must at least in principle be of a kind that we could learn about from experience. Content and source are thus deeply intertwined in our testimonial practices.

3.2. Kinds of reporters

Just as there is a wide range of kinds of testimonial content, there is great diversity with respect to testimonial sources. As is to be expected, the kinds of reporters we encounter in testimonial exchanges will vary with the kinds of reports we expect, or hope, to receive.

A first important class of testifiers consists of our *epistemic peers*. Recall that we earlier identified as one core feature of mundane knowledge that it concerns matters about which we can reasonably expect the vast majority of people to be competent. With respect to mundane knowledge, we are epistemic peers: all else being equal, each of us is as competent and likely to get things right as any other. (Let us ignore, for the moment, that some cases of mundane knowledge are 'indexical', so to speak: each of us is an authority on their own name and, in this sense, we are all on a par with one another, but that does not mean that if I want to know *your* name I can ask just anyone!) The basic idea generalizes to other kinds of knowledge: for example, when it comes to specialist knowledge, it may often be reasonable to ask of putative experts whether they are epistemic peers. Yet it is not immediately clear what we mean when we judge two informants to be epistemic peers. The philosophical literature offers competing definitions of epistemic peerhood. (For a survey, see Gelfert 2011a.) Early definitions stress equality with respect to 'intelligence, perspicacity, honesty, thoroughness, and other relevant epistemic virtues' (Gutting 1982: 83). Other authors have added that, for two informants to count as peers, they must be 'equals with respect to their familiarity with the evidence and arguments which bear on that question' (Kelly 2005: 174). Yet others have opted for a minimalist definition that does away with substantive assumptions about similarities in epistemic virtues, abilities and familiarity. According to one such view, someone is my epistemic peer if, in a hypothetical case of disagreement, I would consider the two of us to be equally likely to be mistaken (Elga 2007: 499).

The question of epistemic peerhood typically arises in cases of disagreement such as the following:

> [PEER DISAGREEMENT.] Suppose that five of us go out to dinner. It's time to pay the check, so the question we're interested in is how much we each owe. We can all see the bill total clearly, we all agree to give a 20 percent tip, and we further agree to split the whole cost evenly. [. . .] I do the math in my head and become highly confident that our shares are $43 each. Meanwhile, my friend does the math in her head and becomes highly confident that our shares are $45 each. (Christensen 2007: 193)

The question of how to react to such peer disagreements – whether to reduce one's confidence in one's own result, or whether to take the fact of disagreement as evidence that the other person is probably wrong – has recently given rise to a new sub-area in philosophy, the epistemology of disagreement. What matters for the purposes of our discussion here is the fact that assessing the testimony of others will often involve determining whether they are our epistemic peers, or whether they are epistemically inferior – or superior – to us.

Where specialized factual knowledge is concerned, it would be misguided to rely on epistemic peers alone: in such cases, we actively seek out experts. *Expert testimony* is fast becoming an important element in policymaking, and even at an individual level we rely on the specialized expertise of others – for example, whenever we see our family doctor for treatment. The specific epistemological problems of expert testimony will be discussed in Chapter 9. For the moment, let us just note that whether or not a given knowledge claim is 'esoteric' (where this is to be understood in the neutral sense of requiring specialized expertise) or is mundane depends on context:

> [EXPERT KNOWLEDGE.] For example, consider the statement, 'There will be an eclipse of the sun on April 22, 2130, in Santa Fe, New Mexico.' Relative to the present epistemic standpoint, i.e., the standpoint of people living in the year 2000, this is an esoteric statement. Ordinary people in the year 2000 will not be able to answer this question correctly, except by guessing. On the other hand, on the very day in question, April 22, 2130, ordinary people on the street in Santa Fe, New Mexico, will easily be able to answer the question correctly. (Goldman 2001: 106)

It is obvious that what requires expertise in this case is not the *verification* of the event as it unfolds, but the successful *prediction* of it, more than a hundred years into the future. An expert, when called upon to make such a prediction, would have to have a good grasp of the laws of physics, access to data of the exact planetary constellations, and the ability to mathematically derive future constellations of the Earth, Moon and Sun from this information.

In addition to testimony from individual people, we also frequently encounter *institutional testimony*. Consider your bank statement informing you that you are approaching your overdraft limit, a corporate press release advising shareholders of an imminent takeover, or a government gazette announcing recently passed legislation. In all of these cases, the truth of the claims in question is vouched for not by a single interlocutor, but by a social institution: even the company's press spokesman is speaking *on behalf of* the corporation, not in his capacity as an individual knower. (It is worth noting that in some cases the issuance of testimony may bring about its truth – as when legislation comes into effect with its publication.) Institutional testimony – or, more generally, *group testimony* – raises important questions for any general account of testimony. Earlier it was noted that one natural, though not unproblematic, way to think about testimony is in terms of belief expression: in presenting a statement as testimony, the testifier represents himself as holding a corresponding belief and vouching for its truth. Yet for the case of institutional testimony such a theoretical framework seems woefully inadequate, since groups and social institutions cannot be said to hold beliefs of their own, and it is far from clear whether it would even be possible, in each case, for there to be a single individual *within* the group or institution who could have the requisite belief.

3.3. Formats and media of testimony

In many of the examples found in the literature on testimony and its epistemological problems, the paradigmatic case of testimony is one of a face-to-face encounter between a single speaker, who makes an utterance, and a single hearer, who understands the speaker and forms a belief on the basis of his say-so. All testimony requires some form of medium, by means of which the 'sender' can relay his message to the 'recipient'; in the paradigmatic case this would be the spoken word, expressed in a language shared by the speaker and the hearer. Testimony, of course, is not limited to verbal testimony, spoken here and now. It also includes written material, recordings, electronic records, sign language, and (some) gestures and facial expressions. If I ask the waiter where the washroom is, and he points to a narrow corridor at the back of the restaurant, there seems to be no significant difference between this action and a full verbal statement.

Artefacts and inanimate objects can likewise be thought of as sources of testimony, such as 'road signs, maps, the measurement markings on rulers, destination-markers on buses and trams', tombstones and so forth (Coady 1992: 51). In many cases there is at least the presumption of human involvement somewhere in the process of the production of such artefacts: road signs are put up by the local council, the accuracy of maps is vouched for by cartographers, and the destination shown on the bus has presumably been keyed in by the bus driver at the start of his shift. Many such cases straddle the boundary between individual and institutional testimony, whereas in other cases – such as the use of measurement instruments – it becomes increasingly questionable whether the information gained by, say, reading off a digital display, is truly 'testimonial' in character, or whether it isn't just a case of technologically mediated observation.

It is perhaps worth flagging a class of testimony that in recent years has become more than just a theoretical possibility: *computer-generated testimony*. With the advent of 'intelligent' algorithms, it is now entirely conceivable that humans can carry on 'conversations' with computers – for example, by posing questions to an automated helpdesk via a web interface – which mimick the experience we would have if we were to email back and forth with a (perhaps not overly enthusiastic) human operator. Similarly, the technological possibilities of massively distributed collaboration have given rise to resources such as *Wikipedia*, which defies traditional notions of authorship and calls for new strategies of assessing the credibility of shared information. (On the epistemology of *Wikipedia*, see Fallis 2008 and Tollefsen 2009.)

3.4. Attributability

What makes the case of *Wikipedia* interesting is not only its character as a form of collaborative testimony, but its status as an *anonymous source*. Although, in principle, every edit to an entry is logged and users can view the history of each page, in many cases it would be *de facto* impossible for a user to identify the first time a particular claim found its way into a Wikipedia entry. And even if, by luck or through sheer determination, the user could identify the corresponding entry in a page's history, more often than not she would find a pseudonymous user name or, quite possibly, an IP address – neither of which contains much information about the epistemic credentials of the user who edited the page. This contrasts sharply with the more standard case of testimony that is uniquely attributable to its originators.

A related distinction concerns *official* versus *unofficial testimony*. Consider the case of rumours. Rumour may be described as 'the propagation of ostensibly informative hearsay, usually on a topic of broader interest, and typically communicated via informal pathways in the absence of independent corroboration by either first-hand evidence or official (authoritative) sources' (Gelfert 2013a: 771; see also Chapter 10 below). Unlike official testimony, which is typically broadcast by a single authoritative source to a large audience ('the general public'), rumour spreads by word of mouth and through other channels, across informal social networks. Calling official sources 'authoritative' in this context does not imply that they must actually be reliable or engage in truthful communication. Rather, it means simply that these are the sources that have been tasked with, or are generally recognized as performing the social function of, disseminating information to the public. There are of course borderline cases: gossip magazines whose main selling point is their indiscriminate dissemination of rumours about the private lives of celebrities, or officially sanctioned rumour campaigns, for example with the aim of undermining political or military adversaries. Notwithstanding such special cases, it seems fair to say that if the content of a rumour is confirmed as true by relevant official sources, it ceases to be a rumour. (See also Chapter 10, Section 2.) Indeed, as many practitioners of the dubious art of 'reputation management' know only too well, confirming a rumour may be the only effective way of ending its persistence *as rumour*, since official rebuttals of rumours – such as official assurances that 'there is no government conspiracy' – tend to only reinforce their circulation.

3.5. The reference class problem

The above ways of classifying testimony, based on content, kinds of reporters, media, and attributability, are neither unique nor exhaustive. Depending on one's epistemic and pragmatic goals in a given context, other ways of classifying testimony might be deemed more useful. In the legal case, for example, it may be important to know – both for procedural reasons concerning its admissibility as evidence, and for epistemic reasons relating to its reliability – whether a given piece of testimony was given voluntarily or was obtained through coercion. Similarly, it may be useful to distinguish between intentional and unintentional testimony. Someone, perhaps under the influence of alcohol, blurts out a secret they had promised to keep – surely in such a case the lack of intention does not prevent the utterance from qualifying as an instance of testimony. Similarly,

> [POSTHUMOUS DIARY.] consider a case in which you learn from Sylvia Plath's posthumously published diary that she was deeply depressed, and then someone asks you what the epistemic source of knowledge is. Isn't the natural answer to this question testimony? (Lackey 2008: 18)

The power of testimony – that it can, in principle, make available to others any propositional content – also carries with it the risk of someone's inadvertently passing on information that they originally intended to keep secret or had wanted to share with only a select few.

Whatever one's preferred way of dividing up testimony into distinct kinds and reference classes, there does not appear to be a fact of the matter as to how a particular case of testimony should be classified. Testimony does not come neatly packaged into disjunctive reference classes. Coady (1992: 84) nicely illustrates this point with the example of the statement 'There is a sick lion in Taronga Park Zoo': Is it to be classified as a 'medical report or geographical report or empirical report or existence report'? These are just some of the possible classes that this particular statement could be filed under, based on its content. And what about classifying the report based on its source and medium? If I see a sign outside the enclosure at Taronga

Park Zoo, informing visitors that the lion is sick, should I group this piece of information under 'institutional testimony', 'testimony from signs', or 'testimony from zoos all around the world'? Statisticians are familiar with this indeterminacy of relevant reference classes; the 'reference class problem', as it is known in statistics, consists in the challenge of finding principled reasons for preferring one way of classifying a given case over another when making predictions or statistical generalizations. One standard recommendation is to consider the narrowest (i.e. most specific) reference class for which reliable statistical data is available. But any actual case of testimony by necessity falls into several reference classes – according to content, kind of reporter, context, format, etc. – and any decision to classify a given report one way rather than another involves an element of arbitrariness.

As we shall see in Chapter 5, the reference class problem poses a challenge to global reductionist accounts of testimony, which attempt to reduce testimonial justification to statistical claims about the relative reliability of different kinds of testimony. The problem is most acute when dealing with descriptions of cases that have been stripped of all contextual and background information. Yet it is worth keeping in mind that such cases are, in fact, relatively rare. Most testimony is received not in a context-free way, but through the combination of habitual patterns of behaviour (e.g. reading the newspaper over breakfast), trusting relationships with others (e.g. friends, family, colleagues, etc.) and active inquiry. A working knowledge of one's social environment, and of the pathways by which we receive the testimony of others, will therefore have an important role to play in deciding whether to accept or reject a given claim.

4. Broad and narrow definitions of testimony

Having presented a number of examples of testimony and having noted some of the peculiarities that afflict different kinds of testimony, let us now look at how philosophers have tried to give some unity to this diversity. In particular, we will be looking at broad and narrow definitions of testimony, and their respective shortcomings, before exploring alternative (intermediate) views in the next section.

Recall our earlier definition of 'testimony-based belief' as referring to any belief that one 'reasonably and directly forms in response to what one reasonably takes to be testimony and which is essentially caused and sustained by testimony' (Pritchard 2004: 326). This immediately raises the further question: What is testimony? Many philosophers, intending to capture the diversity of testimony, have given very inclusive definitions.

Thus, Elizabeth Fricker holds that testimony consists of 'tellings generally', with 'no restrictions either on subject matter, or on the speaker's epistemic relation to it' (Fricker 1995: 396–7). John Mackie speaks of testimony as simply a way of acquiring knowledge 'by being told by other people, by reading, and so on' (Mackie 1969: 254); in a similar vein, Catherine Elgin characterizes the domain of testimony as consisting of 'utterances and inscriptions that purport to convey information and transmit warrant for the information they convey' (Elgin 2002: 292). Ernest Sosa nicely sums up the spirit of this inclusive way of thinking about testimony, when he endorses 'a broad sense of testimony that counts posthumous publications as examples', requiring only 'that it be a statement of someone's thoughts or beliefs, which they might direct to the world at large and to no one in particular' (Sosa 1991: 219).

Following a suggestion by Jennifer Lackey, let us call this inclusive view of characterizing testimony the *Broad View of the Nature of Testimony*, or simply 'the broad view'. One might then propose the following definition of when a speaker *S* may properly be said to be giving testimony:

[THE BROAD VIEW.] *S* testifies that *p* if and only if *S*'s statement that *p* is an expression of *S*'s thought that *p*. (Lackey 2008: 20)

At first sight, this definition would appear to have a lot going for it; it certainly encompasses many of the cases discussed in the earlier part of this chapter. In particular, it is able to account for cases such as that of the posthumous diary. When Sylvia Plath wrote, in 1952, that 'I feel behind my eyes a numb, paralysed cavern, a pit of hell, a mimicking nothingness' (Plath 2000: 149), she is clearly expressing vivid thoughts, which may be accepted by a contemporary biographer as testimony to her mental condition, even if the words were never intended by Plath to be read by anyone else but herself. Furthermore, the definition allows for the very real possibility of insincere testimony. By only requiring the expression of *thought content*, rather than full-fledged belief on the part of the speaker, the broad view includes in its definition the lying testimony of a witness who is committing perjury in order to save his friend's skin.

Unfortunately, by erring on the side of inclusiveness, the broad view appears to overshoot the mark: it declares too many expressions of thought contents to be instances of testimony – including some that, by the lights of our ordinary understanding of the term, should not be counted as testimony at all. As Bertrand Russell puts it:

[MACBETH.] When you hear an actor on the stage say 'I have supped full with horrors', you do not think he is complaining about rationing, and you know that his statements are not intended to be believed. (Russell 1948: 208)

To be sure, the actor does not in fact express a belief of his – if anyone could be said to hold the belief, it would have to be the fictional character Macbeth! – and he does not intend to convey a belief to the audience. But since the broad view explicitly waives the requirements of belief and intention on the part of the speaker, so as to allow for lying testimony and for the possibility of merely overheard testimony, 'adding on' restrictions for special contexts such as theatrical make-believe would seem *ad hoc* at best and incoherent at worst.

An obvious alternative approach would be to make explicit the specific conditions that an act of communication must satisfy in order to count as testimony proper, in contrast to non-testimonial utterances. By tightening the conditions on what constitutes testimony, one might arrive at the following *Narrow View of the Nature of Testimony*, espoused by Coady:

> [THE NARROW VIEW.] A speaker S testifies by making some statement p if and only if:
>
> **(1)** His stating that p is evidence that p and is offered as evidence that p.
> **(2)** S has the relevant competence, authority, or credentials to state truly that p.
> **(3)** S's statement that p is relevant to some disputed or unresolved question (which may, or may not be, [whether] p?) and is directed to those who are in need of evidence on the matter. (Coady 1992: 42)

Although explicitly put forward as a definition of 'natural testimony', intended to capture 'the conventions governing the speech act of testifying', the narrow view remains indebted to formal conceptions of testimony – not least by assimilating testimony to the (legal) category of 'evidence'. Talk of 'evidence' suggests that an objective relationship of support must exist, or must at least be presumed by the hearer to hold, between the act of stating that p and it actually being the case that p. (One must be careful not to demand too close a connection between the two: clearly, the random act of stating that p need not stand in any objective relationship to anything much in the world, including the fact of whether or not p, and certainly need not objectively make it any likelier that p.)

Upon closer inspection, the narrow view in its above formulation might be deemed to contain some redundancy. Clause (3), in particular, is the conjunction of two conditions, since it demands both relevance to an open question and targeted presentation of the testimony to those 'in need of evidence on the matter'. Both of these conditions, as Coady himself admits (1992: 45), could be seen as implicit in clause (1) – that is, as specifications of what it takes for someone *to offer something as evidence* in the first place. Clause (2), with its requirement of 'competence, authority, or credentials to state truly that *p*', likewise needs some unpacking. The requirement of 'authority', Coady argues, is necessary to rule out cases involving, say, a hypnotized subject who has been programmed to make certain statements – truthfully, and seemingly with full conviction – when prompted to do so. Even if we know about the subject's condition, and know about the veracity of the information, such statements could at best be treated by us as mere evidence, not as testimony, since the subject 'has no authority himself to vouch for *p*' (Coady 1992: 45), having been manipulated by a third party.

While the narrow view of testimony is able to rule out cases such as the hypnotized testifier – who, arguably, functions more like a recording device than a responsible witness – it unfortunately also excludes many cases of perfectly acceptable testimony. Plath's diary, a competent and authoritative record (let us assume) of her thoughts and emotions, was not 'offered as evidence' to anyone (except perhaps to a hypothetical audience – which, however, could hardly be said to 'stand in need of evidence' on the matter of Plath's mental life). By contrast, the case of the lying witness seems to be better handled by the narrow view: even when the witness asserts ~*p* (i.e. the negation of what would actually reflect the facts), such a statement would still count as potential evidence and would certainly be relevant to the determination of the defendant's guilt or innocence – except, in this case, in all the wrong ways. However, further trouble for the narrow view comes from the requirement of competence. Recall that clause (3) states that the speaker must *actually* possess the relevant competence to state truly that *p*; yet, it seems obvious that in many cases of testimony – including some cases of putative expert testimony – the testifier merely arrogates to himself the epistemic authority to speak from knowledge, when in fact he lacks the requisite competence.

5. Speaker and hearer testimony

The broad and narrow views of testimony both have significant shortcomings, and in both cases at least some of the problems appear to be the result of overshooting the mark: the broad view is simply too inclusive, and the narrow view too restrictive. This suggests that a workable definition of testimony – one that is true to our intuitions about what properly constitutes testimonial acts of communication, and is at the same time informative – is to be found somewhere in the middle. There is, of course, no guarantee that any single set of conditions will successfully delineate the category of testimony – our intuitions about what is, and is not, testimony might simply be too volatile, or different people might have divergent views on whether a particular example is, or is not, an instance of testimony, or testimony might turn out not to be a unitary category at all. The remainder of this section discusses two such intermediate views of the nature of testimony: one which attempts to steer a middle path between the broad and narrow views while holding on to the unity of testimony as a category, the other sacrificing the unitary character of testimony in favour of a two-fold notion of *speaker* and *hearer* testimony.

The first approach, which has been dubbed the *Moderate View of Testimony* (Lackey 2006a: 184), is due to Peter Graham (1997). Following the structure of Coady's narrow view, but modifying the three clauses in distinct ways, the moderate view arrives at the following definition:

> [THE MODERATE VIEW.] S testifies by making some statement p if and only if
>
> **(1)** S's stating that p is offered as evidence that p
>
> **(2)** S intends that his audience believe that he has the relevant competence, authority or credentials to state truly that p
>
> **(3)** S's statement that p is believed by S to be relevant to some question that he believes is disputed or unresolved (which may or may not be p) and is directed at those whom he believes to be in need of evidence on the matter. (Graham 1997: 227)

In essence, the moderate view weakens the strict conditions of the narrow view by relativizing them to the speaker's beliefs and intentions: no longer does S's act of stating that p have to stand in an *objective* evidentiary relationship, it only needs to be offered as such; in a similar move, the demand for objective competence, authority or credentials on the part of the speaker has been replaced by S's intention to be perceived as competent, authoritative and credible by his audience. This way, the moderate view avoids the narrow view's problems in accounting for testimony by speakers who lack competence, but not confidence: incompetent testimony by those who pass themselves off as knowledgeable may be lamentable, but it is testimony no less. Unfortunately, by including the speaker's beliefs and intentions in clause (3), the moderate view – like the narrow view – is unable to account for cases of unintentional testimony, such as the case of the posthumous diary which cannot plausibly be said to be directed at those whom the diarist believed to stand in need of evidence on her thoughts and feelings.

The persistence of such problems in attempts to square the 'objective' information-bearing character of testimony with the 'subjective' role of beliefs and intentions on the part of the speaker, has led some philosophers to question whether testimony is a unitary category at all. As Lackey puts it:

> What these problems point to is that there are at least two aspects to our concept of testimony. On the one hand, we often think of testimony as a source of belief or knowledge for hearers, regardless of the speaker's intention to be such a source. On the other hand, we often think of testimony as involving the intention to communicate information to other people, regardless of the needs or interests of the hearers. (Lackey 2006a: 181; 2008: 19)

On this interpretation, it would be misguided to expect every act of testimony to involve *both* an intention on the part of the speaker to communicate a specific belief to his audience *and* a desire on the part of the audience to learn from the speaker, yet this expectation is what guides the narrow view (and, to a lesser extent, the moderate view as well). Instead, we should distinguish between *speaker testimony* (*s*-testimony) and *hearer testimony* (*h*-testimony):

> [SPEAKER TESTIMONY.] *S* gives *speaker testimony* that *p* if and only if, by performing an act of communication *a*, *S* reasonably intends to convey the information that *p* (in part) in virtue of *a*'s communicable content.
>
> [HEARER TESTIMONY.] *S* gives *hearer testimony* that *p* if and only if, by performing an act of communication *a*, *S*'s audience reasonably takes *a* as conveying the information that *p* (in part) in virtue of *a*'s communicable content. (Modified after Lackey 2008: 30/32)

Note that in both cases we are dealing with testimony given by the same speaker *S*, who is performing one and the same act of communication *a* (e.g. uttering a sentence, penning a diary entry, etc.). The difference lies in the divergent perspectives of the speaker and hearer, specifically between the speaker's intention to communicate and the audience's interpreting an act of communication as conveying content. Thus, the diarist who keeps his writings under lock and key and has no intention of conveying the information to another person, while not giving *s*-testimony, may nonetheless be said to be giving *h*-testimony, if an (illicit or posthumous) reader reasonably takes the diarist's writings as conveying information in virtue of their communicable content.

Since nothing seems to be able to prevent the speaker's intention and the hearer's interpretation of an act of communication from coming apart in this way, one way to acknowledge this duality of perspectives is to opt for the following *Disjunctive View of the Nature of Testimony*, espoused by Lackey:

> [THE DISJUNCTIVE VIEW.] *S* testifies that *p* by making an act of communication *a* if and only if (in part) in virtue of *a*'s communicable content, (1) *S* reasonably intends to convey the information that *p* or (2) *a* is reasonably taken as conveying the information that *p*. (Lackey 2008: 35–6)

The disjunction 'or' linking parts (1) and (2) should, of course, not be understood in the exclusive sense ('either . . . or'); after all, in those cases where a speaker *S* intends to convey a belief, or piece of information, to the hearer, who in turn takes the speaker's act of communication as conveying the belief or information in question, it will be natural to consider the act of communication a success: the speaker's testimony was received in the spirit in which it was intended.

Study questions

1 From an epistemic point of view, is the exclusion of hearsay from legal proceedings justified? What might be some of the (epistemic) reasons for enforcing such a restriction?

2 In Locke's example (discussed in Section 3.1), was the King of Siam justified in rejecting the Dutch ambassador's testimony? Under what circumstances should we accept (or reject) surprising claims?

3 What are some of the arguments for or against the possibility of testimony-based mathematical knowledge?

4 Does Lackey's distinction between speaker and hearer testimony (Section 5) adequately capture our testimonial practices?

5 Can there be non-verbal testimony?

Further reading

Coady (1992), esp. chapter 2, remains a good starting point for any qualitative characterization of the various kinds of testimony we encounter in different (formal and informal) contexts. In addition to the definitional issues discussed in this chapter, a parallel debate has arisen concerning the status of testimony and knowledge as natural or social kinds. Kusch (2002a) sketches a communitarian theory that views testimony primarily as a vehicle for assigning to others the social status of 'being a knower'; by contrast, Michaelian (2008) argues that testimony is likely a natural kind and that, for this very reason, it is likely necessarily reliable. Frisch (2004) reflects on the ethical dimension of testimony, understood in the sense of *bearing witness*, and brings into dialogue themes from literary and intellectual history, analytic philosophy and Continental philosophy. A useful comparison of the different conceptions of testimony and ideals of knowledge in Western and Indian epistemology can be found in Matilal's and Chakrabarti's editorial introduction to their 1994 collection of papers.

2

The testimonial conundrum

As the discussion in the previous chapter has shown, testimony is a multifaceted phenomenon which manifests itself differently in different contexts. In future chapters, we will frequently refer back to some of the examples and classifications developed in Chapter 1. While it is useful, for descriptive purposes, to have stylized cases and partial taxonomies at hand, it is equally important to develop a qualitative understanding of what holds our various testimonial practices together. Why is testimony so important to us, and what is its place in our epistemic lives? The present chapter approaches this question both from the perspective of the individual hearer – who, in his capacity as the recipient of testimony, is faced with the choice of accepting or rejecting a given testimonial claim – and through a more abstract characterization of testimony as a mechanism of expanding one's belief system. In the final section, we will review the arguments of a number of thinkers who have suggested that, beyond its immediate function of making knowledge available to the hearer, testimony is intimately tied to the very idea of human sociality itself.

1. Ordinary giving and receiving of knowledge

Turning to others for knowledge is as basic an experience for human knowers as responding to other people's questions by proffering relevant information that one takes to be knowledge. You ask me the time – I look at my watch and unhesitatingly pass on what the hands on my watch indicate. Your friend is momentarily unsure about the year the Berlin wall fell ('Was it 1989 or 1990?') – you tell him the date was 9 November 1989. In both cases the inquiring party acquires knowledge by being told. The fact that such testimonial exchanges strike us as trivial – too trivial, perhaps, to warrant the designation 'testimony' – only goes to show just how basic an ingredient in everyday life the ordinary giving and receiving of knowledge is. As Trudy Govier puts it: 'Our way of life includes the social practices of asking and telling', and in particular the 'social practices of *asking questions* and *telling people answers*' (Govier 1993a: 20). Importantly, what Govier calls 'mundane asking and telling' need not be restricted to the category of *mundane testimony* as defined in Chapter 1, that is, to knowledge of the kind that we can expect any functioning interlocutor to be competent and sincere about. Specialist knowledge, too, more often than not is simply there for the asking.

Michael Welbourne, in a series of papers, has argued that underlying our mundane practices of asking and telling is an essential feature of knowledge, which sets it apart from individual belief. This feature is its essential *commonability*: the fact that it can be collectively shared. As Welbourne puts it: 'Knowledge is not, as a belief necessarily is, the unique possession of an individual; rather it is a thing which may be available to anybody' (1986: 6). If we were to think of the communication of knowledge merely in terms of the duplication of the speaker's belief in the mind of the hearer, we would be missing an important difference between the two:

> If you and I both believe that *p*, then there are two beliefs, yours and mine. But if we both know that *p* there aren't two 'knowledges' or two bits of knowledge, yours and mine. There is one bit of knowledge which we both have. (Welbourne 1986: 6)

To be sure, belief and knowledge are typically closely correlated. But against the majority view in epistemology, according to which belief that *p* is a necessary condition of knowing that *p*, Welbourne insists that the two can come apart. For linguistic support, Welbourne turns to a grammatical difference between the verbs *to believe* and *to know*. Whereas *believe* is always followed by a *that*-clause which expresses a propositional content (except when we say of a person that we believe *her* or *in her*), *know* can also be correctly accompanied by interrogative *wh*-clauses (which are introduced by a question word, such as *who*, *what*, *which*, *where*, etc.). Thus, while it would be grammatically correct to say that 'I know where the red fern grows', the corresponding construction with *believe* ('I believe where the red fern grows') would be ungrammatical. 'The upshot of all this', writes Welbourne, 'is that the verb *know*, but not the verb *believe*, has the characteristics which the idea of inquiry requires of any word which is to be capable of expressing the goals and achievements of inquiry' (1986: 11). Unlike 'belief', which refers to an individual's mental state, the word 'knowledge', according to Welbourne, has an essentially social meaning: when we credit someone with knowledge, we do not merely attribute a mental state to them, but instead indicate their membership in a community that partakes in '*what is known*', that is 'knowledge which, once articulated, is available to anybody' (1986: 53).

One need not follow Welbourne's communitarian conception of knowledge to agree with his analysis that, when we rely on other people's testimony, we typically do so on the assumption that they 'speak from knowledge' – however one wishes to define 'knowledge' in this context. And without the tacit assumption that knowledge can be shared, we would hardly have reason to accept at face value what other people tell us – what would we stand to gain? – nor would we expect to find entrenched social practices of asking and telling. Yet, as things stand, the mutual giving and receiving of knowledge is an important ingredient in our epistemic lives – so much so that we often regard others as reliable sources of knowledge, through whom we can come to know things, as if by proxy. (For an exploration of how testimony compares to the 'standard' sources of knowledge in philosophy – perception, memory, reason and inference – see Chapter 3.) This becomes evident in those cases where we do not simply accept what we are told, but instead seek clarification about the source of our interlocutor's claim:

> 'How do you know that *p*?' 'Joe told me so.' This is a very natural answer. It seems to be the case, therefore, that quite often the causal link connecting the fact and the knowing subject consists, in part at least, in the relation of *X*'s telling *Y* that *p*. (Vendler 1980: 283)

Often enough, stating the source of what one believes to be knowledge – 'Joe told me so' – is also meant to address the interlocutor's implicit request for additional justification. After all, when we ask 'how do you know that *p*?', we typically do not wish to merely satisfy our curiosity as to the *causal origins* of our interlocutor's knowledge, but instead wish to find out whether our interlocutor's *epistemic grounds* are indeed sufficient for knowledge. If our interlocutor responds 'Joe told me so', but we independently know Joe to be unreliable on the matter in question, we will typically not credit our interlocutor with knowledge. However, in the absence of such reasons for doubt, unless the claim in question calls for unusually high epistemic standards, stating the source will often suffice as an adequate answer to the question of 'how do you know?' – even when the question is understood in the sense of 'how can you be sure?'

Two caveats need to be added to this general account of mundane asking and telling as the paradigmatic ways of sharing knowledge. First, it is important to note that, like all social practices, the epistemic practices involved in the sharing of knowledge are bound to be culturally modulated: 'We cannot presume that mundane asking and answering as they are understood in *Western* cultures exist in *all* cultures' (Govier 1993a: 21). What might look like a legitimate direct question in one culture, in another culture might be considered rude or inappropriate, depending on the context and content of the question. Many cultures value indirectness and exhibit a preference for inferring information 'from context or behavior rather than asking directly' (ibid.). In some cultures, it is not unusual for an informant to feel obliged to give information – sometimes, if he lacks the requisite knowledge, by fabricating it – lest he 'lose face' by being perceived as unhelpful or non-knowledgeable. (The latter is a frequent complaint from travellers asking for directions in Asian countries, but it applies equally to, say, Western cable news pundits.) Thus, direct asking and telling are ideal types, and each culture and society will develop its own (range of) social practices for the giving and receiving of knowledge, and for its dissemination across relevant communities. Second, it is worth flagging that, even when we do not actively seek out informants and ask them directly about matters of concern to us, we nonetheless remain epistemically dependent on our social environment in various indirect ways. For example, we often trust that, if radical changes were to occur, we would hear about it – through the media, from friends and acquaintances, or via other, presently unidentified sources in our environment – so that we can take the absence of such testimony as constituting support for our belief that things are as we remember them to be. For, 'if it were no longer so, I would have heard about it' (McDowell 1994: 201). Sometimes, epistemically speaking, testimony is silver, but silence is golden.

2. Our epistemic predicament

On the standard view in epistemology, knowledge is a species of justified true belief – even if it turns out to be exceedingly difficult to specify the conditions for when a justified true belief should count as knowledge. While this view has not been without its fair share of critics – recall Welbourne's alternative proposal, discussed in the previous section – it continues to inform many issues in epistemology. Indeed, it is hardly an exaggeration to say that, in essence, most problems in epistemology concern the question of how we should regulate and revise our beliefs.

Why should an epistemic agent revise her beliefs? The short answer is: to eliminate a falsehood, or to add a new true belief. If we think of the agent's beliefs as forming a 'corpus' – that is, an integrated whole – then this system of beliefs 'is modified by expansion as well as by contraction and replacement' (Levi 1983: 34). Beliefs that have been found to be wanting – either because they turned out to be false, or because their justification has been undermined – are constantly being dropped from the corpus, and new beliefs may come to replace or supplant them. Dropping false or contradictory beliefs from one's corpus may seem straightforward: a slight contraction of one's system of beliefs is a small price to pay if what remains is a set of consistent and justified beliefs. But why should an agent expand her corpus, given that the addition of a new belief always carries with it the risk of adding a falsehood or importing inconsistency into her belief system? The answer is as simple as it is obvious: to obtain new error-free information. The fact remains, however, that belief expansion is an epistemically 'risky' move, and for the risk to be worth it, the promise of obtaining new knowledge, from the agent's point of view, must outweigh the danger of acquiring a falsehood.

Human beings, of course, cannot afford to simply refuse belief expansion in the interest of error avoidance. Practical goals and interests quickly force us to adopt new (fallible) beliefs, if only so we can respond to our environment in a way that ensures our survival. When it comes to perceptual beliefs, we seem to be hard-wired to accept (most of) them as true: we cannot, as a general rule, *not* believe our own eyes. Finally, most human beings exhibit some degree of curiosity: quite apart from specific practical interests, we enjoy acquiring beliefs about the world and strive to keep abreast with developments in various areas of life that we take an interest in. We are thus constantly faced with the challenge of having to balance our interest in the acquisition of relevant new beliefs against the need to filter out false or misleading information and to monitor our corpus of beliefs for inconsistencies and unresolved tensions. The need to strike the right balance between striving for new knowledge, while at the same time avoiding error, is at the heart of our epistemic predicament.

Epistemic agents aim to meet this challenge by implementing two strategies of belief expansion which, following Isaac Levi, may be called 'inferential' or 'routine' expansion. In inferential belief expansion, an agent will actively weigh the evidence, consider different alternative interpretations and deliberate on the degree of confidence he should attach to the belief in question. In this sense, inferential expansion may be thought of as 'a species of deliberate decision-making' (Levi 1983: 38). Whereas, in practical matters, deliberate decision-making involves different courses of action, in inferential belief expansion the options are 'potential expansion strategies which qualify as potential answers to the question under investigation, and the aim is to gratify the demand for information occasioned by the question while at the same time avoiding error' (ibid.). Inferential expansion, thus, is cognitively demanding and requires active effort. By contrast, in routine expansion, the agent has already decided, prior to inquiry, to accept the outcome of the chosen routine without further investigation. (If special circumstances arise that call for additional investigation, the belief expansion would cease to be a routine matter.) As Levi puts it, in routine expansion, the agent 'has been conditioned or committed to a program' of adopting certain kinds of new beliefs, depending on past instances of the routine, 'but not depending on his finding out what that outcome is and combining it with the rest of his knowledge to decide upon an optimum expansion strategy' (ibid.: 39).

An interesting situation arises when the belief to be 'imported' into the agent's corpus, contradicts other beliefs which the agent already holds. In such a case, after belief expansion, the agent could no longer consider all of his beliefs to be true. From an inferential perspective, this should count strongly against adopting the new belief in question. As Levi puts it, although 'the informational benefits promised will sometimes warrant risking error, no such benefits should warrant risking certain error' – hence, the agent 'should not deliberately expand into contradiction' (ibid.: 40). Things are different for routine belief expansion. In this case, belief expansion is no longer a matter of weighing the pros and cons of accepting the particular belief into the corpus; instead, the agent has elected beforehand to accept the outcome of the chosen routine. This is simply what committing to a routine means. Few agents are so naïve as to think that their routines are infallible, and following a routine may well, on occasion, lead into contradiction. But, as Levi notes, in such a case the contradiction is due to the agent's following a routine 'which he assumes is highly albeit not perfectly reliable: He has accepted a risk of error for the sake of new information and lost' (ibid.). Unlike inferential expansion (provided it is implemented correctly!), 'routine expansion is capable of injecting contradiction into a corpus even when implemented in a way which respects the desideratum of avoiding error' (ibid.: 41). After all, there are only so many possibilities of error that can be foreseen (and prevented) at the point of committing to a routine. Fallibility, then – that is, the genuine possibility that most of our beliefs may be wrong (though, perhaps, not all at the same time) – is an ineliminable part of our epistemic predicament.

Interestingly, Levi explicitly includes 'appeal to the testimony of competent witnesses or experts' among the routine sources of belief. Testimonial beliefs, like first-hand observations, 'gain entry [into an agent's corpus] through the implementation of a routine' (ibid.: 40/41). The importance of such routines should not be underestimated:

> Neither the testimony of the senses nor of other witnesses added via an expansion routine are, once admitted to *X*'s corpus, distinguishable from theories, laws, statistical assumptions, predictions, or other singular hypotheses with respect to certainty or [subjective] infallibility. (Levi 1983: 41)

The idea that much of our knowledge is due to routine reliance on testimony – in other words, that it is the result of a prior commitment to accept what an informant would tell us – has sometimes been glossed in terms of a generalized trust in our epistemic environment. Thus, Govier argues that 'we are committed by our own judgments, by consistency, and by social practice to the epistemic reliability (in favorable contexts) of other people', and she immediately adds: 'Other things being equal, we are committed to trusting other people for the truth' (Govier 1993a: 22). Trust in the testimony of others may sometimes turn out to be misplaced, but such disappointment is not specific to testimony: all of our sources of belief can let us down. As Levi puts it: 'It is a defect of all modes of routine expansion that they can breed error and, indeed, lead to the contradiction of our most cherished theories' (Levi 1983: 41). Such is our epistemic predicament, and the only appropriate response to it, it would seem, is to look for ways to manage the risk of error, in a way that does not deprive ourselves of the possibility of acquiring new and diverse knowledge.

Is justified true belief knowledge?

An important project within epistemology has been the search for necessary and sufficient conditions of knowledge, with the goal of providing an analysis of the concept of knowledge. An influential and, in many ways, natural thought has been that knowledge is (a species of) justified true belief. The *tripartite definition of knowledge* (sometimes called jtb analysis of knowledge) holds that an epistemic subject S knows that p if and only if:

(1) p is true,
(2) S believes that p, and
(3) S is justified in believing that p.

In an influential paper published more than 50 years ago, Edmund Gettier (1963) showed that these three conditions are not jointly sufficient for knowledge: an epistemic subject may satisfy all three conditions, and yet fail to know that p. For example, I may look at my watch in the morning and form the true belief that it is 9:30 since this is what the hands seem to indicate. Given that I have successfully relied on my watch on many past occasions and have found it to be an excellent source of information about what time it is, my belief is justified. However, unbeknownst to me, as the result of a rare mechanical failure, my watch in fact stopped at 9:30 p.m. the night before and only accidentally displays the correct time. Although my belief is true and justified, it does not constitute knowledge.

Such *Gettier cases* led to the search for what has been called the 'missing fourth condition': a condition that, if added to the tripartite account, would prevent beliefs from being 'Gettiered'. The collective failure to identify such a condition has led to a growing sense of dissatisfaction with the project of conceptual analysis as applied to the concept of knowledge. This has given rise to a number of alternative approaches, some of which are discussed in Chapter 11.

Further reading: Gutting (2009), chapter 3, gives an excellent historical overview of the research programme prompted by Gettier's paper. For a thorough survey of attempted solutions (and dissolutions) of the Gettier problem, see also Hetherington (2005).

3. Trusted acceptance and rational rejection

Epistemology, in essence, studies how we can hope to come to terms with our epistemic predicament and how we should respond to its twin demands of acquiring new knowledge while avoiding error. The general question of how we can successfully expand our corpus of beliefs, without corrupting it by including too many falsehoods among the things we take ourselves to know, becomes especially pertinent in the case of testimony. As we have seen in Chapter 1, testimony covers a vast array of situations and contexts, as well as a range of different subject matters and contents. We often feel, quite rightly, that we are not in a position to check for ourselves whether what we have been told is true or not. Indeed, attempting to verify (or falsify) every single bit of testimony would quickly undermine the very utility of testimony as a shortcut to knowledge: By the time we have ascertained the veracity of a new piece of information first-hand, we no longer need to take anyone's word for it. We rely on testimony not merely out of necessity – as in the case of historical facts, which cannot be ascertained first-hand – but also because it is often more convenient to ask someone knowledgeable than to investigate matters on one's own. First-hand investigation takes time and effort, whereas reliance on the testimony of others frees up individual cognitive resources that may be put to better use elsewhere. Yet, for such reliance on others to be epistemically commendable, it too must strike the right balance between belief expansion and error avoidance.

Belief expansion (i.e. adding to one's belief system a claim thought to be true) and contraction (e.g. by eliminating a belief now thought to be false) have direct analogues at the level of testimonial encounters, in the form of the *acceptance* or *rejection*, respectively, of a piece of testimony. The connection is obvious, insofar as acceptance of a true testimony gives rise to a true belief, whereas rejection of a false testimony amounts to the avoidance of an erroneous belief. As we shall see in Chapter 8 (Section 2), the extent to which we need to consciously *decide* to accept or reject a given testimony is a matter of philosophical controversy. At a descriptive level, however, it seems fair to say that, whereas in many cases acceptance or rejection comes naturally, in some cases we may also remain indifferent towards someone's testimony or may (decide to) withhold judgement. Acceptance and rejection, unfortunately, are only imperfectly correlated with the truth or falsity of the testimonial claim in question – if we were perfect 'truth-detectors', there would be no epistemological problem of testimony in the first place. Instead, we are well aware that we sometimes erroneously reject perfectly valid testimony, whereas on other occasions we take on trust testimony which – intentionally or not – is false. The general question arising from our epistemic predicament – which balance to strike between belief expansion and error avoidance – in the case of testimony becomes the challenge of striking the right balance between testimonial acceptance and rejection. Knowing when, and whom, to trust for knowledge thus are questions that lie at the heart of the epistemology of testimony.

In the case of testimony, belief expansion typically occurs via *trusted acceptance* of what a source tells us, whereas avoidance of error is achieved through the *rejection* of a particular claim. (We do, of course, also try to avoid acquiring erroneous beliefs by simply staying away from sources that are unreliable, in which case the question of whether to accept or reject testimony may simply not arise in the first place.) Both epistemic 'moves' – accepting what another tells us, or rejecting an interlocutor's claim – are clearly appropriate in some situations and inappropriate in others. We should not accept just anything we are told, but neither should we deprive ourselves of opportunities to acquire knowledge by opting for a wholesale rejection of testimony. The problem of whether to accept or reject a given piece of testimony presents itself anew in every single case, and the demand that each case be settled on rational grounds can easily give rise to a host of competing considerations. Perhaps this is why some commentators have felt a sense of puzzlement at how we should respond to testimony. Thus, Fricker writes:

> I find my own intuitions about testimony wildly volatile: consider some cases, and it seems obvious that we must have a default position of trust in what others tell us [. . .] but consider others, and it seems equally obvious that our attitude to others must be critical and skeptical, that we must and do weigh the balance of probabilities against what they say being true, on the one hand, and against their being mistaken or insincere on the other. (Fricker 1995: 406)

Questions of epistemic justification often take the form of asking what grounds we have for holding a particular belief – or, in the case of testimony, why we accepted someone's testimony. But rejection, too, needs to be rationally grounded, lest we descend into a stance of full-on scepticism about the word of others. If belief expansion of the kind that is necessary to secure our knowledge is to be possible, we cannot simply reject without good reason everything we are told. The realization that trusted acceptance and rational rejection are flip sides of our epistemic predicament, as applied to the special case of testimony, has long been captured by recommendations such as H. H. Price's injunction to 'believe what you are told by others unless or until you have reasons for doubting it' (1969: 124).

The stance of simple, trusted acceptance is nicely illustrated by Coady's example of checking one's phone bill (see Chapter 1, Section 3.1). I ring up the company's service number on being unable to locate my invoice, and an anonymous voice tells me the amount and when it is due. I simply accept this information, trusting that this is a valid way of ascertaining how much I need to pay: 'No thought of determining the veracity and reliability of the witness occurs to me [. . .] given that the total is within tolerable limits' (Coady 1992: 143). But how simple is such 'simple' acceptance of testimony really? Arguably, I would not accept just any amount the anonymous voice tells me. If I was told that I owe $349,243.25 by next Friday, I would presumably suspend belief – or suspect that something has gone seriously wrong. (Incidentally, this is the sum a customer in Singapore was initially charged in 2011 for one month's worth of international data roaming, as reported in *The New Paper*, 21 December 2011.) The key phrase in Coady's description of this case is, of course, the caveat that the total be 'within tolerable limits'. Some commentators, notably Fricker, have taken this to indicate that testimonial acceptance is never 'simple', but instead is always subject to our having actively assessed the content of a message for plausibility and is conditional on our continuously 'monitoring' our informant for signs of insincerity or incompetence. (See also Chapter 5, Section 4.) Yet it seems incontrovertible that much of what we take ourselves to know is based on simple, trusted acceptance of what others tell us. Pronouncing all such instances of simple acceptance to be the result of mere 'gullibility' would hardly do justice to the richness of our testimonial practices – not least in light of the fact that modern societies are heavily invested in creating contexts that enable simple, trusted acceptance, for example by setting up schools and other institutions of learning.

Cases of rationally grounded rejection of someone's testimony, like instances of simple acceptance, are a dime a dozen. Sometimes we reject another person's testimony because we know better: we may have better evidence to the contrary, our interlocutor's claim may flatly contradict what we take ourselves to know more firmly, or we may know our interlocutor to be in error on independent grounds. On other occasions, it is not the claim itself, but the circumstances of its production, which lead us to reject a given testimony:

> A man rang my doorbell and claimed that my rain gutters are loose. Should I believe him? They look fine to me, I know that he hasn't been up on the roof to inspect them properly, and I am further discouraged by the fact that he wants me to pay him today to fix them tomorrow. So I infer that the reason why he said what he did is not because he knows that my gutters do need work (though perhaps they do), but because he is hoping to make a fast buck. (Lipton 2007: 244)

In the latter case, what prompts us to reject our interlocutor's testimony is not any intrinsic implausibility of his claim – after all, the gutters *may* stand in need of repair – nor any direct evidence to the contrary, but a mix of contextual factors and background knowledge. It is the combination of the latter which leads us to conclude that the utterance itself – that is, the interlocutor's act of testifying – is best explained by his desire to make a fast buck, and that he has fabricated a story without any basis in fact. Clearly, in situations where we know our informant to be in error or have reason to distrust the speaker, or in which the utterance is best explained by the likely falsity of the claim in question, it will often not only be natural, but also rationally justified to reject the testimony we receive.

Trusted acceptance and rational rejection are flip sides of our epistemic predicament with respect to testimony. This suggests that, for a theoretical position in the epistemology of testimony to be viable, it should be able to account for both types of responses and, ideally, should offer insight into how to deal with intermediate cases. One can make this point more precise by rephrasing it in terms of desiderata. The first desideratum of any epistemological theory about testimony is that it should allow for the possibility of accepting a statement on trust alone and thereby acquiring knowledge. As John McDowell puts it, at 'the core of a good general account of testimony' should be the intuition that, 'if a knowledgeable speaker gives intelligible expression to his knowledge, it may become available at second hand to those who understand what he says' (McDowell 1994: 198). The precise role of 'trust' in the acceptance of another's intelligible testimony of course needs to be discussed (see Chapter 8); all that is being presupposed in calling 'trusted acceptance' a desideratum is that it must be possible, on occasion, to acquire knowledge from testimony without gathering evidence in support of either the claim itself or the general reliability of its source. The second desideratum which any theoretical account of testimony should allow for, in addition to the possibility of trusted acceptance, is the possibility of rational rejection: it must, at least sometimes, be rational to reject what others tell us. A theory of testimony that compelled us to believe whatever we are told would not only do violence to our actual testimonial practices and to values such as intellectual autonomy, but would also lead to irresolvable theoretical problems (e.g. in the case of conflicting testimonies from different parties).

Calling testimonial acceptance and rejection 'theoretical desiderata' amounts to the demand that any viable theoretical account of testimony should admit of the twin possibilities of acceptance on trust, and of rational rejection of testimony. Exactly how trusted acceptance and rational rejection ought to be balanced against each other – either in general or in a particular instance – is a question that each account needs to address on its own terms. It is here that the volatility of philosophical intuitions becomes most evident and the philosophical problem of testimony takes on the character of a conundrum. This sense of theoretical bewilderment is nicely illustrated by a passage in Russell's 1948 book *Human Knowledge*, in which Russell – within a few short pages – moves from a statement of the commonsense maxim 'to accept testimony unless there is a positive reason against doing so in the particular case concerned' (206) to the claim that 'we cannot accept testimony at its face value', and finally to the head-scratching question: 'why should we accept it all?' (208).

4. The conundrum of testimonial dependence

Russell's question – 'Why accept testimony at all?' – has a simple, if somewhat flippant, answer: because we cannot *not* rely on the testimony of others. Our dependence on others for knowledge is so pervasive that, if we are to lead rich epistemic lives, we cannot do without testimony as a source of knowledge. The examples discussed in the previous chapter convey a sense of the diverse range of contents and beliefs that are made available to us by the word of others, all of which would be out of reach if we were to selectively excise testimony from our methods of belief formation. We are, therefore, well advised to accept that testimony is at least sometimes a valid source of knowledge – even if, as discussed in the previous two sections, adding testimonial beliefs to our corpus necessarily carries with it some risk of error. Yet, as Bob Plant notes: 'These risks are, however, constitutive of the possibility of testimony, rather than mere lamentable failings of its actual operation' (Plant 2007: 46).

We would stand to lose much more than just knowledge, if we were forced to give up on the exchange of testimony. Beyond its epistemic function of making knowledge available to the recipient, testimony is intimately tied to human sociality – as is already evident from the discussion, in Section 1, of our social practices of 'mundane asking and telling'. The connection between human sociality and testimonial dependence is nicely brought out in these lines from Kant's lectures on logic:

> We do not only have a propensity to participate [in society] but also to communicate. Man only learns something so as to be able to communicate it to others. . . . The inclination towards sociality and communicating his judgments to others is so natural to man that he cannot move himself to giving up on it without gradually growing grumpy and depressed. (Quoted after Gelfert 2006: 648)

There are at least two aspects to this. First, much of the communication we engage in with others does not primarily aim at imparting knowledge – even if overtly informative speech acts are typically governed by norms of truthfulness, sincerity and accuracy – but instead seeks to strengthen social ties. Even when we volunteer testimony, we often do so not because we recognize the urgency of the informational need on the part of our interlocutor, but because we wish to be recognized as knowledgeable and helpful. There need not be anything disingenuous about behaving in this way, and if, in the process of engaging in such behaviour, knowledge is being transmitted, then it is not only epistemically unproblematic, but beneficial. The wish to be believed as a person – as opposed to being relied upon, in purely instrumental fashion, as a mere source of information – has deep roots in our psychology as social beings. As Stanley Cavell puts it: 'I do not always feel that speaking to someone is making myself handy for them, or always done because something handier is lacking' (1979: 392). The fact that the speaker is personally invested in her testimony is also recognized by the recipient, which is why 'if I accept what you say, on the basis of your saying it, [. . .] I respond by saying "I believe you", not "I believe what you say"' (Cavell 1979: 391).

Second, we often participate in testimonial exchanges in order to put our own judgements to the test – if not explicitly, then at least in indirect ways. Again, Kant puts this point succinctly: 'Man always wishes to test his judgment to others; other people's judgments are to be regarded as *contrôleurs* of our own judgment' (quoted after Gelfert 2006: 644). Modern commentators echo this point, arguing that even perceptual and memorial beliefs need to be put to the test in this way. Thus, Sydney Shoemaker (1963) writes:

> Unless I were willing in some circumstances to accept the utterances of other people as memory claims, and as evidence concerning what has

happened in the past (among other things, what has happened to me in the past), and were willing to do this without first having conducted an empirical investigation to determine whether I am entitled to do it, I would in effect be admitting no distinction between the way things are and the way they seem to me to be [. . .]. (Shoemaker 1963: 254)

In a similar vein, James Ross notes that, not only has much of what we take ourselves to know 'come to be believed simply because we have trusted various reporters', but 'our perceptual observations are themselves conditioned by and dependent upon the authority we accord to the opinions of others' (Ross 1975: 36).

It is part of the philosophical conundrum of testimonial dependence that, by the time we are in a position to ask epistemological questions, we have already been thoroughly infused with the knowledge, beliefs and information gained from the testimony of others. In *On Certainty* (= *OC*), Ludwig Wittgenstein (1969) implicitly notes this when he writes: 'I learned an enormous amount and accepted it on human authority, and then I found some things confirmed or disconfirmed by my own experience' (*OC*, 161). When we call into question specific beliefs – or belief-forming practices – we always do so against the backdrop of an already established 'world-picture':

> But I did not get my picture of the world by satisfying myself of its correctness; nor do I have it because I am satisfied of its correctness. No: it is the inherited background against which I distinguish between true and false. (*OC*, 94)

Among those propositions that are integral to my world-picture, however, are many – for example, the claim that 'the Earth is round' – that I could not have acquired were it not for the testimony of others. This renders many of my judgements at least partly dependent on testimony as a source of knowledge:

> In general I take as true what is found in text-books, of geography for example. Why? I say: All these facts have been confirmed a hundred times over. But how do I know that? What is my evidence for it? I have a world-picture. Is it true or false? Above all it is the substratum of all my enquiring and asserting. (*OC*, 162)

Testimonial practices of asking and telling are thus not just a convenient way of sharing knowledge, but may be regarded as a condition of the very possibility of inquiry. Even those who, as mature reasoners, tend towards caution in their testimonial dealings with others, may find, upon reflection, that they are epistemically indebted to others in more ways than they might have suspected at first.

Study questions

1 Is testimony necessary to human sociality and vice versa? In what sense, if any, could an isolated epistemic agent, for example Robinson Crusoe (before he meets his companion Friday), be said to testify?

2 What is the philosophical significance of the observation that the verb 'to know', but not the verb 'to believe', can be accompanied by interrogative *wh*-clauses (*who*, *where*, *when*, etc.)?

3 Is routine belief expansion intrinsically less reliable than inferential (reasoned) belief expansion? Consider different examples and reflect on the role of our environment in how we form (justified) beliefs.

4 Reflect on each of the two desiderata, trusted acceptance and rational rejection, and think of concrete examples where such a response would be epistemically beneficial. Having done so in each case, how does this influence your general view of testimony as a source of knowledge?

Further reading

An interesting, if idiosyncratic, general introduction to the problem of knowledge, which gives centre-stage to testimony as a way of sharing knowledge, is Welbourne (2001). Faulkner (2006) sheds light on the role of testimony in our epistemic lives by contrasting the traditional case of Cartesian scepticism with scepticism about testimonial knowledge. Elgin (2001) situates testimony as a mechanism for information transfer within a broader account of our epistemic lives that recognizes the importance of the normative relations we stand in. For a discussion of Kant's views on the link between testimony and human sociality, see Gelfert (2006).

3

Testimony, perception, memory and inference

In the previous two chapters, we have encountered the wide range of kinds and contexts of testimony (Chapter 1) and have come to appreciate just how important it is for us to find ways of managing the testimony we receive, if we are to acquire knowledge and avoid falsehood. In order to gain a more fine-grained sense of the place of testimony in our cognitive lives, the present chapter explores the relation of testimony to the other sources of knowledge. As we shall see in the next section, what constitutes a source of knowledge is itself not an easy question. Even entrenched distinctions – such as the one adverted to in the title of this chapter, between perception, memory and inference (reason) – are not without problems. Does perception include introspection, perhaps as a form of 'inner' perception? Does inference exhaust our capacity of reason, or is there room for a form of direct rational intuition? While a full investigation of these questions would go well beyond the scope of this chapter (or, indeed, this book), it is important for a proper appreciation of testimony to examine how testimony fares in comparison with some of those epistemic sources that are most widely regarded as 'basic': perception, memory and inference.

1. Sources of knowledge

For all the attention that philosophers have lavished on the concept of knowledge and its analysis, systematic investigations of the question of what constitutes a source of knowledge are surprisingly rare. Examples of sources of knowledge are easy enough to come by, and many authors even give lists of what they take to be the main sources of knowledge. While there is much overlap between these lists, there remain considerable discrepancies between them – which indicates that much more could be said about what gives each source of knowledge its unity and what sets them apart from one another. (For a discussion of this problem, see Scholz 2004.) Consider this list compiled by Robert Audi:

> If, in the history of epistemology, any sources of knowledge deserve to be called the classical basic sources, the best candidates are perception, memory, consciousness (sometimes called introspection), and reason (sometimes called intuition). (Audi 2002: 72)

Indeed, Audi notes, many writers prefer to simply speak of 'experience and reason' as the major sources of knowledge, which suggests that 'there might be some unity among the first three sources and indeed some possibility of other experiential sources' (ibid.). Other authors differ in their classifications: Sven Bernecker makes a further distinction between reason and inference and adds testimony to the list of 'basic sources', while moving memory to its own category of controversial sources of knowledge:

> Among the basic sources of knowledge and justification are perception, testimony, reason and inference. Whether memory is a basic source of knowledge is a controversial issue. (Bernecker 2011: 326)

Finally, Edward Craig makes a distinction between 'on-board' sources of information ('eyes and ears, powers of reasoning', memory) and the, by extension, 'off-board' testimony of informants; whereas for the former, we ordinarily 'take it that the beliefs they mediate are true', in the case of testimony-based beliefs at least some of the factors that determine their veracity depend on the minds of others (Craig 1990: 11–12).

Implicit in many attempts at giving a taxonomy of sources of knowledge is the thought that they stand in a hierarchical relationship to one another. As Lorraine Code puts it:

> For classical empiricists and their successors, perception, memory and testimony, hierarchically ordered with perception on top, count as the principal sources of empirical knowledge. This ordering maps the relative reliability of the processes, with perception ranking as most stable, reliable and secure, memory coming second on all of these scores, and testimony ranking a poor third, closer to opinion, hearsay and rumor than to the other more respectable sources. (Code 1996: 255)

On this account, empiricists have extended to experience a hierarchical model of knowledge which can be traced all the way back to Plato. In Plato's hierarchical model, *episteme* – absolute knowledge of first principles – can only be acquired by rational intuition, which puts us in touch with the realm of 'ideal forms', of which the empirical world is merely an imperfect reflection. As a result, even our best empirical knowledge, based on careful observation and systematic study, can at best give us justified opinions, not true knowledge. The uneducated senses, more often than not, lead us into error, and reliance on testimony only exacerbates matters by exposing us to the sophistry of others.

One might ask why it was deemed so important to develop a hierarchy of sources of knowledge. If knowledge is the goal of inquiry, should we not embrace all sources of knowledge equally? Depending on context, it may be more practical to rely on one source rather than another, but surely at least in successful cases it should no longer matter, once a piece of knowledge has been acquired, *how* it was acquired. In response to this line of thinking, it is worth noting that, historically, philosophers have operated with more finegrained distinctions between epistemic states than the contemporary focus on knowledge versus (more or less) justified belief suggests. This is evident in the writings of numerous historical figures, including John Locke, who begins *An Essay Concerning Human Understanding* by declaring that it is his goal 'to enquire into the Original [=origin], Certainty, and Extent of humane Knowledge; together with the Grounds and Degrees of Belief, Opinion and Assent' (book 1, chapter 1, section 2). Different forms of assent, ranging from opinion and belief to true knowledge (*scientia*), are appropriate for different epistemic sources. An echo of this can be found in the reluctance of many contemporary epistemologists to allow for an empirical mode of acquiring a priori knowledge; such knowledge, it is often argued, simply requires different grounds for belief than empirical investigation can furnish.

Worries such as these point to an inherent ambiguity in the notion of 'source'. When we speak of someone as relying on a particular 'source of knowledge' for a given belief, we may be referring either to the cause of the belief in question or to its source of justification. These two aspects sometimes come apart, which may lead to confusion, especially when considering the position of an individual knower within a larger framework of knowledge and justification. For example, as we shall see in Section 4, Audi considers memory not to be a basic source of *knowledge* – since we can only remember what we once already knew – but is willing to accept its status as a source of *justification*: after all, we can be justified in believing that things were thus-and-so on the basis of a vivid feeling of remembering that this is how things were, even if our belief is wrong. In the case of testimony, it has been argued that, although each time I accept another's statement, I necessarily rely on perception – I must hear what she says sufficiently clearly to be able to understand it – this does not render perception the source of my belief: perception plays a purely auxiliary role, and my belief owes its epistemic standing to testimony as a source.

2. Testimony and perception

Perception as a source of knowledge occupies a central place in epistemology, and the question of how testimony compares to perception has given rise to a lively and important debate within the epistemology of testimony. All empirical knowledge, at its root, derives from what we – individually and collectively – experience of the world through our senses of vision, hearing, touch, smell and taste. Even when science tells us about unobservables – for example, particles too small to be seen, or forces (such as the magnetic field) which we cannot sense – such knowledge, in the end, is derived from complex scientific experiments that measure, say, subatomic events and translate such data into an observable format (e.g. a particle trajectory displayed on a computer screen). Testimony, too, is often taken to have its basis in perception, both in terms of how we receive it – through *listening to* someone speak or by *reading* printed words on a page – and in terms of its content. (Recall how, in Chapter 1, we encountered a number of proposed restrictions concerning the subject matter of testimony, viz. concerning moral, mathematical and supernatural testimony.) The very idea of 'witnessing' an event is inextricably linked to the idea of first-hand experience: though others may later come to learn about the event on the basis of testimony, at the beginning of each testimonial chain of communication there must be someone who saw things 'with her own eyes'. (Although perception is an umbrella term for all the sensory modalities, each of which has philosophical problems specific to it, for the sake of simplicity – and in line with the idea of the 'eyewitness' – we will be focusing on visual perception.)

Consider a case of everyday perception. Jogging in the park, I see a woman walking her dog, a well-groomed Dalmatian. I see it quite clearly – it is a sunny day, the view is unobstructed, and I have no reason to distrust my eyes – and not a shadow of doubt crosses my mind; this is simply how my perception represents the world as being. But on closer inspection it is clear that the state of affairs I claim to have observed is not a simple one. For one, how can I be sure that the woman is walking *her* dog rather than, say, a friend's? It seems that, in making my earlier claim, I have already relied on inferences based on probabilities ('many more people walk their own, rather than their friend's dog') and assumptions concerning how we individuate the behaviour of others ('a man or woman holding a dog on a leash can be said to be *walking the dog*'). So let us focus on just one element in this state of affairs, the dog. Let us also assume that my perception is veridical: there is, in fact, a Dalmatian in front of me and not, say, a cleverly disguised albino Rottweiler.

In seeing that there is a well-groomed Dalmatian in front of me, I am helping myself to concepts such as *Dalmatian* and *well-groomed*. If I did not possess these concepts, I would not be able to *perceive that* there is a Dalmatian in front of me (and *that* it is well-groomed) – even if, assuming that nothing else in my mental and visual capacities had changed, I would still be able to *perceive* the Dalmatian: a large white dog with black spots and a shiny coat. This latter kind of perception may be called 'simple seeing', as opposed to the (conceptually structured) 'seeing-that' in the former case. Seeing-that (and, by extension, perceiving-that), thus, involves the capacity to apply concepts in a way that is not required for simple seeing. Furthermore, seeing-that is *factive* – that is, it requires that the world be as perceived: I cannot *see that* there is a Dalmatian in front of me if what I am looking at is not, in fact, a Dalmatian. But mistakes are possible, so an intermediate category – somewhere between simple seeing and factive seeing-that – is needed. This may be called 'seeing-as': I might see the white dog with black spots *as* a Dalmatian, when in fact it is not. A more finegrained taxonomy of ways of seeing might further distinguish between seeing-as and 'recognitional seeing', since the latter need not require the application of concepts. (As Jesse Prinz notes: 'Recognition outstrips conceptualization'; Prinz 2006: 437.) Simple seeing, seeing-as and seeing-that all qualify as types of perceptual experience, and at least the latter two tend to issue in perceptual beliefs: all else being equal, when we perceive an object A *as* having quality *x*, we form the belief that 'A is *x*'. Note, however, that this relationship is defeasible: often we have good reasons not to form perceptual beliefs merely on the basis of seeing-as: if I have repeatedly encountered the famous Müller-Lyer illusion – in which two same-length arrows are judged to be of unequal length, depending on whether the arrow's 'feathers' point inward or outward – I will, on future occasions, be reluctant to form a perceptual belief on the basis of my continuing to see one line segment as longer than the other.

The epistemology of perception analyses the source of justification for our perceptual beliefs and the conditions under which they may result in our perceptual knowledge. One puzzle regarding perceptual justification concerns the role of non-conceptual perceptual experience – for example of the kind associated with simple seeing – in conferring justification to some of our beliefs, since it might seem that rational relations (including relations of justificatory support) could only hold between conceptual states. Regarding the question of when perceptual beliefs should count as knowledge, one prominent suggestion has been that, in addition to the actual belief's being true, what is required is that the belief be the output of a reliable perceptual mechanism and that the world must 'cooperate' in such a way that, across relevant alternative scenarios of how equivalent perceptual experiences might have come to pass, the agent would not have formed a false belief. (See Goldman 1979.) Finally, there has been considerable discussion of whether, and under which conditions, ordinary perceptual beliefs might be accorded a foundational role for knowledge generally. (For an introductory, yet in-depth discussion of the epistemology of perception, see Audi 2011, esp. chapters 1 and 2.)

For the remainder of this section, let us concentrate on the relation between testimony and perception as sources of knowledge. How are the two related? We have already seen that testimony depends on perception both for its reception and for (much of) its content. What about the other direction of dependency? If it turned out that perception, or a significant portion of our perceptual knowledge, depended on testimony, this would put pressure on the idea of a fixed hierarchy between the sources of knowledge, specifically between testimony and perception, with the latter being the more fundamental of the two. There is no doubt that sensory perception is causally prior to testimony: each piece of testimony needs to be perceived in order to be understood, and language acquisition – a precondition for testimony – would be inconceivable without reliance on perception. But once we have been inducted into the practice of giving and receiving testimony, it is by no means clear that this causal priority translates into a justificatory advantage of perceptual beliefs over testimonial beliefs. This can be seen by reflecting on the role of defeating beliefs.

Consider the case of optical illusions. The first time you were exposed to the Müller-Lyer illusion, perhaps you took out a ruler and measured the length of the horizontal lines yourself, confirming that, indeed, the lines were of the same length, appearances notwithstanding. Now imagine marvelling, one clear summer evening, at the beauty of the full moon rising over the horizon. Just as you are beginning to wonder why it is that the moon is so much larger this time round than on previous occasions – 'is it perhaps closer to the Earth at this time of the year?' – your companion remarks on the fact that the apparent difference in size is a mere illusion: the combined result of two close cousins to the Müller-Lyer illusion, the Ponzo and Ebbinghaus illusions, which skew our judgements concerning depth and relative size. You accept your friend's testimony – not without a tinge of resentment for his having spoilt the moment – since the explanation is plausible and you have no reason to distrust your friend's testimony. As a result, you acquire a testimonial belief in the illusory nature of your observation, which defeats any nascent perceptual belief you might have formed otherwise. Testimony also appears to sometimes influence perceptual judgements directly. In a series of 'conformity experiments', Solomon Asch (1956) asked groups of subjects to perform simple 'perceptual tasks', such as judging which of three lines matched the length of one that had previously been shown; when the other 'subjects' – who, unbeknownst to the only real participant in each session, were confederates of the experimenter – declared an obviously non-matching line to be the correct answer, 75 per cent of the real participants yielded at least sometimes to the group 'consensus', with a number of participants subsequently reporting that they had come to see the wrong line *as matching*.

The role of testimony in perception, however, goes beyond the occasional testimonial defeater for perceptual belief and the influence of social pressure. Recall that even the clearest cases of perceptual knowledge – namely, successful instances of seeing-that – are at the same time instances of seeing-as and as such require the application of concepts to sensory experience. Yet it is clear that many of the concepts we, in fact, employ could not have been acquired without extensive reliance on the word of others; as Coady puts it, 'many (some would say, all) of the concepts in terms of which we make perceptual judgments are socially provided' (Coady 1989: 241). By analogy with the concept of 'theory-ladenness' in scientific observation, one might be tempted to speak of a general 'testimony-ladenness' of ordinary observation and perceptual knowledge. But let us not go too fast. After all, it is one thing to acknowledge that there can be no thought without language, no perceptual knowledge without concepts, and no concept acquisition without an extensive historical reliance on testimony, but it is quite another to say that a current perceptual belief here and now – although indebted to a person's socially acquired framework of concepts – depends on testimony for its epistemic justification. As Elizabeth Fricker insists, likening the acquisition of concepts to the climbing of a ladder: 'Perhaps, having ascended via the ladder, one can then take hold elsewhere, and kick it away. This possibility deserves exploration' (Fricker 2004: 123).

Among those philosophers who have concerned themselves with testimony, Thomas Reid (1710–96) was perhaps the one who most forcefully argued for a thoroughgoing parallel between perception and testimony. In his *Inquiry into the Human Mind*, Reid writes:

> There is a much greater similitude than is commonly imagined, between the testimony of nature given by our senses, and the testimony of men given by language. The credit we give to both is at first the effect of instinct only. When we grow up, and begin to reason about them, the

credit given to human testimony is restrained and weakened, by the experience we have of deceit. But the credit given to the testimony of our senses, is established and confirmed by the uniformity and constancy of the laws of nature. (Reid 1983: 87)

What grounds this analogy for Reid is the thought that perception and language both are processes of signification; in particular, they involve two kinds of signs: natural (or 'original') signs, which we can understand on the basis of our innate capacities, and artificial signs, understanding of which we acquire on the basis of experience and inductive reasoning. When it comes to perceptions, this is reflected in the difference between original perceptions – through which Nature, as it were, presents to us certain qualities of an object directly – and acquired perceptions, which initially required experience and inductive reasoning (such as the reasoning from cause and effect), but which have since become second nature to us. Although the connection between an acquired perception and what it represents may be causal – that is, furnished by Nature – it is not initially presented to us directly (the way that, say, the hardness of a billiard ball would be presented to us directly, if we were to encounter it through our sense of touch). Depending on the level of sophistication required, beliefs derived from such acquired perceptions may be 'complex convictions in which perception as well as reason plays a role, and though they are not pure cases of perception, they may without abuse of language be called complex perceptions' (Lehrer and Smith 1985: 29).

Against sceptics – and those who, like the rationalists, thought that the deliverances of our senses could not be trusted – Reid insists that perception as a source of knowledge is justified on the basis of the following principle: 'That those things do really exist which we distinctly perceive by our senses, and are what we perceive them to be' (Reid 1872: 445). Human nature is so constituted that perceptual belief comes instinctively; indeed, as Reid puts it, this is 'one of the best gifts of nature' (Reid 1983: 86). And Reid sees no compelling case for privileging reason as the sole source of knowledge, since even the rationalist must assume the existence of thought, and hence of mental contents – of just the sort that perception provides: 'Why, sir, should I believe the faculty of reason more than that of perception? – they both came out of the same shop, and were made by the same artist' (ibid.: 85). If the rationalist is willing to grant the validity of a principle that warrants trust in our innate capacity of reason – as he must, lest his position slide into scepticism – then there seems to be no basis for denying other innate capacities of acquiring knowledge the same privilege.

A structurally identical argument supports our reliance on testimony as a source of knowledge, or so Reid argues. As in the case of perception, we can distinguish between original signs – 'signs in the natural language of the human countenance and behaviour' (ibid.: 91), that is, facial expressions and body language – and artificial signs, which give rise to conventional languages such as English and need to be acquired through experience and inductive reasoning. To be sure, no analysis of written or spoken language will be able to uncover a necessary connection between, say, a particular word and what it refers to; from an abstract standpoint, language is conventional all the way down. Yet it is equally clear, given the fact that humans everywhere acquire language as a matter of course (and different languages at that), that all language ultimately is the product of human nature and its ways of responding to different stimuli and social environments, under the influence of general principles. In the case of testimony, these are the *principle of credulity* – according to which we respond to others on the assumption that 'our fellow creatures will use the same signs in language, when they have the same sentiments' (ibid.: 93) – and the complementary *principle of veracity*, a propensity to speak the truth which manifests itself in the fact 'that truth is always at the door of my lips, and goes forth spontaneously, if not held back' (ibid.: 94). Both principles are 'original principles' of the human constitution and, although modulated by experience, their operation is no more a matter of conscious reflection than is the operation of the principles that underlie perception: 'In the testimony of Nature given by the senses, as well as in human testimony given by language, things are signified to us by signs; and in one as well as the other, the mind, either by original principles or by custom, passes from the sign to the conception and belief of the things signified' (ibid.: 90).

One need not accept every detail of Reid's account to agree with his general point that testimony may be regarded as a 'social operation of the mind'. Both components of this expression are important: the fact that testimony is 'social' in character, and that it is a *sui generis* 'operation of the mind'. This is – of course – not to suggest that testimony could somehow function in isolation from perception, reasoning, and all the other intellectual operations and principles of the mind. On the contrary, all our informational sources exhibit considerable cohesion. As Coady puts it:

> An individual's present perception of something in front of him as an eighteenth-century mahogany architect's desk will be determined not only by the gross perception of certain colours and shapes but by the memories and inferences of both himself and others which are built into the conceptual and perceptual skills with which he approaches this particular cognitive encounter. (Coady 1992: 169)

Synchronic cohesion of this type, along with coherence between different sources – manifesting itself in sustained operation and successful action over time and across different domains – may well amount to the best anti-sceptical argument available, and testimony is as much part of this 'mix' of informational sources as perception. Indeed, if it appears to us that testimony compares unfavourably to perception, this may merely be a by-product of our having continuous access to perception, but only intermittent access to testimony. Peter Graham, contrasting the cases of 'looking at an apple on a table' and receiving testimony to the same effect, makes just this argument: whereas in the visual case 'over a relatively small portion of time, one will have a number of distinct but interlocking experiences of, and beliefs about, the apple', in the case of being told that there is an apple on the table 'all the hearer may have in favor of the belief is this one presentation-as-true' (Graham 2006a: 110). However, this is at best a difference in degree and does not controvert the claim that, by accepting a single piece of testimony, it is often possible to acquire knowledge of matters that would otherwise require careful observation.

3. The role of inference

Inference – our capacity to reason – is an important element in the epistemic toolkit of human beings. It allows us to go beyond what we already know, either by moving deductively from known premises to novel conclusions entailed by those premises, or by inductively inferring from experience what lies beyond it. It is through inference – of the deductive and inductive kind, respectively – that we can come to know complex mathematical truths and can extrapolate from past experience to future events; at the same time, reasoning allows us to reflect on the very processes of belief formation. Such reflection ranges from simple cognitive 'housekeeping' – monitoring my belief system for inconsistencies and withholding belief when confronted with evidence that contradicts what I take myself to know – to the farthest realms of philosophical speculation. At a broader level, the same capacities also allow us to participate in what is sometimes called 'the game of giving and asking for reasons' (Brandom 2000: 195), that is, the keeping track of the argumentative moves and rational commitments of others.

The capacity to reason – including the ability to consider what lies beyond what is given to us in experience – is often taken to be a distinctive feature setting human cognition apart from other animals. As Kant puts it in the *Groundwork*: 'Now, a human being really finds in himself a capacity by which he distinguishes himself from all other things, even from himself insofar as he is affected by objects, and that is *reason*' (AA, IV, 452). To be sure, reason need not manifest itself solely through inference: rationalists famously argued that some truths could be rationally 'intuited' (i.e. seen to be true immediately) without the help of experience or other propositions. Nonetheless, a paradigmatic case of knowledge based on reason – and a clear example of inference as a source of knowledge – would be the derivation of a mathematical theorem from fundamental axioms, using only the laws of deductive logic. In a successful deductive derivation, each step is logically entailed by the previous step and the rational force of each transition can be appreciated by any competent reasoner; as a result, deduction is often called 'truth-preserving': if a reasoner accepts the premises of a (valid) deductive argument as true, she is rationally compelled to also accept its conclusions.

'Inference', if understood along the lines of deductive step-by-step reasoning, suggests a rationalist model of knowledge, according to which we must exclude from our reasoning any uncertain premises or fallible inferential moves. But we also speak of inductive inferences, which are by necessity fallible, and we often reason in qualitative ways, which cannot be readily assimilated to either the laws of deductive or inductive logic. A broader notion of 'inference' would therefore need to relax some of the strict demands of deductive reasoning. A suitably lenient understanding of inference can be found in the works of empiricist philosophers such as David Hume. Much of Hume's discussion concerns inferences from causes to effects, and from effects to causes, where such inferences are to be understood not in a narrow (scientific) sense, but in a broad sense as the kind of inferences that allow us to acquire a working knowledge of our everyday environment. Thus understood, the term 'inference' refers to 'any rule-governed passage of mind from input to output' and 'carries no necessary implication of conscious explicit reasoning' (Welbourne 2002: 412):

> Thus Hume would be happy to say that Pavlov's dogs infer that food is coming (they get to believe it) when they hear the bell. And, in fact, of course, many of our everyday causal inferences have this automatic character; I hear the door-bell ring and thereupon believe that there is someone on the doorstep. (Ibid.)

This suggests that we can learn at least as much about how we form inferential beliefs 'from a cautious observation of human life' (as Hume puts it in the introduction to his *Treatise of Human Nature*) as we can from introspection.

One important point of controversy about the role of inference in our cognitive lives concerns the extent to which perceptual and testimonial knowledge are inferential. Let us turn to the case of perception first. Why might one worry that perceptual beliefs are inferential? On one influential theory of perception, we do not perceive objects in the world directly, but only in a mediated way, through sense data which represent an object (e.g. a stove top) as having certain qualities (e.g. as red, round and hot). While we have direct access to sense data as mental items, available to introspection, we do not have direct access to the kind of relationship that holds between sense data and the world. Under normal circumstances, we do well to place simple trust in the way the world is represented to us in sense data, but cases such as hallucinations or optical illusions serve as vivid reminders that the world and our sensory image of it can come apart. One might think, then, that perceptual knowledge can only be secured via an independent argument that spells out the conditions under which sense data reliably and accurately represent the way the world is. Perceptual beliefs about the world, it would seem on this account, are not only causally mediated (via sense data), but also depend for their justification on an inference to the reliability of our sensory systems.

Philosophers who regard the idea that perceptual knowledge might be inferential as deeply unpalatable have responded in different ways. One could hold, with Reid, that we have no evidence for the existence of sense data (or 'ideas') as 'images' of external objects, nor do we have reason to think that sense data can be 'separated out' as playing a purely internal role in the process of perception; sensations, Reid insists, have no intrinsic properties in and of themselves, but must be understood instead as natural signs standing in a real connection with the things signified. Alternatively, one might argue that, although perceptual beliefs about the world do depend on the reliability of causal processes beyond our immediate cognitive reach, it is simply not the case that our justification for those beliefs takes the form of an argument which has the assumption of reliability as one of its premises. Rather, what justifies a given perceptual belief of mine, all else being equal, is simply my having the requisite sense data. Perceptual beliefs are, of course, fallible – appearances can be deceiving – but the twin facts of fallibility and defeasibility are quite independent of the question of whether perception is inferential or not. The fact that, in the earlier case of the moon illusion, my companion's testimony defeats my nascent perceptual belief (which, in any case, would have been erroneous) that the moon is closer than usual, does not show that the original perceptual belief was inferential. The reverse, of course, also holds: 'The fact that my perception defeats your testimony does not show testimony is inferential and not direct' (Graham 2006a: 102).

If one is committed, in Reidian fashion, to the parity between perception and testimony, then similar considerations as in the perceptual case will carry through for the case of testimony. But even Reid notes that the two cases are not entirely identical and differ in one important respect: testimony, unlike perception, depends on the will of another agent. This renders testimony subject to possible deception, a possibility which does not exist for perception (except metaphorically, as when we say 'my eyes have deceived me'). As Reid acknowledges:

> Men sometimes lead us into mistakes, when we perfectly understand their language, by speaking lies. But nature never misleads us in this way: her language is always true; and it is only by misinterpreting it that we fall into error. (Reid 1983: 102)

Perhaps, then, we ought to actively rule out this possibility whenever we are inclined to accept a given piece of testimony. This suggests that, although we may be naturally inclined to accept what others tell us, we need to supplement testimonial belief with a justification for why, on this occasion, we should regard the testifier as sincere and reliable.

Whether such an inferential justification is indeed required has been a bone of contention among contemporary epistemologists of testimony. Much of the discussion centres on the phenomenology of testimonial acceptance. Recall Coady's example of the phone bill, mentioned in Chapter 1:

> [PHONE BILL.] I ring up the telephone company on being unable to locate my bill and am told by an anonymous voice that it comes to $165 and is due on 15 June. No thought of determining the veracity and reliability of the witness occurs to me [. . .] given that the total is within tolerable limits [. . .] There is nothing hesitant or suspicious about the unknown communicant's response[.] (Coady 1992: 143)

To Coady this suggests that testimonial acceptance typically lacks the phenomenology associated with inferential reasoning: it does not seem to be the case that I need to engage in any inferential activity in order to acquire a valid testimonial belief. Michael Dummett concurs with Coady, noting that 'if someone tells me the way to the railway station' or volunteers a piece of news, such as 'the Foreign Secretary has just resigned', 'I go through no process of reasoning, however swift, to arrive at the conclusion that he has spoken aright': understanding of the utterance and acceptance 'are one' (Dummett 1993: 419). Others, notably Fricker, have argued that 'we know too much about human nature to want to trust anyone, let alone everyone, uncritically' (Fricker 1995: 400); as a result, a responsible hearer will 'always engage in some assessment of the speaker for trustworthiness', by 'continually evaluating him for trustworthiness throughout their exchange, in the light of the evidence, or cues, available to her' (Fricker 1994: 145/150). Valid testimonial beliefs, on this account, are always, at least in part, inferentially grounded. As Fricker sees it, Coady himself implicitly acknowledges this when he spells out an important condition for testimonial acceptance in the case at hand: namely, that 'the total is within tolerable limits' and that 'there is nothing hesitant or suspicious about the unknown communicant' response'. This, Fricker argues, points to 'precisely the active sub-personal monitoring of the speaker by the hearer for signs of lack of sincerity and competence' (Fricker 1995: 405) she herself regards as the norm.

As we shall see in Chapter 5, the dispute between Coady and Fricker regarding the role of inference in testimonial acceptance closely tracks their divergent views concerning the source of justification for testimonial beliefs. But is it even legitimate to accord the question of inferentialism, and the attendant question of the phenomenology of testimonial acceptance, this much significance? It is important to note at least a few dissenting voices. Thus, Martin Kusch has doubted whether talk of a distinct 'phenomenology' of testimonial acceptance can be at all helpful in determining the relative standing of testimony as a fundamental source of knowledge:

> At best, our phenomenology of perception and testimony consists of imagined public scenarios of justification – completely derived from, and secondary to, the real-life settings. There is no determinate phenomenology of testimony over and above imagined talk. And what little phenomenology there is fails to distinguish perception from testimony. (Kusch 2002b: 25)

In a similar vein, John McDowell has doubted whether, over and above a general account of what it takes to be a responsible knower, we even need a specific account of testimony:

> If we are not to explain the fact that having heard from someone that things are thus and so is an epistemic standing by appealing to the strength of an argument that things are that way, available to the hearer by virtue of his having heard his interlocutor say that they are, do we need some other account of it? I would be tempted to maintain that we do not. (McDowell 1994: 212)

Yet, as Miranda Fricker notes, even on such 'quietist' proposals a very real theoretical puzzle remains, for if the hearer's being a responsible knower 'is not a matter of her making an inference, then what *is* it a matter of?' (Fricker 2007: 68).

4. Testimony and memory

Perception and inference would be of little use if knowledge gained on their basis could not be retained by us. Acknowledging that perception and inference are not strictly instantaneous, one might grant the existence of what is sometimes called 'the specious present': in William James's words, 'the short duration of which we are immediately and incessantly sensible' (1890: 631). Perhaps, during this short time period, we could take in some of our perceptual environment and even perform simple inferences, thereby acquiring some knowledge of the world around us. Without a capacity to retain it, however, such knowledge would be fleeting: one moment we would have it, the next moment it would be gone – and we would not even know we ever had it. (If this situation sounds far-fetched, consider the case of patients who have lost the ability to form new memories, yet who are able to orient themselves, and respond, to present stimuli.) As Dummett puts it, without memory 'you will be trapped in a cognitive solipsism of the present moment' (1993: 420).

Compared with perception, inference, and even testimony, memory has received relatively little systematic attention from epistemologists. This is surprising, given the rich empirical findings of the psychology of memory, which has developed a finegrained taxonomy of the different interlocking types of memory. 'Memory', conceived of as an umbrella term for the capacity to retain (and recall) acquired knowledge and abilities, can be divided into declarative (or explicit) memory and procedural (or implicit) memory. Procedural memory refers to the memory of skills, both physical (e.g. playing the piano) and mental (e.g. playing chess), which is typically acquired through repeated performance of particular types of action. Early theorists, including James, sometimes referred to this acquisition of skill as 'habit' (often in contradistinction to 'memory' in the declarative sense). By contrast, declarative memory includes the recall of facts and events that can be explicitly stated (episodic memory) as well as knowledge of meanings and concepts (semantic memory). Both procedural and declarative memory are forms of long-term memory, as opposed to short-term memory, which refers to the ability to keep a limited amount of information readily available, for a brief period of time.

To the extent that epistemologists have concerned themselves with memory as a source of knowledge, their interest has mainly been in declarative memory – that is, in 'remembering-that'. In much the same way that epistemology has traditionally privileged knowing-that over knowing-how, remembering-how (i.e. procedural memory) has taken a backseat to remembering-that in epistemological discussions of memory. Drawing more on the phenomenology of remembering than on firm empirical results, philosophers of memory also tend to distinguish between a narrow and a broad sense of remembering, with the former involving a vivid, sensory way of remembering (which may involve recalling 'memory images') and the latter consisting simply in the ability to report past facts and events. For the most part, the philosophical default position has been to consider memory a purely preservative process – so much so that its standing as a 'source' has sometimes been disputed. Here is Dummett: 'Memory is not a *source*, still less a *ground*, of knowledge: it is the maintenance of knowledge formerly acquired by whatever means' (Dummett 1993: 420–1). Others distinguish between memory's inability to generate genuinely new knowledge and its function of furnishing justification. Thus, Robert Audi writes:

> Memory is not, then, a *basic source* of belief or knowledge, a source that generates them other than through dependence on a contribution by some different source of them. It is, however, a basic source of justification. (Audi 2011: 78)

The idea is that, although memory cannot lead us to form genuinely new beliefs – except when combined with inference and perception – we are nonetheless justified if we form a belief on the basis of remembering that p, even if p is not (or no longer) true.

Empiricist theories of memory have tended to endorse a picture of memory, according to which remembering an event consists simply in conjuring up a mental image, or mental content, identical to one that was originally produced (e.g. by perception) at an earlier stage. For Hume, the main difference is mostly one of vivacity; others, for example Bertrand Russell, demanded that a memory should at least be attended by a feeling of familiarity. However, in an influential argument Charles Martin and Max Deutscher (1966) argued that the empiricist criteria were inadequate and needed to be supplemented by a demand for causal continuity, so as to rule out cases in which beliefs that the subject once had on the basis of perception, but which she has since forgotten, get re-implanted in the subject through, say, hypnosis, and are then mistaken for memorial beliefs. Assuming that the insertion of the belief would have happened irrespective of whether or not the subject originally had the belief, its later recreation could hardly count as a case of remembering, as there is no causal connection between the two instantiations of the belief. Not just any causal connection will do, however: consider a case similar to the previous one, but with the slight modification that the re-implantation of a belief is through the testimony of a friend with whom the subject had earlier shared the belief in question. Although the first occurrence of the belief is part of the causal chain that led to its second occurrence in the subject, that later belief would clearly be testimonial, not memorial, in character. One attempt to resolve the problem has been through positing the existence of memory traces, which must be preserved throughout in the remembering subject's brain, but such manoeuvres gradually lead further and further away from the ordinary concept of memory.

The very idea that memory needs to be preservative for it to function as a source of knowledge and justification has recently been called into question. As psychologists and epistemologists of memory are realizing, memory often operates in a constructive, rather than purely preservative manner. (For an excellent discussion, see Michaelian 2011.) The 'constructive' side of memory may lead to the generation – or transformation – of stored content, either before or during retrieval, and may result in the formation of genuinely new beliefs: that is, beliefs which the subject did not previously accept. A number of psychological processes have been documented which lead to such generation, transformation and reconstruction of memorial beliefs. Thus, when it comes to visual memory, the phenomenon of boundary extension has been robustly demonstrated: when asked to describe, or graphically recreate, an observed scene, subjects routinely and confidently remember seeing a surrounding region that was not previously in view. (See Intraub and Richardson 1989.) Over time, memories also tend to integrate information from other sources, which, upon retrieval, is attributed to the perceived original event. In source monitoring, subjects infer the original source of a memory – not necessarily consciously – from specific features of the remembered content. As two psychologists of memory put it, such processes and imperfections 'provide critical evidence for the fundamental idea that memory is not a literal reproduction of the past, but rather is a constructive process in which bits and pieces of information from various sources are pulled together' (Schacter and Addis 2007: 773).

For epistemologists committed to the purely preservative character of memorial knowledge, such evidence poses a serious challenge, since it suggests that our faculty of memory is far less reliable than traditionally thought. After all, if preservation of content is the ultimate standard by which memory is to be judged, then any transformation or alteration would, by definition, amount to a corruption of memory. However, as Kirk Michaelian has suggested, it is not at all clear that the (re)constructive aspects of memory necessarily lead to a degradation of justification. Take source monitoring as an example. As Michaelian argues, many scenarios are conceivable in which

> the reliability of memory is secured not despite the reconstructive nature of retrieval but (in part) because of it: because they rely on reliable indicators of the origins of [memory] traces, reconstructive retrieval processes tend to come to the right conclusions about those origins. (Michaelian 2011: 329)

In other words, not all transformations that result from constructive memory are epistemically problematic: where such processes (e.g. through selectivity of detail, extrapolation beyond the initial evidence and incorporation of testimonial information) in fact lead to the generation of reliable beliefs upon the retrieval of a memory, we need not regard them as diminishing our status as knowers, but may even regard them as enabling us to have justified memorial beliefs. For the traditionalist, who considers memory as at best a way of preserving knowledge, such a proposal would have an air of paradox to it, for it suggests, as Michaelian puts it with an eye to the phenomenon of boundary extension, that 'we need not and should not say that the subject does not genuinely remember the scene because she did not see the whole of it; we should instead say that she remembers the scene even though she did not see the whole of it' (2011: 334).

5. Content preservation

Even if our actual capacity for remembering is not purely preservative, but has almost always a constructive element, can one perhaps still single out the preservation of content over time as its function, or one of its functions? The idea here would be that making previously stored content accessible may be considered a function of memory, even if the actual outputs of the psychological processes underlying this capacity only imperfectly realize this function. By analogy, one might say that our capacity to reason from premises to conclusions has as its function the preservation of truth through the laws of logic, even if many of us routinely make mistakes when we attempt to perform logical deductions. If one is willing to grant this much, then it may be worthwhile to consider what some of the epistemological consequences of such 'idealized' preservation of content and justification might be. In the remainder of this section, we shall briefly look at a parallel between memory and testimony, insofar as both may be thought of as transmitting justification, before turning to an influential proposal by Tyler Burge, regarding how content preservation itself creates a warrant for accepting the deliverances of either source.

One line of thinking that develops the parallel between memory and testimony takes as its starting point the suggestion that, as Peter Lipton puts it, '[k]nowledge that depends on memory [. . .] might profitably be viewed as the transmission of knowledge from past to present self' (Lipton 1998: 2). In other words, when we retrieve a memory, we are in effect receiving testimony from a former self, and the attendant epistemological questions – concerning the reliability of the belief in question and the generally fallible nature of communication – are not much different in the two cases. As Ernest Sosa puts it, while 'memory is a psychological mechanism that conveys beliefs across stages of a life' of one individual, testimony is 'a social mechanism that conveys beliefs across lives at a time' (Sosa 1991: 218). In both cases, the recipient – the present self – is confronted with a belief that depends for its content and justification on factors that are not (or no longer) immediately available. Just as I implicitly rely on the reliability of my former self's perceptual faculties when I presently remember an event I witnessed, so in the case of testimony I rely on the epistemic justification of others. Hence, if, as Paul Faulkner puts it, 'testimony operates to transmit knowledge and warrant', a natural way to think about the nature of this transmission is in terms of testimony making the 'extended body of warrant' available, where this refers to 'the proprietary justification possessed by the speaker, and the prior sources if the speaker's belief is [itself] testimonial' (Faulkner 2011: 22). On this model, I need not myself have direct access to the prior interlocutors' reasons and evidence in order to be able to 'inherit' the cumulative justification for the belief in question.

Tyler Burge (1993) takes the role of content preservation in knowledge acquisition one step further, arguing that it allows us, all else being equal, to accept the deliverances of (preservative) memory and testimony at face value. Acceptance of testimonial and (certain) memorial beliefs, according to Burge, is warranted, because the following principle holds, at least to a first approximation:

> A person is entitled to accept as true something that is presented as true and that is intelligible to him, unless there are stronger reasons not to do so. (Burge 1993: 467)

Burge is, of course, aware that this principle needs to be qualified, given that certain background assumptions need to be in place about how intelligibility issues in an epistemic entitlement to accept something as true. The full 'Acceptance Principle' will be stated below; first, however, let us retrace how Burge motivates the existence of a link between intelligibility and justification. At the outset, it is worth noting that Burge is not offering a unified theory of testimony and memory at large, but is zooming in on a narrow but significant aspect both have in common. In line with the suggestion that something can be learned from looking at an idealized version of our mental faculties, Burge focuses on *purely preservative* memory, rather than *substantive* memory in all its empirical facets. Whereas substantive memory 'imports subject matter or objects into reasoning', purely preservative memory 'introduces no subject matter' and 'simply maintains in justificational space a cognitive content with its judgmental force' (ibid.: 465). A paradigmatic example of purely preservative memory would be the kind of memory that allows us to move from one step to the next in logical deductions, thereby maintaining the rational force of the previous steps in an argument all the way to its conclusion. In particular, it is what allows the logical deduction of, say, a mathematical theorem to count as a priori knowledge, since one might otherwise worry – given what was reported in the previous section about memory as an empirical phenomenon – that extensive reliance on memory might gradually turn longer deductions into empirical (rather than a priori) results.

In a similar move, Burge argues that we have a non-empirical entitlement for accepting an intelligible piece of testimony at face value – even if the content of that testimony is itself an empirical claim. (Interpreting Burge's account through the lens of Faulkner's, one might say that it is through an a priori entitlement to accept what he is told that the recipient of testimony inherits the 'extended body of warrant' which, depending on the character of the belief in question, may contain empirical as well as a priori elements.) Recall that many epistemologists have noted the dependence of testimony on the senses for its reception. One might think that this dependence on sensory perception necessarily turns any testimonial belief into an empirical phenomenon. Yet as Burge argues, in the case of testimony the function of perception is, in fact, 'analogous to the function of purely preservative memory in reasoning': it simply allows the original justification to be preserved, not across time (as in the case of memory) but across different reasoners. It is, Burge argues, simply not the case that testimonial beliefs are necessarily empirical 'just by virtue of the fact that the beliefs are acquired from others' (ibid.: 466). Instead, the very intelligibility of a piece of testimony – the fact that we can understand it as a meaningful statement that has passed through, and is brought about by, another rational being – gives us a non-empirical (though defeasible) warrant to accept it as true.

The argument for this link between intelligibility and warrant, somewhat underdeveloped in Burge's paper, is a functional one: since 'intelligible presentations-as-true come prima facie backed by a rational source or resource for reason', and since 'reason is a guide to truth' (of which the practice of 'intelligible affirmation is the face'), therefore anything that carries the hallmarks of having originated from a rational source – such as an intelligible piece of testimony – deserves to be accepted (unless the recipient has specific reasons not to do so). This leads to the following full version of the Acceptance Principle (which, admittedly, is a bit of a mouthful):

> A person is apriori entitled to accept a proposition that is presented as true and that is intelligible to him, unless there are stronger reasons not to do so, because it is prima facie preserved (received) from a rational source, or resource for reason; reliance on rational sources – or resources for reason – is, other things equal, necessary to the function of reason. (Ibid.: 469)

A couple of points about the Acceptance Principle are in order. First, it is important to note that Burge's argument is not based on an inquiry into the actual reliability of testimony in general or the empirical circumstances of a given piece of testimony in particular. Indeed, as Burge emphasizes, it 'is not a statistical point about people's tending to tell the truth more often than not', and neither does it turn on assumptions about the innateness of certain principles of testimony (such as Reid's twin principles of veracity and credulity; see Section 2). Second, because of its a priori character, the Acceptance Principle opens up the possibility that a priori knowledge may be preserved through testimony; this sets it apart from the more standard view, discussed in Chapter 1, according to which a priori claims, such as mathematical truths, cannot be known on the basis of the say-so of others.

Burge's proposal is intriguing because it promises something quite extraordinary: the transformation of the fact of its intelligibility into the basis of justification for accepting a message as true. In addition, it dispenses with the need for any empirical investigation of either the circumstances of the testimony or the reliability of the belief in question. It would seem, then, that through mere armchair reflection we could establish that testimony is, by and large, an acceptable source of knowledge. As Burge himself recognizes, one might wonder whether this proposal 'can ever be the last word in the epistemology of acceptance for anyone over the age of eleven' (Burge 1993: 468). In order to see what is so extraordinary about Burge's proposal, consider the scope of its purported applicability. If intelligibility as proof of the rational origins of a message were the only standard by which to judge testimony, then it would seem that we should give as much initial credit to the face-to-face testimony of a friend as, say, to the anonymous inscriptions on the wall of a pharaoh's tomb 4,000 years ago. Burge is, of course, aware that we rarely have only the intelligibility of a message to go on when faced with the choice between accepting or rejecting a given piece of testimony, and that empirical factors will often interfere with the entitlement that derives from the Acceptance Principle alone:

> The epistemic default position articulated by the Acceptance Principle applies at an extremely high level of idealization in most actual communication, especially between sophisticated interlocutors. Social, political, or intellectual context often provides 'stronger reasons' that counsel against immediately accepting what one is told. Given life's complexities, this default position is often left far behind in reasoning about whether to rely on a source. (Ibid.)

This, however, raises a fundamental worry for the Acceptance Principle as the key to a comprehensive theory of testimony: for, if the rational entitlement that arises from the mere intelligibility of a message is so weak that any empirical evidence, whether relating to the circumstances of the act of communication or to the plausibility of the claim in question, is bound to override it, then one would be hard-pressed to find any real-life context – other than philosophical thought experiments – in which intelligibility alone could tip the balance in favour of testimonial acceptance rather than rejection.

Study questions

1   Is testimony more like memory or more like perception?

2   There is an expression, supposedly Russian in origin, that goes 'He lies like an eyewitness.' If we cannot even trust eyewitness testimony, what hope is there for acquiring knowledge on the basis of what others tell us?

3   Is Coady's example of PHONE BILL (Section 3) a case of direct knowledge from testimony or does it have an inferential component? If the latter, how does the inferential activity involved differ from inferential processes that underlie our perceptual system?

4   Does Burge's Acceptance Principle entail that we can obtain a priori mathematical knowledge through other people's testimony?

Further reading

The epistemological literature on each of the non-testimonial sources of knowledge is almost limitless. Audi (2011) is an advanced, up-to-date introduction which devotes a chapter each to perception, memory, consciousness (introspection) and reason; see the references therein. Green (2006), in his encyclopedia article, draws interesting parallels between testimony, perception, and memory, and hints at a broader 'epistemic parity' between these three sources.

4

Testimony and evidence

In the legal arena, the testimony of witnesses, once admitted by the court, is considered evidence. As such, it is to be treated as on a par with other kinds of evidence, for example empirical findings. Much, of course, hinges on the credibility of the witness. But if the witness is judged to be reliable, then her statement that she saw the defendant at the crime scene at the night of the murder should carry the same weight, and should be weighed against, the empirical finding that the bloody footprints at the site of the murder match those of the defendant. Treating legal testimony as of a piece with other forms of evidence is an elegant procedural solution to the problem of integrating and comparing our various sources of information, before arriving at a final verdict. But outside the legal context with its procedural constraints, it is far from clear whether testimony is fruitfully thought of as continuous with evidence. For one, we are forced to rely on the testimony of others precisely when we *lack* evidence ourselves; eroding this distinction between first-hand evidence and second-hand knowledge by assimilating testimony to the catch-all category of 'evidence' may simply not be very insightful. More importantly, however, there appears to be a contrast between the way we process evidence and how we learn from the testimony of others. Forming a belief on the basis of evidence almost always involves some degree of inference and generalization, on which it depends for its justification, 'even if you yourself did not consciously employ any explicit reasoning in the process by which you came to acquire that belief' (Goldberg 2006: 33). By contrast, in the case of testimony – at least when all goes well – we acquire knowledge by accepting what another tells us; we do not reason our way to a conclusion all by ourselves, but remain indebted to our source's reasons for belief. At the heart of the debate about the relationship between testimony and evidence is thus also the question of how inferential our testimony-based beliefs really are.

1. Testimony as legal evidence

In Chapter 1, it was noted that 'testimony' as an umbrella term for offering factual reports as a ground for belief is perhaps most frequent in the legal domain. To the extent that legal proceedings first need to establish the facts – before determining matters of legal and moral responsibility and subsequently deciding on an appropriate legal sanction – they need to base their factual determinations on as complete a range of informational sources as is reasonable in the case at hand. If a defendant is accused of murder, say, the court might take into account biological traces found on the alleged murder weapon, statements of eyewitnesses who were present in the vicinity at the time of the crime, the defendant's cell-phone records that establish his presence in the neighbourhood, and other pieces of evidence, all of which need to be weighed against each other. Thus understood, the testimony of others is simply one type of (legal) evidence among many, and its admissibility is governed by conventional rules concerning the conduct of legal proceedings.

As Coady notes, it is part of the legal status of testimony 'that the speaker is not just offering some statement as evidence but that it *is* evidence' (Coady 1992: 42). To put it crudely, in the formal setting of legal proceedings it is not up to the witness, or her intentions, whether or not her utterance should count as evidence; this is determined by the conventions that govern this particular institutional context. The same, of course, holds for epistemic characteristics of the witness: unreliable, false, or misleading legal testimony, once admitted by the court, is still evidence. In turn, certain kinds of informative speech on the part of the witness – for example, the reporting of hearsay – fail to be legal evidence, even when what is reported is in fact truthful and reliable. Once testimony is admitted as legal evidence, it is to be regarded as on a par with other types of evidence, against which it needs to be weighed. If a judge or jury sides with a witness against a piece of empirical evidence, it must do so on the strength of the witness's testimony (or in light of the weakness of the competing empirical evidence), rather than on the basis of simply taking the witness's word for it.

From the legal standpoint, then, testimony occupies a hybrid position: On the one hand, it is considered as one form of evidence among others, with which it is thought to be on a par. While testimonial evidence cannot claim exemption from critical scrutiny, it can neither be dismissed without good reason. On the other hand, its special status is recognized implicitly in a plethora of rules of evidence, which govern who can be a witness (historically, this category has often been restricted to those of a certain social status), which contents are admissible (declarations of fact, not expressions of opinions; first-hand observations and inferences, rather than hearsay), and which sanctions apply if a witness is found to be making false statements.

For example, in the special case of sworn testimony, intent to deceive is not always necessary for false statements to count as perjury. (In the German judicial system – which relies only in exceptional cases on the swearing in of witnesses – even merely negligent false testimony, provided it has been made under oath, may be punished by up to one year in prison.) Such legal rules reflect the recognition that the evidentiary link between testimony and the facts is more tenuous than, say, the causal link between the blood on a knife and the murder that took place.

2. Epistemological conceptions of evidence

Epistemology employs a broader notion of evidence than the legal domain. For example, in relation to the basis of empirical knowledge, we sometimes speak of the 'evidence of the senses', whereas in connection with scientific knowledge, we routinely speak of evidence for or against a scientific theory. In the former case, what constitutes evidence is sense data – that is, private mental items of an individual – whereas in the second case, the evidence may be distributed across the scientific community (or, increasingly, may exist only as potential knowledge, in the form of electronic data recorded by measurement instruments). At a more abstract level, we may even consider 'evidence' for or against certain philosophical positions – say, whether persistent moral disagreement is evidence against moral realism (i.e. against the view that there are knowable, mind-independent moral facts). Such uses of 'evidence' draw on a more generic understanding of the term than in the legal domain; according to this more general sense, something is considered 'evidence' for a specific proposition p if it counts in favour of the truth of p, makes it more probable that p or simply confirms that p. As this way of putting it already suggests, the specific nature of the relationship between evidence and what it supports can be characterized in a number of ways; indeed, considering the centrality of the concept of 'evidence' across a number of important philosophical debates, one may find it surprising that there is a wide range of competing conceptions of what, exactly, evidence is.

An important strand of epistemological theorizing about evidence takes its lead from an internalist understanding of what it would take for something to 'be evident'. According to epistemological internalism, in order to determine whether one is justified in holding a particular belief that p, 'one need only consider one's own state of mind' (Chisholm 1989: 76). For example, when pondering the justification of a present perceptual belief I hold, it would be enough for me to reflect on my present sensory experience that things are thus and so (perhaps combined with my recognizing that I have no reason to think that I am either hallucinating or being deceived). At least in simple perceptual situations, then, the fact that things are *directly evident* to me is what justifies my corresponding perceptual beliefs. Roderick Chisholm has defined the quality of being evident such that

> a proposition *h* may be said to be *evident* for a subject *S* provided (1) that *h* is reasonable for *S* and (2) that there is no proposition *i* such that it is more reasonable for *S* to believe *i* than it is for him to believe *h*. (Chisholm 1966: 22)

Coupled with certain principles – for example, that if *S* believes that he perceives something to have a certain property, *F*, then it is automatically reasonable for him to believe that there is something that is *F* – it is possible to build a theory of knowledge on the basis of whether propositions are acceptable, reasonable, evident or the opposite. Thus, Chisholm defines knowledge as follows: '*S knows* at *t* that *h* is true, provided: (1) *S* believes *h* at *t*; (2) *h* is true; and (3) *h* is evident at *t* for *S*' (ibid.: 23).

One might worry that, by placing the quality of 'being evident' at the heart of its definition of knowledge, Chisholm's theory of knowledge precludes the possibility of testimonial knowledge. For, whereas it seems plausible that perceptual beliefs can be evident in the sense defined above – that is, more reasonable than any competing beliefs one might hold on the matter – the very fact of the *mediatedness* of testimony might seem to preclude that testimonial beliefs could ever be evident in the same way. And indeed, it would be difficult to see how testimonial beliefs could be *directly* evident to the recipient *S* of testimony (except if they were already so prior to receiving the testimony). Nothing in Chisholm's definition, however, rules out that a belief can also be *indirectly evident*. As James Ross has argued along Chisholmian lines, an informant's act of asserting *h* may well make *h* reasonable to *S*. This is especially obvious in (but is not restricted to) cases when *h* is itself directly evident to *W* – for example in the case of *W* reporting that he has a headache. Surely, if we think that it is possible to acquire knowledge in this situation, 'if *W* believes and correctly reports *h* to *S*, then if it is not more reasonable for *S* to believe that *W* is mistaken or disingenuous than it is for *S* to believe that *W* reports his actual belief correctly, then *h* as reported is at least reasonable for *S*' (Ross 1975: 50). If, furthermore, *h* – through *W*'s asserting it – becomes part of a set of mutually supporting propositions, all of which are reasonable and at least one of which is already evident to *S*, then *S* may very well acquire a testimonial belief that is itself *evident* to *S*, and hence may qualify as knowledge.

In order for a proposition *h* to become (indirectly) evident to *S* on the basis of *W*'s testimony, is it necessary that *W* actually believe *h*? This is an interesting question, which Ross considers using the following example:

> [C]onsider the situation where an authority intends to assert (for some pedagogical reason) something he believes false, but which he is in fact in

error about. Suppose a student 'taking him at his word' finds the statement evidently true, though the student had never given thought to the matter before; may not the assertion become evident to the student? It is not indispensable that W believe what he says (in a particular case) in order for what he says to become evident for S. (Ibid.: 42)

For a testimonial belief to become evident to S, it will often be sufficient if S merely *imputes* knowledge to W – irrespective of whether or not W in fact possesses the knowledge in question. Whether it is possible, in such a scenario, for the recipient to gain testimonial *knowledge* on the basis of the speaker's say-so – given that the speaker believes what he says to be false – is a question that has recently received much attention and will be revisited in Chapter 7 ('Testimonial knowledge: Transmission and generation'). Perhaps all that can be said with certainty is that situations may always arise where we face 'an irresolvable doubt as to whether we have merely a justified true belief or knowledge about something that we have been told' (ibid.: 43).

In contemporary epistemology, the concept of 'evidence' is usually considered to be less a matter of whether a proposition is evident to a reasoner (in the sense of 'being evident' just discussed), but in terms of the effect that one proposition has on the probability of another proposition (or on our assessment of it). If the truth of proposition p (e.g. 'the bloody knife bears the suspect X's fingerprints') would make proposition q more probable ('suspect X is indeed the murderer'), then p is evidence for (the truth of) q. If we call q 'the hypothesis', we can then say that, under conditions of uncertainty, a proposition p is evidence for the hypothesis, q, if p 'raises the probability' of q. (Correspondingly, if p lowers the probability of q, we would say that p is evidence *against* q.) This general idea can be made more rigorous through the framework of conditional probabilities. A *conditional probability* refers to the probability that a particular proposition is true (or that a particular event will occur), when another proposition is known to be true (or another event is known to occur, or to have occurred). In our example, although the *prior* probability $P(q)$ – that is, the probability of X being the murderer – may be quite low, what matters is the probability $P(q|p)$, which is shorthand for: the probability of X being the murder *given the fact that* his fingerprints were found on the murder weapon. Mathematically, the conditional probability can be defined as the joint probability of q and p, divided by the prior probability of p:

$$P(q \mid p) = P(q \& p)/P(p)$$

If there were a perfect correlation between X's committing a murder and his leaving behind his fingerprints, then in all scenarios where p is true, the conjunction $q\&p$ would also be true. (That is simply what it means for q and p to be perfectly correlated.) Consequently, the associated probabilities

$P(q\&p)$ and $P(p)$ would be equal, and the quotient on the right-hand side of the equation would yield 1 — which, in the language of probability, amounts to absolute certainty. No matter how small the prior probability $P(p)$ may have been initially, the conditional probability thus uncovers the close link between p and q. By contrast, if q and p referred to totally independent events — for example to the different outcomes of tossing a fair coin — then the joint probability $P(q\&p)$ would simply be the product of the probabilities of the two events considered independently: $P(q\&p)=P(q)\cdot P(p)$. As a result, the right-hand side in the equation above would reduce simply to the prior probability of q: $P(q)$. The probability of the coin landing heads *given that it previously landed tails* would be exactly the same as its landing heads *simpliciter*: $P(q|p) = P(q\&p)/P(p) = P(q)\cdot P(p)/P(p) = P(q)$ — just as it should for a fair coin.

Perfect correlation and total independence are extreme cases. More typically, at least for two causally related events or findings, q and p, the fact that the former obtains will have some influence on the probability of the latter (and vice versa). If we learn that the murder weapon bears the fingerprints of the suspect, we will not only be psychologically more inclined to believe him guilty, but it will be *rational* for us to adjust our estimate of the likelihood of his guilt accordingly, in the light of the new evidence. To be sure, the deed was done before the bloody knife was discovered, and no one in their right mind would claim that the discovery of the fingerprints 'causes' the suspect's guilt (though it may well cause others to think him guilty). What is at issue is not any absolute probability of how events unfolded, but the question of how likely we should judge the hypothesis q, given that we accept a particular finding p. This allows us to define the concept of 'evidence' in terms of conditional probabilities: p is evidence for a hypothesis q, if and only if $P(q|p) > P(q)$ — that is, if p's occurrence raises the probability of q's occurring beyond its prior probability $P(q)$.

Bayesian epistemologists take this way of thinking about evidence one step further by modelling belief revision along probabilistic lines. The 'probabilities' in question no longer purport to reflect observed frequencies or objective probabilities independently of the reasoner, but instead represent a reasoner's *degree of belief* — that is, her subjective level of certainty as reflected in what she would be willing to rationally bet on. The word 'rationally' here is meant to rule out situations where a reasoner might choose to incur a guaranteed loss: a rational agent will only incur a predictable risk that is at least matched by an equal expected gain. For one's belief system to be rational, it obviously needs to be responsive to incoming evidence. This is where Bayesians turn to a formula developed by Thomas Bayes, which preserves the coherence of our degrees of beliefs (in such a way as to rule out violations of rationality), while allowing us to adjust the strength of our belief in the light of the evidence.

Bayes's theorem relates the conditional and prior probabilities between a hypothesis h and a piece of evidence e in the following way:

$$P(h\,|\,e) = P(e\,|\,h)P(h) / P(e)$$

This simple formula allows one to calculate the conditional probability of the hypothesis *given the evidence* (the left-hand side of the equation) from the prior probabilities of the hypothesis and the evidence considered in isolation, $P(h)$ and $P(e)$, along with the conditional probability *of the evidence* given the hypothesis. The latter, $P(e|h)$, can often be more easily assessed – for example when the hypothesis *entails* the evidence, in which case $P(e|h)=1$. By treating Bayes's theorem as a recipe for updating one's belief system, Bayesians have made significant progress in understanding various problems of confirmation. Yet significant problems remain: for example, Bayes's theorem does not tell us how to assign values for the prior probabilities. Furthermore, any assignments of degrees of belief necessarily take place against the backdrop of background assumptions b. A more complete formulation of the theorem would need to make this explicit:

$$P(h\,|\,e\,\&\,b) = P(e\,|\,h\,\&\,b)\,P(h\,|\,b)/P(e\,|\,b)$$

Background assumptions – for example about the reliability of a witness – can sway our assessment considerably. Thus, one might come to believe the occurrence of an event judged to be objectively unlikely – say, with a low prior probability of $P(h|b)=0.09$ – on the strength of reliable testimony e, say $P(e|h\&b)=0.9$, which the witness would not have given if the event had not occurred, as broadly indicated by, say, $P(e|b)=0.1$. With these numbers $P(h|e\&b)=0.81$, which indicates a reasonably high degree of belief. However, if the witness is moderately more prone to fabricating surprising reports in the absence of unusual events, say $P(e|b)=0.3$, the final estimate of the probability of the event *given the report* and our background knowledge, quickly drops – in this example, to $P(h|e\&b)=0.27$, one third of its earlier value. (This example has been adapted from Coady 1992: 192.) Much, thus, hinges on the appropriate assessment of our informant's credibility if the Bayesian framework is to be of use in treating testimony as a form of evidence. (In particular, if a reasoner S is biased against an otherwise reliable witness W – for example, due to prejudice – not only may S be doing W an injustice, but S may be depriving herself of a potential source of knowledge.)

Epistemological conceptions of evidence differ in peculiar ways from everyday notions. As the attentive reader will have noticed, throughout the past few paragraphs we have been concerned with the truth, or probable truth, of *propositions*. This is obvious when we refer to h as 'the hypothesis', but it equally applies to e. The propositional character of evidence is also being presupposed when we speak of the hypothesis as 'entailing' the evidence, since entailment is a relation that holds between propositions. But, in ordinary usage, 'evidence' is not restricted to propositions: after all, the bloody knife is a physical thing, and whatever information it contains (*qua* physical object) is not due to its expressing a proposition. While it is often easy enough to resolve the resulting conceptual tension, it is worth keeping in mind that not everyone agrees that all evidence is propositional. A second distinction is between evidential internalists who argue that whether or not something is evidence is entirely a matter of a reasoner's mental states and externalists who argue the opposite. Thus, an internalist might argue that all empirical evidence is constituted by (non-propositional) sense data, while an externalist might claim that all knowledge that has been accepted into our corpus – including testimonial knowledge which we could not have experienced first-hand – is available to us as evidence. (See also Kelly 2008: 940.) Timothy Williamson has recently argued that a subject's evidence consists of 'all and only the propositions that the subject knows' (Williamson 1997: 717); on this account, a false belief that *p* could never constitute evidence – though the subject may mistake it for knowledge and wrongly ascribe evidential significance to it. It is generally regarded as a desideratum of a theory of evidence that it should allow for the possibility of *misleading* evidence. This follows, on the one hand, from the general fallibility of all empirical knowledge (according to which reasonable beliefs, based on ordinarily reliable evidence, may yet turn out to be false) and, on the other hand, reflects the very real possibility – not least in the legal domain – that the evidence may have been tampered with. Thus, to take an example from Richard Moran, 'a handkerchief left at the scene of the crime may throw suspicion on someone and perhaps lead to genuine belief in his guilt' (Moran 2005: 13), yet even when it has been deliberately planted in order to frame someone, it nonetheless constitutes genuine evidence for the investigator who is not (yet) in the know. Misleading evidence is still evidence.

Internalism and externalism

'Internalism' and 'externalism' in epistemology refer to general views about what determines a belief's justification. There exist a number of externalist and internalist theories of epistemic justification (as well as a parallel debate in the philosophy of mind, not discussed here, about the source of our mental contents); here we shall look only at the basic idea behind each side in the internalism/externalism debate.

Imagine challenging another epistemic agent *S*'s belief that *p* by requesting justification for why *S* believes that *p*. One response to this challenge will likely come from *S* herself: 'I believe that *p* because I can see it with my own eyes.' Or, 'I believe that *p* because I was told on good authority.' Or, 'I believe that *p* because it follows from *q* and *r*, both of which I know to be true.' Such responses, which come from within *S*'s own perspective, either involve proffering other beliefs that *S* has as *reasons for* her belief that *p*, or they make reference to other factors, such as sense data, which are cognitively accessible to *S* via introspection. Internalism about epistemic justification amounts to the thesis that the factors that contribute to a belief's justification must be available from within the agent's perspective in this way.

However, an external observer, too, can respond to the demand for justification. Such an observer, who may well have a better overall grasp of *S*'s epistemic situation than *S* herself, might point out that *S* formed her belief that *p* in a way that made it highly unlikely that her belief would be false. If the external circumstances and/or causal processes that give rise to *S*'s belief that *p* are such as to ensure the truth, or likely truth, of her belief, it seems reasonable, ceteris paribus, to consider *S*'s belief justified – whether or not *S* herself is aware of the objective facts surrounding her belief formation. Any theory that endorses such objective factors as the basis of epistemic justification, and does not require that the epistemic agent be aware of them, is a species of externalism.

Further reading: For a collection of papers on the internalism/externalism debate and a useful account of its recent history, see Kornblith (2001).

3. Evidentialism and the paucity objection

When trying to come to a judgement on matters that we are not already certain about, we often find ourselves reflecting on the evidence we have: Is the evidence as a whole sufficiently strong to support coming to a conclusion? And if so, which side does the balance of the evidence favour? In situations of disagreement, we might cite some of the evidence we are relying on, in the hope that our opponent will come to recognize its probative force and will be swayed accordingly. In turn, ignoring evidence that is manifestly relevant to the case at hand may either be considered a sign of dogmatism or would indicate that the disagreement runs even deeper, in that what is at issue is the question of whether or not a particular finding constitutes relevant evidence in the first place. When it comes to evaluating our own beliefs, too, evidence often plays an important justificatory role. As David Hume writes in his *Enquiry Concerning Human Understanding*: 'A wise man, therefore, proportions his belief to the evidence' (Section 10.4). The philosophical position that results from turning Hume's recommendation into an epistemological principle that governs all beliefs, at all times, is called *evidentialism*. It is perhaps best summed-up, in slogan-like form, by William Clifford's famous remark, in his essay *The Ethics of Belief*, that 'it is wrong always, everywhere, and for anyone to believe anything upon insufficient evidence' (Clifford 1879: 186).

When stripped of its ethical overtones, evidentialism as a philosophical position amounts to the thesis that beliefs owe their epistemic justification solely to our possessing the requisite evidence. If a belief were held merely on the basis of, say, wishful thinking, such a belief would not be justified. Similarly, whereas some philosophers (e.g. Harman 1986) have argued that, for competent and responsible reasoners, merely finding that we hold a particular belief imbues that belief with some epistemic justification – since we are entitled to assume that we acquired it for good reason – for an evidentialist more is required to render a belief justified. Compare the case of *A* who holds a (well-formed and, at the time of its initial formation, evidence-based) belief that *p*, but has since forgotten all the evidence he once had, and the case of *B* who has forgotten that he originally came to believe *p* on very bad reasons, but continues to hold on to it. Neither *A* nor *B* have any trace of evidence at their disposal, and apart from their different epistemic 'histories' both subjects are alike with respect to their doxastic situation, so evidentialism would seem to demand that both *A* and *B* lack justification for their belief that *p*. Yet many people would argue that, intuitively, there is a justificatory difference between the two cases, with *A* simply continuing to hold a justified belief and *B* never having had a (sufficiently) justified belief in the first place. *Reliabilists*, in particular, argue that, for a belief to be justified, it need only be generated in a reliable (i.e. truth-conducive) way, irrespective of whether a subject has additional evidence supporting the belief in question. On this account, if *A*'s belief was reliably formed and assuming his faculty of memory is likewise reliable, he is justified in holding on to his belief that *p*, even though he may not be able to give reasons or to recall his original evidence; by contrast, *B* lacks justification, since his belief had originally been formed in an unreliable way. According to reliabilism, having evidence – although desirable for independent reasons – is not a necessary condition of our holding justified beliefs; often, simple *de facto* reliance on truth-conducive ways of belief-formation will be sufficient for justification and knowledge.

How specific must evidence be, if it is to boost our degree of belief or make a robust contribution to our epistemic justification? As a rule of thumb, the less specific our evidence, the less 'epistemic mileage' we can expect to get out of it. One reason why finding the suspect's fingerprints on the murder weapon constitutes such convincing evidence for the suspect's guilt is that we think of fingerprints as being highly specific to an individual. By contrast, claiming that one has evidence that the murderer – just like the suspect – is human, would hardly count in favour of the suspect's guilt, although it is of course entirely consistent with it. In short, the claim that a particular proposition is supported by the evidence more often than not carries with it the tacit assumption that it is based on relevant evidence that is sufficiently specific to the case at hand. In the sciences, where evidence is often construed as confirmation along probabilistic lines, it is common to demand that, in one's inductive reasoning, one should focus on the narrowest class of cases for which one has reliable evidence. Thus, if a medical drug is found to be efficacious in 80 per cent of the cases, except for diabetic patients where the efficacy drops to 10 per cent, a doctor choosing medication for a diabetic patient should obviously consider the lower figure; he would not be acting on the best available evidence, and indeed would be irresponsible, if he were to simply go ahead and prescribe the drug in light of the overall figure of 80 per cent efficacy. The more specific the evidence one is aiming for, the more difficult it is to come by; finding evidence that speaks to the specifics of a given case may take considerable effort, yet if one wishes – on the basis of evidence – to distinguish that case from other, equally plausible scenarios, providing such evidence is what is required. In other words, for a claim to be justified on the basis of evidence, there must exist a sufficiently strong connection between the kind of evidence provided and the kind of claim that is at issue.

In the legal domain, testimony is treated as a *species of* evidence; once formally admitted by the court, the statement of a witness is considered to be on a par with empirical evidence, and all forms of evidence are to be weighed against each other. By contrast, philosophers often draw a line between testimony and evidence, and they do so in at least two ways. First, as will be discussed in the next section, it has been argued that treating testimony as merely another form of evidence does not respect the character of the relationship between speaker and hearer, even in successful cases of passing on knowledge. Second, whereas empirical evidence is typically the result of non-arbitrary causal patterns in the world (e.g. 'fire is usually the cause of smoke, therefore smoke is good evidence of there being a fire'), testimony for the most part is the result of a speaker's free (and, in this sense, arbitrary) decision to offer a factual statement as a ground for belief. This suggests that, rather than treat testimony as a species of evidence, it may be more appropriate to attempt to ground testimonial belief in empirical evidence. What kinds of empirical evidence would be required? The obvious kinds to look for would be either evidence that directly supports (or disconfirms) the truth of the claim in question or evidence for (or against) the reliability of the speaker. Given that testimony often concerns matters beyond what we can ascertain first-hand, and given further that, even where such first-hand verification is (at least in principle) possible, making it a requirement would undermine the usefulness of testimony as a shortcut to knowledge, in many cases all a hearer can hope for is the latter: evidence for (or against) the competence and sincerity of the speaker. (There are, of course, other resources the hearer can help himself to – such as background knowledge and considerations of plausibility – but, although a useful tool for screening out some information, these will often lack the specificity required of evidence: typically, in situations of genuine epistemic dependence, we have to rely on the speaker to tell us whether p or not-p, simply because both p and not-p cohere equally well with our background knowledge.)

An influential objection to the idea that reliance on testimony can be fully grounded in empirical evidence arises from the thought that there simply is not enough evidence to go around. To put it a little less crudely, the claim is that people often acquire justified beliefs and knowledge via testimony, even in situations and contexts that are characterized by paucity of evidence: what little evidence is available in such situations tends to be too unspecific or too inconclusive to justify any evidence-based judgements concerning the sincerity and competence of the speaker or the veracity of the claim in question. As Laurence BonJour notes:

> I receive information via testimony on a very wide range of subjects: it would be practically impossible for me to check firsthand about very many of these, and quite a few involve matters that I am unable to check on my own even in principle. (BonJour 2010: 158)

Coady, too, insists that there are many areas 'in which we rightly accept testimony without ever having engaged in the sort of checking of reports against personal observation' (Coady 1992: 83) that would be required if we were to look for evidence for the truth or falsity of the claim in question. If evidence for the truth or falsity of the claim itself is elusive, then what about evidence for the sincerity and competence of the speaker? This too seems elusive:

> [W]hen I ask a stranger on the street for directions to the Empire State Building, do I have enough information about her to justify my accepting her testimony that it is six blocks north? (Lackey 2008: 180)

The intuitive answer is, of course, no. How could I claim to have sufficient evidence about my interlocutor's sincerity and competence when I have had no previous experience of her conduct in similar situations? Yet if, as it turns out, I lack evidence both about the claim itself and about the speaker, there seems to be little hope of grounding my reliance on a particular instance of testimony in empirical evidence pertaining to the encounter in question.

But perhaps the argument in the previous paragraph is moving too quickly. Recall the trade-off noted earlier, between the specificity of evidence and its ease of availability: the more specific the evidence we demand, the more difficult it usually is to come by. Perhaps, then, we can increase the range of available evidence by lowering our expectations regarding how specific the required evidence must be. Doing so would mean having to content ourselves with a more qualitative assessment of the testimony we encounter, but this may be a small price to pay if the only alternative – at least within the framework of evidentialism – would be to suspend testimonial belief for lack of 'hard evidence'. What might some of these more general considerations consist in? One important example is our background knowledge about people and their psychology. After all, when explaining how others behave, we not only appeal to observable evidence, but we typically attribute internal mental states to people – often on the basis of 'simulating', in our imagination, how we would behave if we were in their place. Such 'folk psychology', it may be argued, can supply additional grounds for testimonial belief, even in situations marked by paucity of empirical evidence. Thus, assuming that my interlocutor does not want to deceive me about the location of the Empire State Building (what would she stand to gain from doing so?), I may reason from my own experience of trying to be helpful towards tourists that she is probably intending to give me the correct information. As Jack Lyons argues:

> When trying to figure out whether to believe a particular report, we consider not only (not even primarily) the sort of report being given; we also take into account the mental states of the person doing the reporting (e.g., the speaker's possible motives for lying, the speaker's background experience etc.) (Lyons 1997: 171)

An alternative strategy of circumventing the paucity of evidence problem would consist in seeking out testimonial encounters of a kind that ensures that sufficient evidence is, in fact, available. As a number of critics have pointed out, the standard presentation of testimonial interactions in the epistemological literature tends to overstate the paucity of evidence. Situations such as asking directions from a random stranger whom one knows nothing about – what Jonathan Adler refers to as the 'null setting' – is, in fact, quite rare. As Tim Kenyon notes:

> Of the various people you see on the street, presumably you would not ask directions of the badly sunburned man wearing the new-looking but ill-fitting T-shirt that features a weak, irrelevant pun and the name of that

city printed on the front. That man's bad sunburn radiates *information*. [. . .] He may be a stranger to you, in the ordinary sense of the term, but he is festooned with informational cues that comprise a rich testimonial context. (Kenyon 2013: 75)

In pre-selecting our sources of information – at the level of individuals as well as at the level of, say, media outlets – we rely on a number of 'filters', even before an actual testimonial encounter comes to pass. The testimonial contexts we seek out are thus not as inscrutable as the standard presentation might suggest, but instead incorporate a great many things we know about the social world we live in. The standard way of presenting testimonial exchanges as isolated one-off encounters devoid of context, one might argue, misdescribes our actual testimonial practices. As Paula Olmos notes, through such decontextualization

we [lose] much of the intuitive 'grounds' we normally assume as the everyday explanation of our trust – information about the speaker or the speaker's type and/or characteristics of the specific practice of testimony in which we are involved, with its own, more or less institutionalized, model of authority, etc. (Olmos 2008: 58)

Jonathan Adler nicely captures the spirit of these responses to the paucity objection when he argues that 'no additional specific evidence concerning the informant is necessary to warrant the acceptance' of her testimony, since we already have at our disposal 'our vast collection of *well-founded background beliefs*' (Adler 2002: 159/163). On such a 'relaxed' form of evidentialism, it seems plausible that much of our reliance on testimony can indeed be grounded in some form of evidence, even if the evidence in question will often be fairly unspecific and will include much background knowledge that was itself acquired on the basis of past testimony.

4. The perversity argument

The thought that testimonial acceptance should be evidence-based has been criticized not only for its alleged infeasibility, but also on the grounds that the very idea of treating testimony as derivative from empirical evidence is problematic. Exaggerating only slightly, the suggestion has been that it is 'perverse' to treat testimony *as* evidence, or to (attempt to) reduce it *to* other forms of evidence. This 'perversity argument' (Keren 2012: 700) comes in at least two forms. First, one might object that assimilating testimony to evidence violates the intuition that, when we accept someone's testimony, we are *taking their word for it*. On this view, withholding trust until sufficient independent evidence is available would, in a sense, amount to not trusting our interlocutor at all: instead of treating our interlocutor as a person, capable of vouching for the truth of a matter, we would effectively be reducing them to the status of being a mere instrument for gathering evidence – much like, say, a measurement instrument in science. Second, it has been argued that, while it may be possible to adopt such an instrumentalist stance towards others – even if it comes at the price of undermining trusting interpersonal relationships with them – one cannot in good faith adopt this perspective towards how one would like one's own testimony to be received.

The idea that an evidence-based view misses something vital about the specific character of testimonial knowledge is, perhaps not surprisingly, most popular among those who grant testimony a fundamental status among the sources of knowledge. Thus, Welbourne writes:

> To receive testimony as *evidence* is precisely not to receive it as testimony. [. . .] If, hearing you assert that *p*, I *take it on trust* from you that *p*, I do not treat your assertion as evidence. I take it that you were speaking from knowledge and that I now know that *p* myself through your say-so. (Welbourne 1981: 312)

If, as Welbourne claims, 'commonability' via testimony is the hallmark of knowledge (as opposed to belief; see the discussion of Welbourne's framework in Chapter 2), then it would be quite misguided to interpret our reliance on testimony in terms of evidence-based belief. Other authors have emphasized that the very fact that testimony is typically given intentionally should count against its value *as evidence*. Consider Moran's example (briefly mentioned at the end of Section 2) of the handkerchief that was left behind at the scene of the crime: finding out that it was left there *intentionally* surely would make us more doubtful about whether things are really as they seem. Hence, Moran argues,

> If speech is seen as a form of *evidence*, then once its intentional character is recognized (that is, not just as intentional behavior, but intentional with respect to inducing a particular belief), we need an account of how it could count as anything more than *doctored* evidence. (Moran 2005: 6)

Far from assuring us of the reliability of testimony, so the argument goes, an evidence-based view should make us *less* trusting. Note, though, that Moran's example operates once again with a 'narrow' notion of evidence as being specific to the situation – in this case, specific to the intentions of the speaker. Drawing on general background knowledge would presumably be a more acceptable practice – although explicitly engaging in such reasoning from background knowledge might, of course, itself be interpreted as a sign of doubt, or distrust, on the part of the hearer.

Other critics of the evidence-based view have questioned whether it is even possible to consistently adopt such a view with respect to *all* testimony – including our own. What is at issue, of course, is not whether we have sufficient grounds to rely on our own testimony: after all, if we are in a position to sincerely testify that *p*, we must already be in a position where we take ourselves to have good reason to believe that *p*. Instead, what is being called into question is whether we can look upon our own act of testifying as merely a convenient way of offering nothing more than evidence. Such a self-image of making oneself available as a source of evidence, to be weighed against other kinds of evidence, rather than of oneself as someone who vouches for the truth, does not match the phenomenology of giving testimony. As Cavell notes, 'I do not always feel that speaking to someone is making myself handy for them, or always done because something handier is lacking.' Testifying, so the suggestion goes, is more than a way of offering substitute evidence in support of a claim, but instead is an act of vouching for the truthfulness of one's claim with the integrity of one's person: in turn, for you to accept my assertion *qua testimony* is to believe 'that the words are mine to say, that I have taken them from myself' (Cavell 1979: 392). An even stronger expression of this sentiment is given by Angus Ross, who argues that, although one can – at least temporarily – treat other people's testimony as evidence, one cannot in good faith adopt this stance towards the testimony one freely chooses to offer:

> What I cannot do is see the words I now choose to utter in that [evidentialist] light, for I cannot at one and the same time see it as up to *me* what I shall say and see my choice [. . .] as determined or constrained by facts about my own nature. [. . .] Any attempt to read my choice of words as evidence for the existence of the state of affairs they report will need to make some assumptions about my nature [. . .], but these are not things *I* can see as a constraint on my choice of words. (Ross 1986: 72–3)

Adopting an external ('third-person') viewpoint with regard to one's own act of testifying, Ross argues, is tantamount to an instance of 'bad faith' – a particular 'form of disengagement from my own actions' (ibid.). On at least one interpretation of the view of critics of the evidence-based approach, then, testimony is at its heart an interplay between the first-person and the third-person standpoint and cannot, without loss or serious distortion, be assimilated entirely to one or the other.

Study questions

1 If, as Ross (1986) suggests, it is problematic to treat one's *own* testimony as merely a species of empirical evidence, is it then also problematic to treat other people's testimony as evidence? Why, or why not?

2 It is certainly *possible* to treat our interlocutors' utterances as evidence. For example, I might come to learn that my friend has a cold by inferring it from her hoarse voice. Given that most testimonial interactions are accompanied by *some* relevant circumstantial evidence, is it ever epistemically responsible to discard such evidence and not consider it in our evaluation of the testimony we receive?

3 Does the intentional nature of testifying undermine its value as evidence?

Further reading

Brewer (1998), although mainly concerned with the status of expert testimony as legal evidence (see also Chapter 9 below), gives a philosophically well-informed survey of the connections between legal theory and the epistemology of testimony. Walton (2007) applies the concepts, tools, and methods of argumentation theory to the conceptual triad of witness, testimony and evidence. For an application of Bayesian epistemology to the problem of testimony, see Bovens and Hartmann (2004), chapter 5.

5

Reductionism and anti-reductionism

In Chapter 2, I argued that, for a theoretical account of testimony to be viable, it must be able to accommodate instances of unproblematic acceptance as well as cases of rejection. We are often right to believe what others tell us, but on occasion have reason to reject what we are told. As we shall see, competing philosophical theories differ in where they draw the line between warranted acceptance and warranted rejection of testimony, but no serious theory can afford to be silent on the issue. In particular, a viable theory of testimony should address the question of what justification we have for either accepting or rejecting an instance of testimony – since, without such an account, there would be no way of ruling out illegitimate cases of rejection (e.g. due to prejudice) or instances of gullible acceptance of testimony. The aim of this chapter is to survey existing proposals and, in the course of doing so, shed light on why developing a theory of testimonial justification is often seen as an especially vexed task. Much of the discussion will revolve around the question of whether testimonial justification must ultimately reduce to non-testimonial justification (i.e. to justification that is based on other epistemic sources such as perception, memory and inference). The reductionism/anti-reductionism debate about testimonial justification dominated much of the early phase of recent epistemology of testimony, with reductionists making the case that testimony is a purely derivative epistemic source, while anti-reductionists insisted on its status as a *sui generis* source of knowledge and justification. The next four sections will discuss what a successful reduction would involve (Sections 1 and 2) and which theoretical positions along the reductionist/anti-reductionist spectrum have been defended (Sections 3 and 4); the final section reexamines the question of whether Hume was a reductionist about testimony, and if so, to what extent.

1. Testimony and the problem of justification

Some of the difficulty of developing a theory of testimonial justification stems from the fact that the notion of justification – or at least our 'ordinary' understanding of it – is not without ambiguity. When we speak of *justifying* a belief, we typically imagine this to be an active process of giving reasons, reflecting on the evidence and (possibly) engaging in further inquiry. However, when describing someone as being *justified* in believing that *p*, we do not normally require that the subject must have engaged in any special activity of justifying, prior to our labelling her as justified. Indeed, contemporary epistemology often takes the *state* of being justified to be the primary notion requiring analysis, with the *activity* of justifying being relegated to an afterthought. For beliefs based on perception, memory and inference, this distinction can often be elided without serious consequences: All else being equal, my perceptual beliefs are justified in virtue of their being the output of my (properly functioning) perceptual apparatus, and, when asked to give a justification of my perceptual belief that *p*, I can successfully discharge this burden by simply pointing to my *having seen* that *p*. Barring special circumstances, I do not need to separately justify why I was relying on my senses in the first place.

The case of testimony is different in character. The justifications we can give for accepting the speaker's word – for example, that we judge her to be trustworthy, or that her past testimony has often turned out to be true – do not usually speak directly to the specific claim that *p*. Imagine consulting a scientific expert on a narrow question in a subject area about which we know next to nothing. The reasons we can cite for accepting what the expert is saying – her scientific credentials, say, or her past track record as a reliable testifier – do not in and of themselves tell us whether *p* or not-*p* (where *p* is a specialist claim, for example 'substance XYZ is a powerful carcinogenic'), although they may make it more likely that she knows the answer. Let us assume the expert does, in fact, know the answer, testifies truthfully that *p* and I subsequently form the testimony-based belief that *p*. What justifies my belief that *p*? Two possible answers suggest themselves. The first answer takes seriously the observation that, more often than not, what justifies my *uptake* of the testimony is neutral with respect to the justification *of the corresponding claim* that *p*: for all I know, had the expert asserted not-*p* instead of *p*, I would have with equal conviction formed the testimony-based belief that not-*p*, even though (or rather: precisely because) my grounds for testimonial acceptance were the same as in the actual case. According to this interpretation, my justification for testimonial uptake is not alone sufficient, but needs to be combined with additional specific beliefs about the speaker's testimony – for example the observation that, *on issues relevantly similar to the present one*, the speaker has in the past been a reliable testifier. Only such specific additional information can guarantee, or at least make sufficiently probable, not only that my belief is based on good reasons (in our example, on the testimony of someone I take to be an expert), but also that the reasons I can cite stand in the right sort of relation to the world. This, in essence, is the basic tenet of the reductionist view of testimonial justification.

Alternatively, one might reject the reductionist demand that a hearer must have additional beliefs – in particular, evidence specific to *this* speaker's reliability on the point in question – for the corresponding testimonial belief to be justified. One will then need to identify other mechanisms and sources of justification, both for testimonial acceptance and for the beliefs thus acquired. For example, one might argue that what justifies my testimonial belief that p is not a matter of further facts about my belief system (in conjunction with my initial reasons for accepting the speaker's testimony), but instead is the fact that the speaker is speaking from knowledge, combined with my recognition that this is so. Recall McDowell's remark that at 'the core of a good general account of testimony' is the intuition that, 'if a knowledgeable speaker gives intelligible expression to his knowledge, it may become available at second hand to those who understand what he says' (McDowell 1994: 198). By trusting the speaker, the hearer essentially 'taps into' whatever justification the speaker may have had – even though he may not be able to engage in the activity of *justifying* his beliefs in quite the same way as the speaker. If someone were to challenge my testimony-based belief that XYZ is a powerful carcinogenic, I would be unable to give a detailed biochemical explanation in defence of that claim – the way my expert source might – but this need not mean that I lack justification or knowledge; it merely means that some of *my* justification is, in fact, due to beliefs and evidence possessed by *other* people, notably by the speaker (and, if applicable, her sources). This, in broad outline, is the basic structure of the anti-reductionist model of testimonial justification. The exact mechanism by which we can 'tap into' the speaker's justification – or, as Hardwig puts it, by which we can 'know vicariously' – is a matter of debate among anti-reductionists: thus, one might posit that the rational force of the speaker's justification is communicated via testimony (even when the details are not), or one might argue that the hearer acquires a right to deflect any challenges by referring them back to the original speaker (thereby effectively 'outsourcing' the task of justifying his testimonial beliefs).

Testimony is an indispensable source of knowledge for finite social beings like us; as we have seen in Chapter 2, it is not easy to imagine what our epistemic lives would be like if we could not routinely rely on the testimony of others. As long as there are others who know better, and whom we sometimes rely on for information, the question of testimony – what justifies our testimony-based beliefs? – is a live concern. For an omniscient being, the question of when to accept (and when to reject) testimony simply would not arise – after all, there is nothing it could learn from others. By contrast, finite knowers like us are faced with the need to manage incoming testimony, assess its trustworthiness and either accept or reject it as the basis for our own beliefs on the matter in question. In light of the enormousness of our dependence on testimony, this may seem a daunting task, and yet the overall success of our testimony-based practices suggests that, on the whole, we do well on that score. No prospective theory of testimonial justification that aims at capturing our epistemic predicament can afford to ignore the perspectival element that comes with the need of finite knowers to manage the incoming social flow of information. In particular, this requires that we treat testimonial justification not merely in abstract terms, but with an eye towards the recipient's need to accept or reject a given piece of testimony. This is not to say that considerations beyond the recipient's perspective do not matter to the justificatory status of his testimony-based beliefs: clearly, there are many external factors that are of utmost importance, such as the reliability of the hearer's social environment. Rather, it is to point out that any such considerations raise the further question of what, if any, bearing they have (or ought to have) on the hearer's first-person perspective. As Leslie Stevenson put it, when we look at the problem of epistemic justification in the context of testimony, we are not so much looking 'for conditions for the transmission of knowledge from A to B (formulated from the point of view of a third person, C), but asking from B's point of view what, if anything, can justify B in believing what A says' (Stevenson 1993: 429–30).

Before delving into the details of the various kinds of reductionist and anti-reductionist theories of testimonial justification, it is worth noting the connections between the debate about testimony and the more general internalism/externalism debate in epistemology. This is because, as we shall see, internalist and externalist concerns are often simultaneously present, and preferences along this dimension will also shape one's view regarding testimonial justification. Indeed, the case of testimony can be expected to bring any internalist or externalist leanings into sharp focus since, as noted in the previous paragraph, successful acquisition of testimonial knowledge is the result of an interplay between factors internal to the hearer and facts about the social environment (including, importantly, the speaker). Even generally reliable (external) social environments cannot normally ensure that a hearer is exposed only to (individually) reliable testimony, so a hearer will have to bring his (internal) critical faculties to bear on the assessment of at least some of the testimony he receives. Likewise, even the most diligent and responsible epistemic agent could hardly expect to be able to bootstrap his way to testimonial knowledge all by himself, were he to be immersed in an epistemically hostile environment populated by unreliable, manipulative or outright deceptive interlocutors. The justificatory status of an agent's testimony-based beliefs thus usually depends on conditions in the broader social environment as well as on the agent's epistemic conduct. For example, a stance of universal acceptance might work well in a perfectly reliable social environment, but would result in many objectively unjustified beliefs in an environment that falls short of such high standards of reliability. An internalist, in response, might insist that an epistemic agent must always 'have *some* access to the warranting force of the testimony' (Gerken 2013: 540) and should not simply surrender control of the epistemic status of his testimony-based beliefs to external factors alone. The exact extent to which an account of testimony is indebted to internalism or externalism about epistemic justification depends crucially on the details of the proposal and cannot easily be prejudged; for the moment, it is important to keep an open mind – and also allow for the possibility that a theory of testimonial justification might end up combining features of internalism and externalism. (On this point, see Gerken 2013, and also the hybrid views discussed in Chapter 6.)

2. Reductionism and anti-reductionism

Much of the debate about the source and character of testimonial justification has revolved around the antagonism between reductionism and anti-reductionism. 'Anti-reductionism', although ostensibly defined in opposition to reductionism, may in fact be understood as the more basic epistemological position, in that it treats testimony as on a par with perception and memory. Testimony, thus understood, is one among a number of fundamental sources of knowledge, and it is not surprising that anti-reductionism is therefore sometimes also referred to as 'fundamentalism' (Kusch 2002b: 37). As discussed in Chapter 3, there obviously are significant differences between all the major sources of knowledge, so it is important to be clear about the sense in which testimony is thought to be as fundamental as, say, perception. A hint may be gleaned from the earlier remark that, when it comes to perception, the fact that it perceptually seems to me that p is, all else being equal, sufficient for me to consider my perceptual belief that p to be justified. Unless I have reason to believe my senses are deceiving me, I do not need separate justification for relying on my perceptual apparatus in the first place. On the contrary, the fact that my belief is based on how my perceptual system represents the world to me imbues it with a kind of justification that, at least under normal circumstances, requires no additional argument or independent corroboration from other sources.

Fundamentalism about testimony extends this model to the case of testimonial justification. Testimony, on this account, is a *sui generis* source of justification and knowledge: a testimonial belief is imbued with epistemic justification – of a kind that, given favourable circumstances, is sufficient for knowledge – merely in virtue of the hearer's understanding the speaker's utterance to be an instance of telling. In other words, all that is required for the hearer's belief to be justified is that it be based on the speaker's testimony; no other considerations – such as additional supporting arguments or extraneous evidence – are needed to generate testimonial justification. The anti-reductionist is not claiming that this initial testimonial justification is always sufficient for knowledge: testimony is fallible, and a belief's initial testimonial justification may be defeated by other considerations the hearer might bring to bear on the trustworthiness of a particular claim. But while additional considerations may be able to strengthen – or undermine – a testimonial belief's justification, this does not detract from the fact that, on the anti-reductionist model, a testimonial belief enjoys an initial irreducible justification simply in virtue of the fact that it is based on the say-so of others. Anti-reductionism comes in degrees. An 'unrestricted version' might hold that 'whatever anyone says about anything is, in the absence of contra-indications, worthy of belief', whereas '[a]ccording to a more restricted version, it is only in certain appropriate circumstances that *A*'s asserting that *P* gives a good reason for believing it' (Stevenson 1993: 430). As Faulkner summarizes the anti-reductionist position, 'a testimonial belief that *p*, acquired through accepting a bit of testimony to *p*, does not need to be supported by further beliefs about testimonial appearances' in order for it to be justified, nor does it require 'beliefs to the effect that the bit of testimony was sincere and competent, or otherwise likely to be true' (Faulkner 2011: 8). In other words, the very fact of its testimonial origin confers justification on a belief and may suffice for the hearer to acquire testimonial knowledge.

In Chapter 3 (Section 5), we already encountered a recent example of anti-reductionism in the form of Burge's Acceptance Principle, which holds that a hearer 'is entitled to accept as true something that is presented as true and that is intelligible to him, unless there are stronger reasons not to do so' (Burge 1993: 467). The very fact of its intelligibility, Burge argues, speaks in favour of a given piece of testimony and confers a weak form of justification on a belief formed on its basis. As a result, when confronted with an intelligible message, the recipient is entitled to accept it as true – unless other considerations tell against doing so. Reid, who is often credited with being the modern originator of anti-reductionism about testimony, comes to a similar conclusion by a different route. As discussed in Chapter 3 (Section 2), Reid posits that 'the general principles of our constitution' (Reid 1983: 92) include two complementary principles regarding the giving and receiving of testimony. The first – the principle of veracity – states that we have 'a propensity to speak truth' (violations of which, as in the case of lying, require effort and discomfort that comes with doing violence to our nature); the second, the principle of credulity, is 'a disposition to confide in the veracity of others, and to believe what they tell us' (ibid.: 95). (This might explain why Reid-style anti-reductionism about testimony is sometimes referred to as 'credulism'; see Pritchard 2004: 328.) Both principles 'tally with each other' (Reid 1983: 93), in that they render our reliance on testimony rational and confer justification upon the beliefs formed on its basis. Despite their different argumentative strategies – with Burge arguing for the reason-giving role of mere intelligibility, and Reid essentially positing a 'testimonial faculty that disposes us to believe credible testimony' (Faulkner 2000a: 128) – both arrive at what has been called a 'presumptive right' thesis:

[PRESUMPTIVE RIGHT (PR) THESIS.] A hearer has the epistemic right to believe testimony merely on the ground that it has been asserted. (Insole 2000: 46)

In her original formulation, Fricker – who, as we shall see, is an ardent critic of any form of presumptive right to accept testimony – notes more specifically that the PR thesis affirms the right 'to assume, without evidence, that the speaker is trustworthy, i.e. that what she says will be true, unless there are special circumstances which defeat this presumption', which in turn amounts to 'a kind of irreducibility thesis, since the hearer's right to believe what [he] is told, on this view, stems from a special normative epistemic principle pertaining to testimony, and is not a piece of common-or-garden inductively based empirical inference' (Fricker 1994: 125). In summary, anti-reductionism includes two theses – first, an affirmation of the distinctiveness of testimony as a fundamental source of knowledge, and second, a presumptive right to default acceptance in the absence of defeating circumstances – which combine in such a way that testimonial beliefs are thought to possess default justification simply in virtue of their being formed on the basis of testimony.

Let us turn our attention from anti-reductionism to its competitor, reductionism about testimony. Before discussing specific reductionist proposals, it will again be worthwhile to consider what, in general, reductionism about testimony would amount to. First, reductionism – like anti-reductionism – is a thesis about the justification of our testimony-based beliefs. As such, it is not primarily concerned with the content or subject matter of our testimonial beliefs. This is not to say that content is never important as a criterion for when to accept testimony. As we saw in Chapter 1 (Section 3.1), testimony as a source of knowledge has historically often been taken – by reductionists and anti-reductionists alike – to be restricted to empirical matters. As Kant puts it: 'Holding something to be true on the basis of testimony is always something empirical; and the person who I am supposed to believe must be an object of experience' (VT, AA 08: 396). One rationale for this restriction is the exclusion of alleged supernatural testimony, which people might otherwise fall for and which – to the extent that it has any basis in fact – can usually be explained in perfectly naturalistic terms. (Russell gives the amusing example of 'the Scotch ghost in the eighteenth century, which kept on repeating: "Once I was hap-hap-happy but noo I am meeserable", which turned out to be a rusty spit'; Russell 1948: 208.) But even if one were to broaden the range of permissible testimonial content to include, say, moral or mathematical testimony, reductionists and anti-reductionists can both grant that, although a particular testimonial claim may be new to the recipient, every chain of testimony must begin with content initially derived from other sources, such as perception, memory and reasoning. As Adler puts it: 'In this regard, we are all reductivists' (Adler 2002: 158).

The real bone of contention between reductionists and anti-reductionists, then, is the source and character of testimonial justification. Reductionists hold that the mere fact that a belief is based on the say-so of others does not, in and of itself, confer epistemic justification: whatever justification a testimony-based belief has must ultimately be due to more basic epistemic sources such as perception, memory and reasoning. Reductionists do not deny that many of our testimony-based beliefs are in fact justified – after all, reductionists and anti-reductionists alike are committed to the commonsense constraint that we can acquire justified true beliefs and knowledge via testimony. Instead, what reductionists deny is that a testimony-based belief can be justified *merely* in virtue of the fact of someone else's having asserted the claim in question. There exists, according to reductionism, neither a distinctively testimonial kind of epistemic justification, nor does the mere fact that an interlocutor has asserted a particular claim issue in a presumptive right on the part of the hearer to accept this claim. Of course, as Stevenson notes, 'this cannot exclude the assembling of evidence that some *kinds* of testimonies are reliable and hence, justifiably believable on inductive grounds' (Stevenson 1993: 430). In order for the fact that the speaker has asserted a particular claim to result in justification on the part of the hearer, the hearer must have available to him an appropriate inductive argument, based on relevantly similar past instances, or he must have additional first-hand evidence at his disposal that speaks in favour of accepting the claim in question.

What kind of additional evidence is it reasonable for the reductionist to demand? Most of the time, evidence that directly confirms (or disconfirms) the claim in question will be out of reach, and even when some such evidence is available it will typically be inconclusive – otherwise there would be no need for us to take anyone's word for it in the first place. But even if the hearer lacks evidence that would speak directly to the claim in question, he may nonetheless have considerable evidence pertaining to the trustworthiness (or lack thereof) of the speaker and the credibility of her testimony. Such evidence might include the speaker's past track record, her present behaviour or demeanour, or specific features of the circumstances of the testimonial encounter. Hence, while the hearer may not be able to amass sufficient first-hand evidence in direct support of the truth of the claim in question, he may nonetheless be able to make up for it by gathering sufficient evidence in support of the trustworthiness of the hearer and the credibility of her testimony. This opens up the possibility that evidence of the latter kind may result in sufficient non-testimonial justification for the corresponding testimony-based belief to count as knowledge. The hearer will, of course, still depend on the speaker in important ways – not least for the content of what is being asserted – but he no longer needs to take her word for it, having instead convinced himself on the basis of first-hand evidence that she is a trustworthy witness and that her testimony is credible.

As a final preparatory step, it may be useful to get a clearer understanding of what constitutes a successful reduction. Generally speaking, reduction is the process of accounting for a 'higher-level' concept or phenomenon (which is typically seen as more complex) in terms of 'lower-level' concepts or phenomena, which form the 'reduction base'. A reduction is considered complete if anything that happens at the higher level can ultimately be accounted for, without loss or residue, in terms of the concepts or phenomena at the more basic level. In particular, a successful reduction must do more than merely make plausible that the higher-level phenomenon does not violate (and in this sense, is compatible with) what happens at the purportedly basic level. As an example, consider the relation between biology and physics. No serious contemporary biologist denies that biological organisms are ultimately composed of molecules and atoms, which in turn are governed by the fundamental laws of physics. But very few, if any, contemporary biologists would think it feasible – or even desirable – to embark on the Sisyphean task of reducing, say, the empirical laws of population biology to the more fundamental laws governing elementary particles and fields. It is one thing to acknowledge that, at an ontological level, biological systems are just 'physical stuff'; it is quite another to claim that our biological theories and explanations could only be considered justified to the extent that they have been successfully 'reduced' to physics. If the latter were the case, we could hardly claim to know a single biological fact. The – admittedly imperfect – analogy with the case of testimonial knowledge should be clear. Testimony, too, depends – causally, and for much of its content – on supposedly more basic processes such as perception, memory and inference. But this does not entail that a complete reduction is either feasible or desirable. Insisting that a reduction is possible 'in principle' – perhaps in an ideal world where we would enjoy much greater access to first-hand evidence than we in fact do – is a moot point if there are principled reasons why, under any actual circumstances, it turns out to be impossible in practice. Recall that, according to reductionism, our testimony-based beliefs are justified precisely to the extent that we are able to justify them on the basis of more fundamental (perceptual, memorial and inferential) beliefs. The mere promise of a successful reduction simply cannot play the kind of reason-giving role demanded by reductionism. As this makes clear, any reductionism that is true to its name sets itself the formidable task of showing how testimonial justification can be fully accounted for in terms of the more basic epistemic sources. At the same time, any attempt to alleviate this burden of proof, for example by broadening the 'reduction base' to also include non-basic elements, would jeopardize the rigour that motivated reductionism in the first place. How various versions of reductionism have attempted to navigate this tension is the topic of the next two sections.

3. Global justification

The problem of justification can be approached in different ways. One strategy is to aim for a *global* account which, for a given source of knowledge, would consist of general arguments justifying our reliance on it in a wholesale manner. A particular belief would then be justified simply in virtue of being an instance of a more general type of knowledge, whose overall validity and reliability have already been established. By contrast, a *local* account of justification would examine the question of justification anew for each individual belief. On this account, whether or not a belief is justified needs to be determined on a case-by-case basis and is not decided by simply recognizing the belief as the output of a more general belief-forming mechanism. In this section, we shall focus on the global justification of testimony – that is, on general arguments aiming to provide a wholesale justification of testimony as a source of knowledge.

Global reductionism denies that testimony is a *sui generis* source of justification. Any justification we have for relying on testimony as a source of knowledge must ultimately be due to, and reducible to, considerations involving only non-testimonial sources. As such, global reductionism rejects any argument in favour of the distinctness of testimonial justification and seeks to assimilate testimony to the more basic epistemic sources of perception, memory and inference. Inductive reasoning is accorded special significance in this endeavour, for it is only by drawing on one's own past experience that one can gradually establish a track record of testimony as a reliable source of knowledge:

> If one finds that reports on certain kinds of topics or made in certain sorts of circumstances or by certain kinds of people tend to correlate well with the facts of the relevant matters whenever one investigates them for oneself, one might reasonably come to rely on those kinds of testimonies thereafter. (Stevenson 1993: 430)

On the global reductionist picture, the term 'testimonial justification' is best understood as shorthand for a diverse set of inductive arguments, background knowledge, and first-hand observations, which in favourable circumstances may come together to render reliance on certain types of testimony justified. Although global reductionism is often referred to as the 'standard view of testimony' (ibid.) or 'the more traditional position' (Shogenji 2006: 332), it is in fact not easy to find explicit endorsements of it in the relevant literature. Among recent analytic philosophers, J. L. Mackie comes closer than most to professing sympathies for global reductionism, when he expresses his hope that, '[a]lthough the greater part of what each one of us knows comes to him by testimony, even this is in principle open to being supported indirectly by the knower's own experience' (Mackie 1969: 257). Mackie also provides a sketch of how an individual might go about supporting testimony by first-hand evidence. As Mackie argues, beliefs

> that one acquires through testimony, that is, by being told by other people, by reading and so on, can indeed be [considered knowledge], but only if the knower somehow checks, for himself, the credibility of the witness. And since, if it is a fact that a certain witness is credible, it is an external fact, checking this in turn will need to be based on observations that the knower makes himself – or else on further testimony, but, if an infinite regress is to be avoided, we must come back at some stage to what the knower observes for himself. (Ibid.: 254)

The prospects of global reductionism, thus, depend crucially on the hearer's having amassed a sufficiently rich (non-testimonial) reduction base consisting of all those things he knows 'off his own bat' (ibid.).

How might a reasoner go about establishing the requisite inductive relationships which, according to global reductionism, are the source of the justification of our testimony-based beliefs? Two strategies suggest themselves. First, the hearer can look for first-hand evidence in order to determine whether what is reported is really the case; second, he can turn to past observations of reports and their correspondence to reality as a basis for extrapolating to future instances of testimony. The first strategy has obvious limitations: Besides being merely impractical, it will often be impossible, as a matter of principle, to directly establish the truth or falsity of the claim, for example when the testimony concerns past events. The second approach, which is aimed at checking not the reported fact itself but the conditions under which the report was made, fares only marginally better. For, given the wide variety of testimonial interactions, inductive generalization seems feasible only for one reference class at a time, where each reference class contains reports of a certain kind. Testimony, however, does not come neatly packaged into disjunctive reference classes. Recall how Coady illustrates this point with the example of the statement 'There is a sick lion in Taronga Park Zoo': Is it to be classified as a 'medical report or geographical report or empirical report or existence report' (Coady 1992: 84)? Given that any estimate of the inductive support of the statement will depend on which reference class it is assigned, and given further that the choice of reference class is underdetermined, it seems that no non-arbitrary global reduction of testimony to inductive reasoning on the basis of non-testimonial evidence is possible. (The reference class problem is, of course, entirely general and also applies to, say, the problem of predicting individuals' behaviour on the basis of social information about them.) Even when a classification seems to naturally suggest itself, for example in contexts where one is dealing with *witnesses* of a certain kind, such as expert witnesses in a court of law or historians writing about past events, this does not guarantee that an inductive generalization will eventually be successful: We may, for example, be unable to make a first-hand assessment of the track record of certain expert witnesses, or we may be unable to seek out other members of the same reference class of testifiers without relying on further testimony:

> [W]e cannot use the idea of a *kind of report* as equivalent to *report of a kind of speaker* and then proceed to validate testimony along the lines of [global reductionism] because the kind of correlation situation whose existence we would supposedly be investigating would have to be known by us to exist already before we could set up the terms of the investigation. (Ibid.)

While these objections do not rule out that, in isolated instances, it may be possible to give a reductionist justification of a *specific* testimony-based belief – though, in most cases, even this would involve considerable effort – they do tell against global reductionism as a general model of how testimonial justification works. It is for this reason that the wholesale reduction of testimony to more basic epistemic sources – as demanded by global reductionism – is regarded as a non-starter by most contributors to the debate.

The failure of global reductionism might be seen as opening up space for a thoroughgoing anti-reductionism, which would place simple, trusted acceptance (of the kind described in Chapter 2) at the heart of its account of testimony as an irreducible source of knowledge. Given that anti-reductionists are committed to the distinctiveness of testimonial justification, one would expect them to have a preference for general arguments in support of testimony as an irreducible source of knowledge – that is, for accounts that aim at global justification. And indeed this is what one finds. Burge's Acceptance Principle, which entitles a hearer to accept as true anything that is presented as true and is intelligible to him (unless he has stronger reason not to do so), is just one such example. Another much-discussed attempt to establish testimony as a fundamental source of knowledge that does not stand in need of reduction is due to Coady, who considers whether a global argument may be given that would provide us with, in some sense, a 'guarantee of truth' (1992: 173). Coady's preferred argument draws on Donald Davidson's 'interpretationism', which in turn is intended as a solution to the problem of radical interpretation. According to Davidson, in order to interpret any interlocutor correctly and to understand what he says, we need to apply a *principle of charity* – that is, we must assume overwhelming agreement, at the level of beliefs, between ourselves and the speaker. Since this applies to *any* interpreter and *any* interlocutor, Davidson argues, it must also apply to the hypothetical case of an omniscient interpreter:

> [I]magine for a moment an interpreter who is omniscient about any sentence in his (potentially) unlimited repertoire. The omniscient interpreter, using the same method as the fallible interpreter, finds the fallible speaker largely consistent and correct. By his own standards, of course, but since these are objectively correct, the fallible speaker is seen to be largely correct and consistent by objective standards. [. . .] Once we agree to the general method of interpretation I have sketched, it becomes impossible correctly to hold that anyone could be mostly wrong about how things are. (Davidson 1986: 317)

Introducing the theoretical device of an omniscient interpreter is thought to provide the important link between mere overlap of belief systems and truth. Coady uses Davidson's belief-centred arguments and applies them, with some modifications, to testimonial utterances. Where Davidson argues that interpretation can only take place against the backdrop of a largely shared 'system of belief', Coady speaks of a fundamental 'communality of constitution [which] gives rise to some basic similarity of outlook and hence a considerable communality of beliefs and interests'. This, Coady argues, 'strongly suggests a reasonable degree of reliability about the testimony of others' (Coady 1992: 167–8).

Although Coady's argument is intriguing, it is by no means clear whether his move from overlap between belief systems (which, if one accepts Davidson's point, may be a necessary presupposition to make) to the reliability of testimony (which is entirely a matter of one's actual epistemic environment) is warranted. For Coady's argument to be successful, and for it to establish that the majority of testimony we encounter could not be false, the principle of charity, too, would have to apply not at the level of beliefs, but instead at the level of assertive speech acts. But what is true of beliefs, need not be true of assertions (and vice versa): sometimes assertions deliberately misrepresent beliefs, and often beliefs go unreported. As Davidson himself notes: 'What is shared does not in general call for comment; it is too dull, trite, or familiar to stand notice' (Davidson 1984: 200). Hence, truthful testimony at best represents a small subset of a person's beliefs – one that is 'filtered' by the speaker, who need not have his interlocutor's best epistemic interests at heart. Thus, it is doubtful that the transition from beliefs to testimonial statements can be made as smoothly as would be required for Coady's Davidsonian argument to work. Yet even if one found the argument acceptable, a further problem would remain: all it would establish is that testimony, *by and large*, could not be mostly wrong about how things are. The impossibility of global error, however, does not rule out that any testimonial claim, considered singly, might turn out to be false. (On this point, see Lipton 1998.) These criticisms make plain that the interpretationist defence of trust in testimony lacks specificity: it can neither distinguish between relevant or irrelevant testimony, nor does it give any indication as to when it would be rational to reject testimony. While it may succeed in making plausible that not all testimony could be false all the time, more than the mere impossibility of global error would be required for a wholesale justification of testimony as an irreducible source of knowledge.

As a final example of a global anti-reductionist defence of testimony, let us consider a transcendental argument due to Stevenson, which is intended to show that the general reliability of testimony is, in fact, presupposed by global reductionism itself. The argument is in the same ballpark as Coady's and Burge's, insofar as it too relates to issues of intelligibility and interpretation, but it adds an interesting theoretical twist by aiming to show that the very process of assigning determinate content to our interlocutors' utterances – a necessary precondition of any reductionist project of testing our interlocutors' testimonial claims against the facts – depends on a prior endorsement of testimony as a reliable source of knowledge. If successful, the transcendental argument would leave reductionists in the awkward position of having to argue that, as Tomoji Shogenji puts it, 'our trust in testimony can be justified by perceptual and memorial evidence *before* we even assign meaning to utterances'. This would be a hopeless position to be in, since it would seem to require that we be able to 'justify our trust in testimony [. . .] without even knowing the propositional contents of the utterances' (Shogenji 2006: 336). Stevenson's argument begins with a significant concession to the proponent of reductionist individualism, by granting the possibility of a 'completely self-taught idiolect'; however, it then goes on to build a case against the possibility of global reductionism:

> If our lone enquirer is to begin to amass the inductive evidence which [the global reductionist] says he needs before he may begin to accept even one piece of testimony, he has to establish correlations between *others' assertions* that *p*, and the fact of *p* as observed by himself. But to do this, he has to know which noises or marks made by others constitute assertions that *p*, and so he has to be able to know that some other minds are using symbols with certain meanings. [. . .] How could our lone enquirer know that someone means 'That is bitter' by a pattern of sounds they sometimes emit? Only, surely, by finding that that noise is (fairly reliably) made only when tasting samples which the enquirer himself recognizes as bitter. Thus one cannot justify interpreting certain performances as observation-statements, i.e., as testimony about what someone perceives, without already committing oneself to the assumption that such statements are reliable, likely to be true. (Stevenson 1993: 441–2)

The transcendental argument places the onus on the reductionist to show how one can assign determinate content to utterances without already assuming the general reliability of (testimonial) observation statements. Some recent defenders of reductionism have taken up this challenge, arguing that the puzzle can be resolved if one treats the claim that observation statements are generally reliable not as a necessary presupposition, but as itself a testable hypothesis. The hearer would, in effect, be continuously testing both 'the hypothesis that a certain utterance is to be interpreted in a particular way' (Shogenji 2006: 338) *and* the hypothesis that testimony is generally credible. (For a detailed argument along these lines, see Shogenji 2006.) Whether or not one considers the transcendental argument for anti-reductionism 'an almost impregnable defence against the reductionist' (Insole 2000: 48), this much is clear: along with the various objections discussed earlier, it exerts considerable pressure on reductionists to move from global attempts to reduce testimony to perception, memory, and inference, to more sophisticated versions of reductionism – including those that allow for a limited role of (previously acquired) testimonial beliefs in carrying out the reduction of new testimonial beliefs and their justification.

4. Local reductionism

Not all attempts at reduction, however, have to be global. Even if global reduction of testimony to perception, memory and inference – 'without remainder', as it were – is not possible, it may still be possible to provide a *local* reduction in cases of testimonial beliefs formed by a mature recipient. Elizabeth Fricker has developed just such a 'local reductionism', which acknowledges both that any attempt to reduce the justification of testimonial beliefs to non-testimonial sources of evidence must proceed on a case-by-case basis, and that, in investigating the justificatory basis of our beliefs as mature reasoners, we must necessarily rely on some conceptual, linguistic and other background knowledge that we acquired as children, unreflectively, on the basis of other people's testimony. Keeping these assumptions in mind, here is how one might summarize the central thesis of local reductionism (this formulation is based on Christopher Insole's summary of Fricker 1987; 1994; 1995; see Insole 2000: 45):

> [POSSIBILITY OF LOCAL REDUCTION THESIS.] In cases of knowledge by testimony gained by a mature recipient, it is possible to reduce the epistemic status of the testimonial beliefs thus formed to other epistemic resources such as perception, memory and inference.

Initially, there is a lot that is intuitive about this modification of the more general reductionist position. By referring to individual instances of testimony-based beliefs, rather than to testimony as a category, it makes reduction a case-by-case affair, thereby avoiding the sort of overgeneralization that undermined global reductionism. By restricting the demand for reduction to mature recipients of testimony, it both acknowledges our 'general and irredeemable debt to past testimony' (Fricker 1995: 404) and preserves the idea that, as *mature* reasoners, 'one should trust what one is told only when one has adequate evidence that the speaker is trustworthy' (Fricker 2004: 126). In the case of children, blind trust may be excusable, even necessary for acquiring language and concepts, but for us as mature reasoners, different standards apply:

> Does not mere logic, plus our common-sense knowledge of what kind of act an assertion is, and what other people are like, entail that we should not

just believe whatever we are told, without critically assessing the speaker for trustworthiness? (Fricker 1995: 400)

In demanding a critical assessment of the evidence of a speaker's trustworthiness, for each case of testimony received by a mature reasoner, local reductionism rejects any form of presumptive right thesis, according to which the recipient, all else being equal, has a prima facie entitlement to believe what he is told. A presumptive right to believe testimony 'without any investigation or assessment', so the argument goes, would constitute 'an epistemic charter for the gullible':

> We know too much about human nature to want to trust anyone, let alone everyone, uncritically. [. . . W]e know too well how, and how easily, what we are told may fail to be true. (Ibid.)

In order to avoid being misled by insincere testifiers (or being led into error by those who are merely incompetent), 'a hearer should always engage in some assessment of the speaker for trustworthiness' (Fricker 1994: 145). The assessment envisaged by local reductionism requires more than the merely interpretative act of 'recognising an utterance by a speaker as a speech act of serious assertion' (ibid.: 148) – even if, as Fricker argues, the two tasks are continuous with one another:

> The theme of my account is: the *epistemically responsible hearer* will do *a bit more of the same*. She will assess the speaker for sincerity and competence, by engaging in at least a little more interpretation of [the speaker]. (Ibid.; italics added)

More specifically,

> she [=the hearer] should be continually evaluating him [=the speaker] for trustworthiness throughout their exchange, in the light of the evidence, or cues, available to her. This will be partly a matter of her being disposed to deploy background knowledge which is relevant, partly a matter of her monitoring the speaker for any tell-tale signs revealing likely untrustworthiness. (Fricker 1994: 150)

Both the active deployment of background knowledge (by which we might, for example, come to judge certain testimonial claims as too implausible to warrant belief) and the monitoring of the speaker (by which we may hope to detect the speaker's intention to deceive, irrespective of the actual testimonial content) serve as 'filters', allowing only trustworthy information to pass through while rejecting potentially untrustworthy testimony. On this account, testimonial beliefs derive whatever justification they possess from the fact that they have been appropriately monitored and screened by the recipient. Furthermore, the reliability of *acceptable* testimony is directly linked to the *rejection* of unsupported, or suspicious, testimony. It is important, therefore, that instances of rejection be themselves rationally justified, and that, in rejecting a given instance of testimony, we can appeal to resources – such as evidence of the speaker's insincerity – that would render such rejection rational. Providing a defense of the rationality of rejection is crucial given the fact that local reductionism is expressly directed 'against gullibility' (Fricker 1994), urging instead that withholding of belief may be rational more often than we would like to think. In light of the importance that local reductionism attaches to the duty to monitor one's interlocutors' testimony, as well as to the corresponding right to reject such testimony if it fails to meet the required standards of trustworthiness, the rational defensibility of instances of rejection turns out to be a crucial theoretical ingredient of local reductionism.

In summary, local reductionism demands that the justification we have for relying on testimony must be earned anew in each case, by exercising our critical abilities, 'scrutinising' our interlocutor for signs of insincerity or incompetence, 'engaging' in interpretation, 'constructing' explanations of his behaviour and so forth. Assessing the speaker's trustworthiness, on the local reductionist account, is an achievement and must issue in reasons for belief or disbelief that are accessible to the hearer: testimonial justification cannot simply be assumed, but must be actively established, which typically involves an act of inference. 'Monitoring' our interlocutors and constructing an 'explanatory mini-theory' for each new piece of testimony is crucial to this process. (All of these locutions are taken from Fricker 1995: 404–5.) As Fricker puts it in a more recent paper, 'the hearer's right to trust the speaker must be earned by her possession of enough evidence to ground an empirically justified belief that the speaker is trustworthy' (Fricker 2002: 379). In order not to make this requirement too burdensome on the hearer, Fricker argues that the evidence a hearer, H, must have of a speaker S's trustworthiness, need not be stronger 'than whatever property of S it takes' to bridge 'the logical and epistemic gap between "S asserted that p", and "p"' (Fricker 1994: 129). In other words, the hearer need not himself establish the truth, or likely truth, of what S asserts, but he needs to be able to determine, on this particular occasion, 'that S possesses this weakest gap-bridging property', in order for his acceptance of S's testimony to be justified. While this may look like a move that relaxes the demands on the hearer, it is still a formidable requirement – since it requires that H must *take herself as having knowledge* that S is trustworthy. This brings out a strong internalist element in local reductionism: merely being placed in a favourable epistemic environment and habitually accepting reliable testimony is, by the lights of local reductionism, never in itself sufficient for testimonial knowledge – the recipient must always be able to give reasons why *this* interlocutor, on *this* occasion, is to be trusted.

In Chapter 3, we already encountered a criticism of one of the core ingredients of local reductionism: inferentialism about testimonial acceptance. Whereas local reductionism insists that acceptable testimonial beliefs must always be inferentially grounded in specific reasons the hearer has for believing the speaker 'to be trustworthy on this occasion independently of accepting as true her very utterance' (Fricker 1995: 404), anti-reductionists like Coady have pointed out that we often appear to form justified testimony-based beliefs without engaging in inferential reasoning or conscious monitoring of our interlocutors. The example Coady gives is that of calling up a company hotline to inquire about an outstanding bill and trusting an anonymous voice to tell us the correct amount. (See Chapter 3, Section 3.) In the remainder of this section, I shall build on this earlier discussion and offer three further criticisms, each of which attacks a core element of local reductionism. The first line of criticism casts doubt not on the psychological plausibility of local reductionism's account of 'monitoring', but on its ability to establish a rational basis for testimonial acceptance and rejection. (See Gelfert 2009: 176–81.) The second criticism concerns local reductionism's distinction between a 'developmental' phase that allows for simple trust and a 'mature' phase that requires careful screening of one's interlocutors; although initially plausible, such a distinction cannot be consistently maintained across the various epistemic domains. The final line of criticism explores whether it is possible to amend local reductionism, for example by weakening its demands for evidence, before concluding that structural features of local reductionism render such amendments unsuccessful.

Turning to the first line of criticism, it will be useful to begin by reflecting on the character of the evaluative mechanisms that, according to local reductionism, enable us to arrive at reasoned judgements concerning the trustworthiness of *this* interlocutor, on *this* occasion. According to Fricker, much of our evaluative activity 'may be automatic and unconscious' (Fricker 1995: 404) and is directed at analysing our interlocutor's behaviour and demeanour:

> the specific cues in a speaker's behaviour which constitute the informational basis for this judgment [concerning the speaker's trustworthiness] will often be registered and processed *at an irretrievably sub-personal level*. (Fricker 1994: 150; italics added)

Much hinges on the question of whether such a conception of inferential processing is robust enough to achieve the kind of reduction that is required in order to regard testimonial justification as merely derived from more basic epistemic resources. Furthermore, to the extent that local reductionism is intended as a defence of epistemic autonomy against the dangers of gullibility, it must leave room for an exercise of one's critical faculties. If our knowledge 'of what other people are like' is to be at all compelling, then we must be in a position to convince ourselves, on the basis of that 'commonsense knowledge' (Fricker 1995: 400), to withhold simple acceptance whenever it would be epistemically advantageous to do so. If, however, the crucial act of monitoring is accomplished by subconscious processes, then this is not much of an epistemic accomplishment: *sub-personal* monitoring, strictly speaking, does not amount to any critical assessment at all, since critical judgement requires that the mechanisms and standards by which we judge be open to scrutiny – which, by definition, is not the case if they operate 'at an irretrievably sub-personal level'. In any case, merely positing the *existence* of sub-personal mechanisms does not guarantee that they are indeed sources of epistemic justification – at least not the kind of (internalist) justification required by local reductionism, which demands that the hearer be able to credit himself with specific knowledge of whatever quality of the speaker makes her trustworthy *on this occasion*.

Fricker anticipates some of the problems arising from the rational inscrutability of subconscious judgements, yet insists that her account succeeds nonetheless in giving a 'justificationist account' of knowledge (Fricker 1994: 141) and in demonstrating that, as far as testimonial justification is concerned, '"local" reduction is possible' (Fricker 1995: 403):

> [I]nsisting that subjects be able to retail the details of the cues they have responded to is demanding the impossible; but we may insist, compatibly with the sub-personal character of these perceptual or quasi-perceptual capacities, that the subject's beliefs must not be opaque to her, *in that she must be able to defend the judgement which is the upshot of this capacity with the knowledge precisely that she indeed has such a capacity* – that 'she can tell' about that kind of thing; though she does not know how she does it. (Fricker 1994: 150; italics added)

This passage points to an inherent instability in Fricker's account: If testimonial knowledge depends on the brute reliability of 'sub-personal' mechanisms, about whose workings we must remain ignorant, then this leaves little room for the sustained defence of epistemic autonomy as which the position was originally advertised. By making acceptance of testimony a matter of sub-personal mechanisms, local reductionism jeopardizes not only its strong claim to preserving autonomy, but also deprives itself of the resources necessary to make the speaker's response rationally justifiable.

But is this conclusion too hasty? After all, Fricker insists that the subject's critical capacity, and her beliefs about it, 'must not be opaque to her' – she must be able to defend her critical assessments 'with the knowledge precisely that she indeed has such a capacity'. However, the assumption that such knowledge is readily available to us is implausibly optimistic: many people consistently overestimate their ability to pick up on signs of insincerity or incompetence, while others tend to underestimate their critical capacities even if these are *in fact* on a par with those of their more confident counterparts. Given how widespread mismatches of this sort are, surely one should not be too quick to declare that a recipient cannot possibly acquire testimonial knowledge merely on the grounds that he lacks such rather arcane self-knowledge. In any case, the kind of knowledge posited by local reductionism – that is, knowledge of one's own monitoring abilities – is not nearly sufficient to lend inferential support to testimonial acceptance and rejection. This is nicely illustrated by Fricker's own examples of how sub-personally derived judgements can be 'fished up into consciousness and expressed' (ibid.). These include such utterances as

I didn't like the look of him;
Well, she seemed perfectly normal. (Ibid.)

While these are indeed familiar expressions of attitudes of trust and distrust, they are hardly paragons of critical assessment and autonomous judgement. The first example in particular sounds more like an epistemic charter for the cavalier dismissal of others' opinions, which may well be the result of prejudice on the part of the hearer. If inferential judgements were registered at the conscious level only in such a crude way, they could hardly provide us with sufficiently robust reasons to render rejection of testimony rationally defensible.

Unlike global reductionism, which aims at a wholesale reduction of all testimonial knowledge to non-testimonial grounds for belief, local reductionism allows for the use of beliefs acquired from past testimony in assessing new instances of testimony. Testimonial beliefs that were acquired during the 'developmental phase' are exempt from the demands of reductionism, which apply only to testimony received by mature hearers:

Acknowledging *my general and irredeemable debt to past testimony*, I may nonetheless want to trust no new informants unless I have grounds to believe them trustworthy. [. . .] My reliance on a particular piece of testimony *reduces locally* just if I have adequate grounds to take my informant to be trustworthy on this occasion independently of accepting as true her very utterance. (Fricker 1995: 404; first italics added)

While this move significantly broadens the reduction base available to mature reasoners – which now includes testimonial beliefs acquired during the developmental phase, in addition to non-testimonial beliefs and evidence – the rigour of subsequent reductions depends on there being a clear demarcation between the mature inferential phase and the formative developmental period. This raises the question of exactly where to draw the line, and on what basis. As Insole notes:

> Presumably the vital feature of the developmental phase here cannot *just* be calendar age: it is not just in virtue of being eight years old that someone is not required to monitor and assess a speaker of trustworthiness [. . .]. It must be in virtue of an *epistemically relevant feature* of the subject's epistemic capacities and experience, which is, often but *not exclusively*, due to youth. (Insole 2000: 51–2)

Anyone studying a new subject, learning a new language, or finding his way around a new community with its own rules and conventions, will sometimes find himself in a 'developmental' phase, irrespective of calendar age. This raises the worry that 'the developmental and mature phases do not run one after the other, but concurrently and in parallel' (ibid.: 52), depending on individual level of expertise and abilities. This would make it exceedingly difficult for the hearer to keep track of which instances of testimony are properly 'developmental' (and may thus be accepted on trust) and which need to be scrutinized and monitored carefully. (One could even imagine the somewhat paradoxical case of a speaker's mistaking his lack of critical assessment for a sign that the testimony in question must therefore be of a kind that can be legitimately trusted.) When the reduction base is a continually shifting target, because of concurrent developmental and mature phases, carrying out a successful reduction may become a nigh impossible feat.

In response to this criticism, the local reductionist might argue that what matters to the 'developmental phase' is not the acquisition of new types of factual content, but the acquisition of, on the one hand, a certain basic ('commonsense') conception of the way the world is and, on the other hand, the ability to identify those tell-tale signs of insincerity and incompetence that the mature hearer is supposed to look out for in his interlocutors. There is some evidence that this is what Fricker has in mind when she writes about the developmental phase that '[s]imply-trusted testimony plays an inevitable role in the causal process by which we become masters of our commonsense scheme of things' (Fricker 1995: 403). Yet this simply pushes the problem back one step: What counts as a tell-tale sign of insincerity and incompetence varies across (sub)cultures, disciplines, professions and their associated idioms and behaviours, mastery of which cannot be assumed to be 'locked in' during a single initial phase of development. Regarding the suggestion that what matters is only the 'commonsense' part of the knowledge one has acquired early in one's development, it is worth noting that this leads to another unfavourable trade-off for local reductionism, since '*either* what we learn in the developmental phase can have a substantial factual content, in which case we are pushed towards admitting that the mature and developmental phases run concurrently [. . .]; *or* what we learn in the developmental phase has a vanishingly small substantial content, so limited that it is dubious that this is something we learn at all rather than something which is a prerequisite to learning' (Insole 2000: 52–3) – in which case it would likely be too narrow a reduction base for the mature reasoner to rely on for the justification of new testimonial beliefs.

Finally, let us consider whether local reductionism can be modified in a way that would address the worries raised so far. One response to the obvious difficulty of separating out a stable reduction base from among the many testimonial beliefs an individual acquires throughout successive phases of intellectual growth, would be to give up on the strict distinction between a 'developmental' and a 'mature' phase. Perhaps what makes a hearer epistemically 'mature' is the fact that he, unlike an immature reasoner, does not simply trust what he is told, but seeks to inferentially integrate new testimonial beliefs into his overall belief system by checking for coherence. Such a modified account would no longer be very reductionist in spirit – since coherence would now be checked against one's belief system as a whole, including testimonial and non-testimonial beliefs – but it would preserve the intuition that testimonial acceptance must be *reasoned* acceptance, on the basis of evidence available to the recipient (in this case, evidence of coherence between the speaker's testimony and the recipient's beliefs). How might such an internal check for coherence work in practice? For any given new testimonial claim, there are three possibilities: A) the claim bears no obvious relation to one's belief system; B) the claim does not cohere with, but instead is in tension with, one's belief system; and C) the claim is coherent with one's belief system. (See Maltzahn 2006: 101–2.) Scenario A describes a situation where we have no prior beliefs and have had no prior experiences of a relevant kind, so considerations of coherence are of no help in determining whether to accept or reject the testimony in question. A test for coherence, under such conditions, would not license belief on an inferentialist picture that demands positive reasons for acceptance. As a corollary, this would rule out the possibility of acquiring knowledge from radically unfamiliar testimony. Whether this tells against a coherentist picture depends on how inclusive one's views are with regard to the commonsense constraint that we can, in fact, acquire broad – perhaps even radically novel – knowledge on the basis of testimony. Scenario B may seem more straightforward, since recognizing a tension between our beliefs and the testimony gives us a reason to reject the latter. In this case too, however, relying on coherence alone would deprive us of an important function of testimony: that of allowing others to correct our misconceptions. Far from furthering a critical stance, such a coherentist version of inferentialism would appear to play into the hands of dogmatic self-reliance. The final scenario, C, although perhaps the most common, is likewise problematic. After all, even when the testimony coheres well with our belief system, this usually says little about the likely truth of the claim, since often the exact opposite of what has been asserted would cohere just as well. As Igor Douven and Stefaan Cuypers note: 'If we ask someone about Tom's whereabouts, then "He has been abducted by aliens" may make us suspicious about the speaker's trustworthiness, but most "normal" answers ("He is visiting his mom", "He is on vacation", etc.) may cohere perfectly well with our background beliefs, even though most of those answers will be false' (Douven and Cuypers 2009: 40). Given that the three scenarios are exhaustive, it seems clear that coherence alone is too weak a criterion to warrant acceptance or rejection of specific instances of testimony. A watered-down version of inferentialism, which replaces the goal of reducing testimonial justification to non-testimonial sources with the goal of achieving integration through checking for coherence, therefore does not look very promising.

Local reductionism, even in its unmodified form, finds itself caught between a rock and a hard place: either it insists on the mature hearer's having access to specific (non-testimonial) grounds that justify testimonial acceptance or rejection *on this occasion*, in which case it could claim to defend epistemic autonomy – but only at the expense of feasibility; or, it could relax the reductionist demands on the hearer – by allowing sub-personal monitoring to take the place of conscious reflection, or by permitting multiple 'developmental phases' – in which case 'local reductionism' would increasingly come to resemble Reidian credulism. In fact, Reid himself acknowledges that our dependence on testimony is greatest in our early development, and that we gradually become more discriminating in our testimonial dealings with others:

> Reason hath likewise her infancy, when she must be carried in arms: then she leans entirely upon authority, by natural instinct, as if she was conscious of her own weakness [. . .]. When brought to maturity by proper culture, she begins to feel her own strength, and leans less upon the reason of others; she learns to suspect testimony in some cases, and to disbelieve it in others; and sets bounds to that authority to which she was at first entirely subject. But still, to the end of life, she finds a necessity of borrowing light from testimony [. . .]. (Reid 1983: 96)

The only part of this quote that one could imagine local reductionists to take issue with is the claim that testimony remains constitutive of rational authority 'to the end of life'. According to Fricker, the constitutive part of testimony is restricted to an early developmental phase, yet in the absence of a principled way of drawing a line between the developmental phase and the mature stage – for the reasons discussed above – it is difficult to see how the goal of 'full epistemic maturity' could be anything other than the pursuit of an ever-receding ideal.

5. How reductionist was Hume?

No discussion of the reductionism/anti-reductionism debate about testimony would be complete without at least a brief discussion of Hume's position on the matter. This is especially the case given that a number of authors attribute to Hume a global reductionism of the kind discussed in Section 3 – so much so that the latter has sometimes been called (including, *mea culpa*, by this author) 'Humean reductionism'. But this is a mistake, in that it grossly exaggerates Hume's reductionist tendencies which, although present in some of his writings, are tempered by a keen awareness of our dependence on others for knowledge and the need for a stance of trusted acceptance of what others tell us. While this is not the place for a detailed textual exegesis of Hume's arguments, it is nevertheless important to summarize his views and contextualize them in a way that explains why Hume's position has sometimes been mischaracterized. (For a detailed reconstruction of Hume's actual views, see Gelfert 2010a.)

Those who have interpreted Hume as a global reductionist about testimony usually turn to Section 10 of his *Enquiry Concerning Human Understanding* ('Of Miracles'), where he writes:

> The reason why we place any credit in witnesses and historians, is not derived from any *connexion*, which we perceive *a priori*, between testimony and reality, but because we are accustomed to find a conformity between them. (*Enquiry* 10.8)

Hume's target in 'Of Miracles' is a very special kind of testimony: reports of alleged miracles. As Hume sees it, *miraculous testimony* does not merit belief. Given that a miracle, by Hume's definition, is a violation of the observed laws of nature – which have been found to hold on the basis of 'firm and unalterable experience' (*Enquiry* 10.12) – any testimony that asserts such a violation must be at least as secure as that which it claims to disprove. In other words, when we encounter an instance of miraculous testimony, we must always weigh the (less than certain) probability of the witnesses' testimony – who, as human beings are known to be fallible – against the remote possibility of a violation of the law of nature. But, given the uniform empirical backing enjoyed by the laws of nature, such a comparison will always come down against the merely probable testimony from imperfect, fallible human witnesses. Thus, miraculous testimony, although not logically incoherent, can never suffice to establish belief in the occurrence of a miracle, understood as a violation of the laws of nature.

Miraculous testimony is, of course, a very special case, and not much follows from it for ordinary cases of relying on others. However, Hume's argument illustrates a clear difference between his view of testimony and Reid's. By putting empirical considerations at the heart of his account, Hume places himself in direct opposition to those anti-reductionists who – like Reid – posit that we can ascertain, through a priori reflection on the principles of our understanding, that we are justified in relying on other people's testimony. For Hume, all of our knowledge of states of affairs in the world around us is 'founded merely on our experience of their constant and regular conjunction', and he takes it to be 'evident, that we ought not to make an exception to this maxim in favour of human testimony' (*Enquiry*, 10.5). Since, in general, there is nothing about an instance of *telling* that necessitates the truth of *what is told*, our only grounds for relying on testimony – as for empirical knowledge in general – are of an inductive nature. Many authors, in their reading of Hume, have combined this general constraint on empirical knowledge with Hume's specific insistence that we must have perceived a conformity between testimony and reality, and on this basis have attributed to Hume an inductivist version of global reductionism. As Lipton characterizes Hume's position, 'any warrant we have for believing a particular piece of testimony must rest on some sort of enumerative induction' (Lipton 1998: 15). Unless we have specific inductive grounds to trust *this* speaker on *this* occasion, testimony should not be accepted: 'I should only believe what someone says if I know that they have a good track record, that is, if I know they have reliably told the truth before' (Bailey and O'Brien 2006: 139). On this interpretation of Hume's inductivist proposal, 'each individual is to rely on her own observations' and 'she must observe not only the occasions of testimony, but also the facts which are testified to' (Webb 1993: 263). Coady summarizes the Reductionist Thesis (RT) he attributes to Hume as follows:

> We rely upon testimony as a species of evidence *because* each of us observes for himself a constant and regular conjunction between what people report and the way the world is. More particularly, we each observe for ourselves a constant conjunction between kinds of report and kinds

of situation so that we have good inductive grounds for expecting this conjunction to continue in the future. (Coady 1992: 82)

It is obvious, for the reasons discussed in Section 3, that such an approach to testimony would not get us very far. Establishing the track record of a speaker first-hand, without reliance on further testimony, is often impossible, and even in those rare cases where it is possible, demanding that we do so would defeat the utility of testimony as a shortcut to knowledge.

However, a moment's reflection shows that Hume could not have endorsed such a global-reductionist proposal. For one, Hume explicitly claims that 'there is no species of reasoning more common, more useful, and even necessary to human life, than that which is derived from the testimony of men' (*Enquiry*, 10.5). So either Hume is unaware of the fact that testimony is useful *precisely because* it relieves us of the need to check the facts first-hand, or the individualistic thesis (RT), which so many authors have attributed to him, does not reflect his actual position. And, indeed, Hume does not think that, for each kind of report, type of reporter, or class of situations, we need to individually establish – through direct observation that what is said corresponds to the facts – an inductive track record to the effect that future testimony of the same kind is likely to be true. Hume recognizes, of course, that testimony is a fallible source of knowledge, and that in any situation where 'the conjunction between any particular kind of report and any kind of object' has been found to be 'variable', the question of the reliability of a new testimonial report is a live one. But precisely because such cases have already been empirically found to exhibit non-constancy, further empirical investigation – by attempting to compare testimonial claims directly with the facts in question – will not usually settle the matter. If, as Hume claims, in such situations 'the ultimate standard, by which we determine all disputes, that may arise concerning them, is always derived from experience and observation' (*Enquiry*, 10.6), he cannot have in mind the daunting task of settling all empirical disputes through first-hand ascertaining of the facts.

What, then, grounds our successful reliance on testimony and justifies our practice of accepting other people's testimony according to Hume? Here is what Hume has to say elsewhere in Section 10 of the *Enquiry*:

Were not the memory tenacious to a certain degree; had not men commonly an inclination to truth and a principle of probity; were they not sensible to shame, when detected in a falsehood: were not these, I say, *discovered by experience* to be qualities, inherent in human nature, we should never repose the least confidence in human testimony. (*Enquiry*, 10.5; italics added)

It is clear from this passage that Hume does not think that each of us, before accepting a new piece of testimony, must individually establish, through direct observation, that testimonies in a given reference class correspond to the facts. Instead, we can rely on indirect evidence and background knowledge – of aspects of human nature ('an inclination to truth') as well as of social pressures ('shame when detected in a falsehood') – to take the place of direct comparison of testimony with the facts. It is such general knowledge of human nature and the social world – not of the truth or falsity of the testimonial claims in question – that must be 'derived from experience and observation'. In his *Treatise of Human Nature*, Hume makes this point even more explicitly:

> When we receive any matter of fact upon human testimony, our faith arises from the very same origin as our inferences from causes to effects, and from effects to causes; nor is there any thing but our *experience* of the *governing principles of human nature*, which can give us any assurance of the veracity of men. (*Treatise*, 1.3.9.12; second italics added)

By appealing to human nature, and our knowledge of it, as the source of justification for relying on the testimony of others, Hume reduces considerably the burden of proof that the recipient of testimony must bear. No longer does the hearer face the Sisyphean task of assessing individual speakers' track records with respect to a plethora of possible reference classes of 'kinds of reports' or 'kinds of situation'. In particular, Hume does not defend the global reductionist view that, in every case of testimony, our corresponding testimony-based belief must derive its justification exclusively from non-testimonial sources of evidence. Instead, when faced with an interlocutor's testimony, the hearer can draw on his background knowledge of human nature and the social world – much of it itself due to testimony – and in many cases can simply trust his tacit understanding of the various practices of giving and receiving information. Unlike Reid, Hume does not think that there is a priori knowledge of human nature, nor does he think that we can give an a priori argument in support of the overall reliability of human testimony. All such knowledge is ultimately acquired from experience. But, once we have convinced ourselves that our social environment is conducive to the acquisition of second-hand knowledge, we can trust the testimony of others just the same. Ironically, then, Hume appears to take a more optimistic view of testimony as a source of knowledge than even some contemporary epistemologists. Whereas local reductionists would have us believe that 'we know too much about human nature to want to trust anyone, let alone everyone, uncritically' (Fricker 1995: 400), Hume holds that our knowledge of human nature can assure us of our fellow human beings' overall 'probity' and their general 'inclination to truth'.

Study questions

1 Must every testimonial chain that communicates knowledge necessarily begin with content derived from other sources such as perception, memory and inference? What about testimony that is involved in the creation or sustainment of social facts, such as wedding vows, oaths or a country's declaration of independence?

2 What are the prospects of giving a global justification of testimony as a source of knowledge?

3 Does the rational inscrutability of the sub-personal monitoring posited by local reductionism undermine its value as a defence against the dangers of gullibility?

4 How might one draw a principled line between the 'developmental' and the 'mature' phases posited by local reductionism?

5 Hume, in the context of his rejection of miraculous testimony, speaks of the 'firm and unalterable experience' of the laws of nature, an exception to which 'has never been observed, in any age or country'. In doing so, he is implicitly relying on the cumulative experience of others which, presumably, is only known on the basis of their testimony. What does this tell us about his account of testimony?

Further reading

Lipton (1998) conveys a sense of the overall shape of the reductionism/anti-reductionism debate in the mid-1990s, while siding with reductionism. Kusch (2002b), in chapters 2 and 3, pays special attention to the dialectic of the debate between Fricker and Coady, and calls into question some of the shared assumptions of reductionists and anti-reductionists. Some of the criticisms of local reductionism discussed above, in Section 4, have been developed more fully in Gelfert (2009). Goldberg and Henderson (2006) build a case against Fricker's slogan 'Against Gullibility' (Fricker 1994) by distinguishing between different context-dependent types of (objectionable and unobjectionable) gullibility, while Weiner (2003) defends a version of the presumptive right (PR) thesis against Fricker's criticism. Graham (2006a) develops a useful taxonomy of possible positions along the reductionism/anti-reductionism spectrum.

6

Hybrid theories of testimony

In the previous chapter, we discussed the long-standing debate between reductionists and anti-reductionists about testimonial justification. As we saw, certain theoretical positions in the reductionism/anti-reductionism debate are best understood in relation to the more general internalism/externalism debate in epistemology. For example, local reductionism's insistence that, in order for a mature hearer to be justified in forming a testimony-based belief, he must have access to non-testimonial evidence that *this* speaker, on *this* occasion, is trustworthy, may be understood as an internalist commitment. By contrast, anti-reductionism's affirmation of a presumptive right of the hearer to accept what he is told (unless there are specific reasons not to do so) may be considered a good fit with externalism, insofar as it would render the success of our reliance on testimony entirely a matter of the trustworthiness of our epistemic environment. However, in spite of such affinities, it would be hasty to assume that internalism necessarily entails reductionism, or that externalists about epistemic justification need to be committed to anti-reductionism about testimony. (On this point, see Pritchard 2004, who devotes ample space to the discussion of internalist as well as externalist versions of credulism, i.e. anti-reductionism.) Not only is there a continuum of theoretical positions – which is what made the reductionist's move away from 'global' towards 'local' reductionism possible – but there are also powerful reasons for thinking that a successful account of testimony needs to include both internalist and externalist elements. In this chapter, we will discuss several such 'hybrid' theories of testimonial justification.

1. Hybrid theories of justification

Internalists about epistemic justification hold that our beliefs can only be justified by mental states that are cognitively accessible to us; whether or not an agent's belief that *p* is justified depends entirely on factors internal to the agent. In particular, no agent could be said to know that *p* merely in virtue of having acquired that belief in a reliable way; knowledge always requires some degree of cognitive access on the part of the agent, who must be able, in principle, to give adequate reasons for holding *p* to be true. In its most general form, internalism allows for considerable latitude regarding which internal factors are seen as acceptable grounds for belief: prior beliefs of the agent, memories, sense data and so forth. More restrictive versions of internalism might limit the range of internal states that qualify as sources of justification, for example by giving priority to what is immediately given in experience and to what can be ascertained through conscious reflection, while excluding prior beliefs of more dubious origin. Reductionism about testimonial justification thus results only if the demand for cognitively accessible reasons for belief is coupled with a restrictive interpretation of what constitutes such reasons – namely, first-hand experience and beliefs (or memories) formed directly on their basis.

Externalists, by contrast, deny any requirement that, for an agent to have knowledge that *p*, he must have cognitive access to reasons for believing that *p* or must be able to engage in reflection on why, or how, he came to believe that *p*. All that is required of the agent is that he came to form the belief via a reliable method – that is, a method that reliably produces true beliefs (and reliably avoids false beliefs). What matters to reliabilist externalism is *objective* reliability: the agent's belief-forming mechanisms must be *de facto* properly attuned to his normal epistemic environment, and it is quite immaterial to the epistemic status of the beliefs thus generated whether or not the agent knows (or could know) that he is so attuned to his environment. As an example, consider Reid's epistemology of testimony. According to Reid, our testimony-based beliefs are justified as the result of the interplay between two innate principles: the principle of credulity, which disposes us to accept what we are told, and the principle of veracity, according to which we have a natural tendency to tell the truth. For us to acquire justified testimonial beliefs, it is enough that these principles *in fact* govern our testimonial exchanges; we do not need to *know that* they are in operation. As Reidian philosophers, we may of course take pride in having identified the inner workings of testimony as a source of knowledge, but such philosophical knowledge neither adds to the justification of our testimonial beliefs, nor does the lack of such knowledge in a less philosophically inclined audience detract from the justification of their testimony-based beliefs. (While its externalist elements have been widely acknowledged, a case can be made that closer examination of Reid's epistemology reveals a number of internalist components; see Van Woudenberg 2013.)

As already hinted at in the previous chapter, the problem of testimony throws the respective merits of internalism and externalism into sharp relief. This can be seen by looking at how each position might respond to the other. Thus, against the externalist, the internalist might point out that even a generally reliable epistemic environment cannot ensure that a hearer is exposed only to individually reliable testimony. This is partly because, even where circumstances are such that testimony is by and large reliable, this is compatible with individual acts of insincerity: there is, in general, no law-like relationship that guarantees that an individual act of testifying will always be truthful. As a result, a hearer would be well-advised to bring his (internal) critical faculties to bear on the assessment of at least some of the testimony he receives. This, in short, is the internalist case against purely externalist testimonial justification. In response, the externalist might reply that, unless there is some 'cooperation' from the epistemic environment (which, importantly, includes the speaker), no amount of conscientiousness and justificatory work on the part of the hearer alone can guarantee that beliefs acquired from testimony will be reliable. This suggests that the actual reliability of our external epistemic environment will often trump factors that are internal to the agent, which would speak in favour of an externalist account of testimonial justification.

'Hybrid' theories of testimony acknowledge the force of both internalist and externalist considerations, but hold that the attempt to construct a unitary account of testimonial justification entirely on the basis of one or the other is misguided. Instead, what is needed is a theory that combines internalist and externalist elements in such a way as to do justice to the fact that, in relying on testimony as a source of knowledge, we depend as much on the reliability of the speaker (and, quite possibly, that of the extended epistemic environment) as on the rationality of our own response to the speaker's testimony. Depending on one's view of the relative importance and role of internal and external factors, one can conceive of many different hybrid theories, several examples of which are discussed later in this chapter. It is worth noting that the meaning of the term 'hybrid' in this chapter is construed somewhat more broadly than in the existing literature. In particular, it refers not only to what a theory says about the nature and source of testimonial justification, but also to the management of testimony – that is, to the question of how a hearer should respond to a new instance of incoming testimony. As discussed in Chapter 2 (Section 3), trusted acceptance and rational rejection are both flip sides of our epistemic predicament with respect to testimony, and a hybrid theory of testimony may be in a better position to account for this aspect of testimonial practice than unitary accounts, since it can more easily explain why the justification we have for accepting testimony so often seems to be different *in kind* from the reasons that justify our rejection of certain other instances of testimony. The twin questions of the *justification* and the *management* of testimony are, of course, not separate issues, but are intimately connected – precisely because our justification for the uptake of a given piece of testimony is usually a precondition of our being justified in holding the corresponding testimony-based belief. In what follows, we will therefore also need to look at what kind of guidance each prospective hybrid theory has to offer to the hearer faced with the challenge of whether to accept or reject a given piece of testimony.

2. 'It takes two to tango'

The first of the hybrid positions to be discussed is Lackey's 'dualism' about testimonial justification, which is explicitly motivated by a dissatisfaction with the standard way in which reductionism and non-reductionism have traditionally been pitted against each other and have tried to account for the interaction between the participants in a testimonial exchange:

> My diagnosis of what has gone wrong in the epistemology of testimony is this: reductionists and non-reductionists alike have attempted to place all of the epistemic work on only one or the other of these participants and, in so doing, have ignored the positive justificatory contribution that needs to be made by the other. (Lackey 2006b: 169–70)

From the stalemate that has ensued between 'unitary' versions of reductionism and non-reductionism about testimonial justification – with reductionism imposing the burden of verification and testing on the hearer, and non-reductionism delegating all epistemic responsibility to the speaker – Lackey concludes 'that it takes two to tango: the justificatory work of testimonial beliefs can be shouldered exclusively neither by the hearer nor by the speaker' (ibid.: 170).

What is needed in order to overcome this impasse, according to Lackey, is a view of testimonial justification that acknowledges 'that the justification of a hearer's belief has dual sources, being grounded in both the reliability of the speaker and the rationality of the hearer's reasons for belief' (ibid.). Lackey's proposed 'dualism' therefore demands that, in order for a testimony-based belief to be justified, not only must the hearer have (cognitively accessible) positive reasons for accepting the speaker's testimony, but the speaker's testimony must also be (externally) reliable:

> For every speaker A and hearer B, B justifiedly believes that *p* on the basis of A's testimony that *p* only if: (1) B believes that *p* on the basis of

the content of A's testimony that *p*, (2) A's testimony that *p* is reliable or otherwise truth-conducive, and (3) B has appropriate positive reasons for accepting A's testimony that *p*. (Ibid.)

When formulated in this way, dualism purports to state only necessary conditions for justification (and, by extension, testimonial knowledge), to which other conditions may need to be added. (Having said that, it is worth noting that conditions (2) and (3) already set the bar very high for what should count as justified testimony-based belief.) In more recent work, Lackey has proposed two further conditions in an attempt to give a fuller account of when internal and external conditions cooperate to make testimonial knowledge possible. The first of these concerns the environment in which the testimonial exchange takes place and which must be 'suitable for the reception of reliable testimony'; the second condition relates to the epistemic outlook of the hearer, who must not have any 'undefeated (psychological or normative) defeater for A's testimony' (Lackey 2008: 177–8).

With its emphasis on necessary conditions only, and in light of its evolving character (e.g. as the result of adding further conditions), dualism is perhaps best understood as a theoretical programme, rather than as a complete theory. A complete theory would need to address in more detail what makes certain environments more suitable for the reception of reliable testimony than others, and how a hearer may be able to tell what sort of environment he finds himself in. This is important since, arguably, part of what renders the hearer's response to testimony rational is the fact that it is well-calibrated to the kind of environment he is immersed in. It also points to a potential weakness of dualism, since the examples Lackey gives of how a hearer should go about acquiring positive reasons for accepting the speaker's testimony – by observing first-hand the general conformity between the truth and 'reports delivered in [certain] contexts' (or certain 'types of reports', made by certain kinds of speakers; see Lackey 2006b: 172–4) – appear to leave dualism vulnerable to the reference class problem and related criticisms that proved decisive against 'unitary' reductionism about testimony. (On this point, see Mößner 2011.) Although Lackey claims that the required positive reasons need only 'render it *not irrational* for the hearer to accept the testimony in question' (Lackey 2006b: 175) – since the likely truth of the testimony is guaranteed by the reliability condition imposed on the speaker – it is not clear how this would address the problem of managing incoming testimony. At the very least, for a hearer confronted with the need to either accept or reject a given piece of testimony, it would be desirable to have more to go on than merely a reasonable belief that it is not irrational to accept what the speaker tells him. Thus, although dualism is a hybrid theory insofar as it accepts that testimonial justification is neither reducible to nor entirely independent of (the hearer's) perception, memory and inference, it does not speak as directly as one might wish to the question of how to manage testimony. Instead, it essentially advises the hearer to accept, whenever possible, only reliable testimony. Yet unless the hearer's positive reasons to accept the speaker's testimony can somehow be intelligibly connected to the testimony's actual reliability, this advice rings hollow.

3. Faulkner's trust theory of testimony

Another influential 'hybrid theory of testimony' is due to Faulkner, who coined the phrase (see Faulkner 2000b). Faulkner begins by acknowledging the 'antecedent plausibility' (ibid.: 593) of the intuitions that lead to reductionism and anti-reductionism, both of which may be interpreted as attempts to square established epistemological theories (e.g. of perception and memory) with the distinctiveness of testimony as a source of knowledge. This distinctiveness derives from the necessary involvement, in the giving of testimony, of the mind of another agent, who need not have the hearer's best epistemic interests at heart. This opens up the possibility of lying, deception, manipulation and other forms of 'artfulness' (ibid.: 586). Whereas fallibility and lack of reliability affect all epistemic sources (though perhaps not all of them to the same extent), artfulness has no equivalent in perception, memory and reasoning. When attempting to extend epistemological theories of perception and memory to the case of testimony, certain modifications are therefore required. For example, if one posits the existence of a 'testimonial faculty', which takes the speaker's utterance as input and produces as an output in the hearer 'the disposition to believe credible testimony and the disposition to disbelief otherwise' (ibid.: 593), one will naturally want to demand that this faculty should monitor for signs of insincerity and lack of trustworthiness; the result is a form of reductionism. By contrast, if one takes inspiration from accounts of knowledge that regard, say, having an apparent perception – that is, the mere fact that it seems to me, perceptually, that p – as providing a defeasible reason for the perceptual belief that p, then one will perhaps be more inclined, in the case of testimony, to also regard mere intelligibility as providing a (defeasible) reason for belief.

Whereas Lackey starts with a broadly reliabilist framework of justification, to which an internalist 'positive reasons' account is added, so as to allow for the uptake of (independently reliable) testimony, Faulkner starts with a critical appreciation of Burge's Acceptance Principle. The Acceptance Principle states that a hearer is entitled to accept as true any intelligible message that is presented as true, unless there are stronger reasons not to do so. (See Chapter 3, Section 5.) The basic idea is that the proper function of testimony, like that of memory, is to 'preserve content'; hence, as in the case of memory, the mere fact that a propositional content presents itself to us as so preserved should count in its favour. Relying only on the Acceptance Principle for an account of testimony, however, 'gets its epistemology drastically wrong', Faulkner claims (2000b: 582). This is because it ignores the possibility of artfulness and, by extension, the distinctiveness of testimony as a source of knowledge. It would simply be 'doxastically irresponsible to accept testimony without some background belief in the testimony's credibility or truth'. Unlike in the case of perception and memory, where the mere absence of defeating background beliefs is enough to inspire trust in their deliverances, in the case of testimony 'rational acceptance requires the presence of supporting background beliefs' (Faulkner 2000b: 587). What is needed, then, is a *principle of assent*: 'An audience is justified in forming a testimonial belief if and only if he is justified in accepting the speaker's testimony' (ibid.: 588).

In spite of his disagreement with Burge over the validity of the Acceptance Principle, Faulkner adopts some of Burge's terminology when he distinguishes between different kinds of positive epistemic status or standing. In particular, whereas the term 'justification' is often used as a generic umbrella term for all forms of positive epistemic status, in what follows it will be reserved for reasons-based arguments that 'must be available in the cognitive repertoire of the subject' (Burge 1993: 459). For a belief to be 'justified' in this narrower sense, it is not enough that an argument be available in principle – perhaps from a 'God's eye' point of view – but that it must be articulable from the particular viewpoint of the reasoner in question. 'Justification', so understood, is clearly an internalist notion. By contrast, 'entitlement' is the 'externalist analog of the internalist notion' (Burge 1998: 3), and derives from our legitimate reliance on *bona fide* sources of knowledge. Thus, I am entitled to trust my memory, even when I am unable to give specific reasons why *this* particular memory, on *this* occasion, is likely to be accurate: the brute reliability of memory (coupled with the fact that it seems to me that I am remembering that p) confers positive epistemic status on my belief that p. As a new umbrella term, Burge and Faulkner use the term 'warrant', which encompasses (internalist) justification and (mostly externalist) entitlement.

The value of distinguishing between warrant in general and its two subclasses, argumentative *justifications* which are cognitive accessible by the agent and *entitlements* which derive from characteristics of the epistemic source in question, becomes evident once one contrasts the reasons that justify accepting a speaker's testimony that p with the overall support that the corresponding proposition enjoys. For, many of the factors that determine whether we consider a speaker credible are manifestly irrelevant to the objective question of whether or not *p*. Yet our testimonial beliefs are not limited to, or even primarily concerned with, reasonable assessments of our various interlocutors' credibility, but are typically about facts and states of affairs in the world. If we take ourselves to have sufficient warrant for many of our testimonial beliefs to count as knowledge, such warrant must draw on additional resources. As Faulkner puts it: 'The warrant of a testimonial belief cannot be equated with the warrant that is possessed for the associated judgment of credibility' (Faulkner 2000b: 594). This is where, according to Faulkner, a hybrid theory of testimony can elegantly close the gap between, on the one hand, the limited justification that judgements of credibility can confer and, on the other hand, the kind of warrant required for knowledge. The account of testimony Faulkner proposes comes in the form of two principles:

(A) An audience is warranted in forming a testimonial belief if and only if he is justified in accepting the speaker's testimony.

(B) If the audience is warranted in forming a testimonial belief, then whatever warrant in fact supports a speaker's testimony continues to support the proposition the audience believes. (Ibid.: 591)

Note that the first principle (A) simply restates, in more precise language, the earlier principle of assent. For a hearer to be warranted in forming a particular testimony-based belief, he must have (cognitively accessible) reasons for trusting the speaker's testimony in the first place. To this internalist requirement is added a second – 'social externalist' (ibid.) – principle, which states that, once the internalist requirement has been satisfied, the hearer effectively 'inherits' whatever warrant the speaker had for her belief. If the speaker is reporting knowledge for which she herself has first-hand evidence (or could give an argumentative justification), then these considerations will continue to support *the hearer's* testimonial belief – even though the hearer may himself be unable to rehearse the speaker's reasons for *her* belief. If, by contrast, the speaker is merely reporting something which she herself took on trust, and for which she has no internalist justification (beyond what is necessary for her to be warranted in accepting *her* informant's testimony), then this does not preclude her passing on that knowledge to her audience: the hearer may still acquire a warranted testimony-based belief by accepting what she tells him. As long as the 'extended warrant' – that is, 'the conjunction of the warrant possessed by the original speaker [. . .] together with any further warrant provided by the chain(s) of communicators' (ibid.) – is sufficient for knowledge, the hearer can 'tap into' the justificatory resources of the community and acquire testimonial knowledge from the speaker, provided he can give positive reasons for trusting her testimony in the first place. (For a more recent statement of Faulkner's hybrid view, which elaborates on several of these aspects, see Faulkner 2011: 201–4.)

Before turning to potential criticisms of Faulkner's trust theory of testimony, it is worth comparing it with Lackey's dualism (see previous section). Both theories include an internalist element, insofar as they require that the hearer have positive reasons for accepting the speaker's testimony, and both theories acknowledge the ineliminable role of the speaker's contribution to the hearer's warrant. But whereas for dualism the justificatory role of the speaker is exhausted entirely by the reliability of the speaker's testimony, on Faulkner's account the speaker's warrant – and, where applicable, the extended warrant of the chain of previous interlocutors – is transmitted wholesale to the hearer. On this account, what matters is the transmission of the – potentially richly structured – extended warrant from hearer to speaker, not just the statistical reliability of the speaker's testimony at the point of information exchange. As Faulkner puts it, 'if the *only thing* that a speaker contributes is being a vehicle for reliable testimony, the speaker's contribution is nominal; it is comparable to that made by a thermometer in telling the temperature' (Faulkner 2011: 45).

The possibility of the wholesale transmission of the speaker's warrant to the hearer, provided a hearer has (cognitively accessible) positive reasons to trust the speaker, is a central pillar of Faulkner's trust theory of testimony. However, it is also a potential source of problems for his account. By tying the social externalist element of his hybrid theory exclusively to the speaker and her warrant, Faulkner may be underestimating the importance of the epistemic environment beyond the speaker. Consider the following counterexample (which has been adapted from Gerken 2013). Imagine two hearers, H and twin-H, in indistinguishable environments and with exactly the same background beliefs and causal histories. Both go through exactly the same 'individualistically indiscernible talk exchange' (Gerken 2013: 552) with their respective interlocutors, S and twin-S, who make the exact same statements (and, in doing so, give off the same cues as to their credibility and sincerity). Both S and twin-S testify to a highly specialized subject matter, for example the prevalence of malaria in a remote region. It just so happens that, whereas S is an expert epidemiologist in full possession of all the relevant scientific information, twin-S is a layperson who has come to the same conclusion on the basis of an isolated report he has come across. Since the testimonial exchange between H and S is *ex hypothesi* indistinguishable from twin-H's encounter with twin-S, both H and twin-H will share the same first-hand justification for accepting their interlocutor's testimony. On Faulkner's account, this would mean that each hearer inherits his interlocutor's (extended) warrant for the belief in question. Yet S's warrant, given his expert status, is vastly superior to twin-S's warrant as a layperson, although both testify to the same conclusion. As a result, H's warrant for belief would be greatly 'boosted' beyond that of twin-H – implausibly so, one might argue, given that, as the scenario has been described, H and twin-H should really enjoy the same degree of testimonial warrant.

What does this purported counterexample show? One interpretation, suggested by Mikkel Gerken, is that Faulkner's account exaggerates the justificatory contribution that 'specific properties of the *particular speaker*' make to the hearer's testimonial warrant. Instead, Gerken argues, it is '*generalizations about epistemic properties of a hearer's normal environment* that constitute the central externalist determiner of testimonial warrant' (ibid.: 553). To put it slightly differently, rather than conceiving of testimonial warrant as something that can be passed on in a wholesale fashion from speaker to hearer, perhaps we should think of it as being constituted, at least in part, by the epistemic environment in which the testimonial exchange takes place. Such a modification of the trust theory would fit well with calls for acknowledging the role of context in the acquisition of testimonial knowledge. As Elgin puts it: 'Testimony takes place within a context framed by a variety of practices and institutions that affect both its content and the level of warrant it purports to deliver' (Elgin 2002: 307).

4. Dual pathways of acceptance

Paul Thagard has recently proposed a model of testimonial acceptance which, although not overtly 'hybrid' in the same sense, is nonetheless helpfully grouped with Faulkner's and Lackey's accounts, since it starts from an acknowledgement of the twin desiderata of routine acceptance and reasons-based rejection of testimony: 'A general theory of testimony has to be able to explain both how testimony is usually accepted automatically but also how it sometimes provokes extensive reflection about the claim being made and the claimant who is making it' (Thagard 2005: 297).

According to Thagard, testimonial acceptance and rejection are the result of the interplay between two pathways governing our response to testimony: a *default pathway* 'in which people more or less automatically respond to a claim by accepting it, as long as the claim made is consistent with their beliefs and the source is credible', and a *reflective pathway* 'in which they evaluate the claim based on its explanatory coherence with everything else they believe' (ibid.: 296). If an instance of testimony passes the initial screening for consistency and credibility, the hearer justifiedly forms a corresponding testimonial belief; only 'if the claim is inconsistent with what the person believes or if the source is known to lack credibility then reflection is triggered' (ibid.: 297). Once the reflective pathway has been triggered, the hearer needs to construct an explanatory network for the utterance; this may require considerable inferential activity on the part of the hearer, since the speaker's making a claim can always be explained in different ways – for example, as the honest expression of a competently formed belief, or as an attempt to deceive the hearer. It is against the backdrop of such an explanatory network that the overall coherence of the speaker's claim needs to be assessed: A claim should only be accepted if its truth would maximize coherence with the rest of one's belief system, otherwise it should be rejected.

What triggers suspension of the default pathway of acceptance and sends a piece of testimony along the reflective pathway? Drawing on results from psychology, Thagard distinguishes between four types of reflection triggers: 'lack of credibility of the source, non-credible behavior of the source, inconsistency of the claim with other beliefs, and incompatibility of the claim with the hearer's goals' (ibid.: 298). It is, of course, one thing to note, at a descriptive level, that certain characteristics of a testimonial encounter trigger conscious reflection on the part of the hearer, but it is quite another to claim that this suffices for epistemic justification. In particular, it leaves open the question of whether testimonial beliefs that have been formed on the basis of the default pathway – that is, without conscious reflection – should be considered justified: 'perhaps it would be epistemologically better always to use the reflective pathway, for the sake of obtaining fewer false beliefs' (ibid.: 299). This is where an appeal needs to be made to the equal importance of error avoidance and belief expansion: 'If we tried to reflect about every one of the statements that we encounter, we would be greatly restricted in the number of beliefs we could acquire.' (Ibid.; see also the discussion in Chapter 2, Section 2.)

Interestingly, Thagard claims that his dual-pathway model 'is reductionist, in that both pathways depend prescriptively on kinds of inference that are broadly used in domains other than testimony' (ibid.: 312). This echoes the Humean position that testimonial knowledge should not be exempt from the overall demand that all justification must ultimately derive from experience. However, as in Hume's case, this at best expresses a general constraint on the kind of knowledge and justification we can expect to gain from the testimony of others; it does not entail any strong form of global reductionism. To be sure, once the reflective pathway has been triggered, a testimonial claim will be subjected to further examination by the audience, which may involve a considerable amount of reflection and inference. Even then, however, the audience can draw on 'everything else they believe' (ibid.: 296) – which, more often than not, will include a substantial number of testimony-based beliefs. This casts doubt on the reductionist credentials of the account, in that it may simply be unable to achieve much in the way of reduction of testimonial knowledge to other forms of knowledge. (For further problems with replacing reductionist inferentialism with its coherentist analogue, see the discussion towards the end of Section 4 of the previous chapter.) It is also worth noting that by describing the initial screening of new testimony as 'an unconscious assessment of the claim and its source', the dual-pathway model is effectively positing testimonial acceptance 'without reflection' (ibid.: 297) as the usual mode of operation of the *default* pathway. As far as the management of incoming testimony is concerned, Thagard's model thus clearly combines trusted acceptance (as the default response to testimony) and rational rejection – as one of the likely outcomes, once the reflective pathway has been triggered – in a way that merits classifying it with other 'hybrid' theories of testimony.

5. Testimony and inference to the best explanation

The dual-pathway model discussed in the previous section makes accepting a speaker's testimony conditional on the testimonial claim's contributing to the overall coherence of one's belief system, where the latter also includes beliefs about what best explains the speaker's utterance. This section will further develop the suggestion that explanatory considerations should play a central role in testimonial acceptance and rejection. In particular, we will be looking at two closely related accounts of what has come to be called 'testimonial inference to the best explanation' (or TIBE, for short). The first account, due to Lipton (2007), attempts to steer a middle path between the more extreme versions of reductionism and anti-reductionism, while holding on to the idea that a unitary account of testimonial justification is possible. By contrast, the second account (developed in detail in Gelfert 2010b), although inspired by the first, is 'hybrid' in character, in that it proposes different sources of justification for instances of trusted acceptance and cases of rejecting testimony.

Lipton gives a nice sketch of the basic idea of TIBE when he claims that 'a recipient of testimony ("hearer") decides whether to believe the claim of the informant ("speaker") by considering whether the truth of that claim would figure in the best explanation of the fact that the speaker made it' (Lipton 2007: 238). At this level of generality, this statement is more of a programmatic idea than a detailed theoretical proposal. Other authors have posited a more elaborate sequence of inferential steps, according to which

> the recipient of testimony is seen as making an inference to the best explanation of why her source – say, John – said that p: she infers that John believes that p in part because p is the case. (Malmgren 2006: 230)

It is worth noting that most contributors to the debate seem to take it for granted that the hearer's inference to the truth of the testimony must always involve a prior inference to the belief of the speaker. As Adler puts it:

> The best explanation for why the informant asserts that p is normally that, first and most relevant here, he believes it for duly responsible reasons and, second, he intends that I shall believe it too (by virtue of recovering this intention from his assertion). (Adler 1994: 274)

Consider this somewhat complex example by Stephen Schiffer, which features a speaker, Sally, who informs her interlocutor, Abe, that it is snowing outside:

> Thus, when Sally informs Abe that it's snowing by uttering 'It's snowing', Abe acquires the knowledge that Sally believes that it's snowing, and this knowledge is crucial to Abe's coming to know that it's snowing, and this is in part because part of the explanation of the fact that Sally believes that it's snowing is that it is snowing. The rest of the story – the extent to which Abe's knowledge is inferential – is a matter of debate [. . .]. (Schiffer 2003: 303)

As Schiffer sees it, 'when we come to know p on the basis of having been told p, it is crucial both that we believe that the speaker believes p and that the best explanation of the speaker's believing p essentially includes the fact that p is true' (Schiffer 2003: 303); denying the necessity of either of these two crucial assumptions, Schiffer claims, would be a 'mistake' (Schiffer 2001: 2315).

Let us call the view that testimonial inference to the best explanation must always proceed via an inference to the speaker's belief the 'narrow view' of TIBE. According to this narrow view, every instance of TIBE is an instance of consciously making inferences about another's belief system. Note, however, that the general framework of TIBE, as outlined in the earlier quote by Lipton, is compatible with a much broader range of explanatory inferences on the part of the hearer. Indeed, Lipton himself construes TIBE simply as 'an abductive inference from the fact of utterance to the fact uttered'

(Lipton 2007: 243). On this broader construal, the hearer need not engage in speculations about the speaker's psychology, but can help himself to any relevant background knowledge and information – including assumptions about the context in which the testimony was offered. This broadening of the range of admissible explanatory considerations is deliberate, since Lipton takes TIBE to be primarily a *descriptive account* of our testimonial practices, which is concerned with 'whether the account illuminates the way we in fact go about deciding whether to believe what we are told' (ibid.). For example, many of us routinely accept the testimony of newscasters on radio and TV, but it seems far-fetched to think that, in every such case, we must first infer that the newscaster believes what he says, before we can legitimately infer that the truth of what he says features in the best explanation of his utterance. If anything, we rely on the professionalism of the newscaster not to let his personal beliefs influence the way he presents the information put together by the programme's editorial team. The broad view of TIBE allows such general explanatory considerations to take the place of inferences pertaining to the speaker's psychology. At the same, though, it remains committed to the view that, in every instance of testimonial acceptance, the hearer must have performed an inference to the effect that the truth of the informant's claim features in the best explanation of the fact that he made it.

The account of TIBE sketched so far is 'unitary' insofar as it explains both acceptance and rejection in terms of the hearer's act of determining whether the truth of the speaker's claim would figure in the best explanation of his utterance. While it is similar to Thagard's account in that it aims to show, in line with reductionism, 'that warranted testimonial beliefs are based on rules of inference or mechanisms of belief acquisition that apply to the beliefs from various sources, not just the source of testimony' (Lipton 1998: 24), it differs in that it does not propose the coexistence of two separate pathways, one for routine cases of default acceptance, the other for cases that require reflection and assessment. Unlike more radical versions of reductionism, it does not require gathering first-hand evidence in order to establish a track record for the speaker: as Lipton puts it, 'judgements about the truth of a particular questioned utterance may be prior to judgements about the general reliability of the informant' (Lipton 2007: 248), given that the hearer can draw on his background knowledge for constructing and comparing possible explanations of the informant's utterance. While Lipton's version of TIBE is thus able to sidestep some of the problems afflicting other versions of reductionism, it also raises new problems of its own, including one that emerges from the universal demand that, for every instance of testimonial acceptance, the hearer must be in a position to judge that the truth of a claim figures in the best explanation of why it was uttered. Consider the case of scientific testimony, in particular the communication of any sufficiently fundamental fact (say, the law of gravity) to a hearer. What would it mean to say, as the basic criterion of unitary TIBE would have it, that the instance of testimony in question is best explained by an account that makes the truth of the testimonial claim – in this case, the statement of the law of gravity – probable? Whereas in the case of eyewitness reports and other ordinary empirical testimony we can easily conceive of many causal stories that would link the circumstances of its production – including the mere fact that it has been produced – to the truth of the claim in question, in the case of scientific testimony (as well as in any other sufficiently general domain of knowledge) these connections are far less obvious and more difficult to assess. As a result, the hearer may simply be unable to tell whether the asserted fact (e.g. that a certain fundamental law of physics obtains) is part of the best explanation of *why someone asserted it*.

If TIBE is to be turned into a workable framework for the justification and management of testimonial knowledge, what is needed is a 'middle ground' of considerations which are explanatorily relevant to the testimony in question, but which neither require engaging in speculations about the speaker's psychology, nor make excessive demands on the hearer's ability to trace the connections between the truth of a claim and the specific circumstances of its utterance. Luckily, it is quite plausible that, under normal circumstances, we do have access to such considerations, in the form of background knowledge of the various social conventions, contexts and institutions that govern our testimonial practices. Thus, we believe what the newscaster says, not because of any assumptions we make about his belief system or psychology, nor because we can claim any special insight into how *this* particular utterance is best explained by the truth of the claim in question, but because we believe that news programmes – at least the ones we take to be trustworthy – are designed to be reliable sources of information about current affairs. Similar in the case of science: While we are often in no position to assess exactly how the truth of a given scientific claim would feature in the best explanation of the production of a specific instance of scientific testimony, we do know a lot about the *kinds* of processes that are responsible for our encountering such scientific testimony. Whereas the former would require specialist scientific knowledge (and detailed knowledge of the social organization of science), the latter merely requires a certain degree of familiarity with how science operates and how it communicates its results (e.g. through peer review and publication in highly competitive journals); the latter is easy to obtain, the former is not.

The unitary account of TIBE thus faces a structural problem. It posits a line of abductive inference – from the fact of the utterance to the truth of the speaker's claim – that may be available to us *in principle*, but whose merits we are rarely in a position to assess. But without the ability to *actually* formulate the various potential explanations of the utterance and assess their connection to the truth of the claim in question, the thought that the best among those explanations entails the truth of the speaker's testimony becomes little more than an article of faith. By extension, judgements concerning the acceptability of a given piece of testimony would appear to lack a robust justificatory basis. In order to remedy this situation, I propose a 'hybrid' account of testimonial inference to the best explanation, one that recognizes that the justification we have for accepting testimony is typically different in kind from the reasons that justify our rejection of (certain other instances of) testimony. The account I am proposing (which is developed more fully in Gelfert 2010b) makes dual use of inference to the best explanation, but applies it in complementary ways to the cases of testimonial acceptance and rejection. In particular, it inverts the role of explanatory inferences in specific cases of assessing a speaker's testimony: Rather than insist that, for a testimonial claim to be *accepted*, its truth must figure in the best explanation of the circumstances of its production, I want to propose that we should *reject* a claim when the best explanation of the fact of its assertion makes the claim improbable or unreliable. Thus, on the account I am proposing, specific explanatory inferences do not justify the acceptance of a particular piece of testimony, but serve as 'filters' that screen out unreliable or untrustworthy claims. Justification for accepting testimony derives instead from a different source, namely from a prior inference that takes the success of our testimony-dependent projects and practices – such as education, science, history, journalism, etc. – as evidence of their overall reliability. The latter is, of course, itself an inference to the best explanation, but is not tied to any specific instance of testimony; instead, it is based on our prior experience of relying on testimony and on our background knowledge of the social world around us. Its success depends on contingent facts about our epistemic environment – including prevalent levels of trustworthiness and reliability among our potential interlocutors – and so does not derive from any a priori epistemic principle special to testimony. Yet, its overall effect, given favourable social-epistemic conditions, is that of justifying a stance of *default acceptance*, whereas *rejection* of testimony requires special reasons that override the hearer's default justification to accept what he is told.

When is a hearer justified in rejecting a speaker's testimony? On the account I am proposing, the answer is: when the best explanation of an assertion renders what is asserted improbable or unreliable. A good example would be (certain kinds of) unsolicited testimony that promises a (deferred) profit in exchange for a (present) cost. Consider the following example offered by Lipton:

> A man rang my doorbell and claimed that my rain gutters are loose. Should I believe him? They look fine to me, I know that he hasn't been up on the

roof to inspect them properly, and I am further discouraged by the fact that he wants me to pay him today to fix them tomorrow. (Lipton 2007: 244)

Clearly, in this case, it is rational to reject the testimony in question, and we are justified in rejecting it precisely because the best explanation of the testimony entails that it is probably false. The point is this: the very factors that, in Thagard's terminology (see previous section), function as 'reflection triggers', also provide abductive evidence for the falsity, or unreliability, of the testimony they accompany. Another obvious example would be the unsolicited denial, from a child, of a misdeed that has not yet been found out: the child's 'I didn't do it' may be the best initial evidence that something is wrong. In other words, we typically reject testimony for reasons that are different in kind from those that underlie our overall tendency to accept what others tell us. This is precisely what the proposed hybrid account of TIBE acknowledges when it demands that we reject testimonies on the basis of likely deficiencies – that is, when the best explanation of its utterance renders the claim in question either false or unreliable.

But rejection of testimony takes place against the backdrop of our pervasive reliance on testimony, for which trusted acceptance is indispensable. Whereas instances of *rejection* occur as the result of a specific inference concerning the case at hand, our *acceptance* of testimony, as suggested earlier, is based on a more general inference, from the success of our testimony-dependent projects and practices to their likely reliability. Indeed, some of the most powerful abductive evidence for the overall reliability of testimony consists in the coherence among the various (at least partially independent) sources we draw on; further support derives from the coherence of new testimony with our observations and background beliefs. The case of science is again instructive in this context. As Douven and Cuypers argue:

> Testimony plays a key role in the practice of science; [. . . the] results of this practice are, by and large, very successful, at least instrumentally (that is, in terms of predictive accuracy and technological applicability). This means that scientific practice, including the part testimony plays in it, is efficacious. The best explanation of this efficacy comprises the assumption that scientists are mostly sincere and competent testifiers; if they were not, the successes of scientific practice would be miraculous. (Douven and Cuypers 2009: 41)

Even though other areas of knowledge – such as history, geography, or more mundane pursuits – may lack the predictive accuracy of science, this does not invalidate the overall structure of the argument, which hinges less on criteria such as precision and accuracy, and more on considerations of coherence between the information gained from different sources and mutual support across different sets of claims. Not only does coherence among independent sources (e.g. in history) or across different areas of knowledge – say, archaeology and geography – confer justification in its own right, but the very fact that it is exhibited in heavily testimony-dependent collective endeavours speaks in favour of the efficaciousness of testimony as a source of knowledge.

On the *hybrid* account of TIBE I am proposing, inference to the best explanation thus has a dual role to play: on the one hand, the coherence and success of our various testimony-dependent collective projects – such as education, science or history – abductively sustain a stance of *default acceptance*, whereas, on the other hand, we are justified in *rejecting* specific instances of testimony whenever the best explanation of the circumstances of its production, including the fact that it has been produced, casts doubt on the reliability of what we are told. Hence, when construed as a hybrid account that acknowledges the dual role of explanatory inferences in the management and justification of testimonial knowledge, TIBE can help us see why we can often take on trust what others tell us, without thereby falling into the trap of gullibility.

Study questions

1 To what extent does each of the hybrid accounts of testimony accommodate internalist and externalist considerations?

2 Compare and contrast Faulkner's 'trust theory' and Lackey's 'dualism' with respect to the role that the speaker's reasons for belief might play in justifying the hearer's testimony-based belief.

3 Think of a recent case where you acquired a belief on the basis of testimony. What are some of the possible explanations of the fact of the telling, and how does the truth of the claim in question feature in what you consider the best explanation?

4 Think of a recent case where you rejected someone's testimony, even though you did not know the claim to be false. Was your rejection based on explanatory considerations involving the likely falsity or unreliability of the claim in question?

Further reading

A clear statement of what the search for a hybrid view would involve can be found in Pritchard (2004). Gerken (2013) combines a hybrid theory of testimony with pluralism about epistemic justification. Fricker (2008), from a genealogical perspective that will be the focus of Chapter 11, argues that the dual need for, on the one hand, relying on others for knowledge, and, on the other hand, convincing oneself of the reliability of one's informants, may account for the persistence of both internalist and externalist intuitions about knowledge more generally.

7

Testimonial knowledge: Transmission and generation

In the previous chapters we have encountered a range of theoretical proposals regarding the nature of testimonial justification and the character of testimonial knowledge. Most of these accept the 'commonsense constraint' that, at least on occasion, testimony can function as a source of knowledge. In other words, given favourable conditions, a listener who forms the belief that *p* on the basis of a knowledgeable speaker's say-so may be properly credited with knowledge that *p*. If the listener's knowledge (that *p*) mirrors that of the speaker, it seems natural to speak of the speaker's having passed on her knowledge to the listener. Testimony, on this account, functions as a source of knowledge for the hearer precisely because it is a way of *transmitting* the relevant epistemic characteristics of a particular belief from the speaker to the hearer. The present chapter discusses various challenges that have been mounted to this 'transmission model' of testimony. One line of inquiry concerns the question of whether testimony can not only *transmit* existing knowledge, but can also *generate* knowledge. If it could be successfully shown that testimony is indeed a generative epistemic source, this would establish testimony even more firmly as an important source of knowledge alongside perception and inference; however, before such implications can be explored more fully, it is important to look more closely at purported cases of testimony as a generative source of knowledge.

1. The transmission model of testimony

A powerful intuition that drives philosophical interest in testimony as a source of knowledge is the thought that, through testimony, we can come to learn what another person already knows. Testimony 'transmits' knowledge from the speaker to the hearer, and it is precisely because testimony allows for knowledge to be passed on in this way that it functions as a source of knowledge for the hearer. The 'transmission model' of testimony places this idea at the heart of its account of testimony. The model, however, can be read in at least two ways. On a weak reading, the model asserts the *possibility* of knowledge transmission via testimony:

1   Testimony can transmit knowledge from the speaker to the hearer (and, thus, can function as a source of knowledge for the hearer).

On a stronger reading, the model demands that whenever testimony functions as a source of knowledge, it does so in virtue of transmitting knowledge from the speaker to the hearer:

2   In order for a hearer to acquire testimonial knowledge that *p* on the basis of a speaker's say-so, the speaker herself must have the knowledge in question.

On the strong interpretation of the transmission model, although the hearer, upon receiving the speaker's testimony, might come to know something the speaker does not know, no such additional knowledge could be acquired *on the basis of* the speaker's testimony. Instead, it would have to be based on extraneous information, such as additional empirical evidence or background knowledge. For example, a hearer might learn, from listening to the speaker's testimony, that she has a soprano voice (of which the speaker herself is unaware), but such knowledge would not be based on the content of what she says. According to the strong transmission model, if a hearer is to acquire genuine testimonial knowledge that *p* – that is, knowledge based on accepting the speaker's say-so that *p* – he can only do so if the speaker herself has the requisite knowledge.

Different versions of the transmission model have been implicitly or explicitly presupposed by a number of contributors to the debate. Ross gives a clear expression of the strong reading of the transmission thesis when he proposes the following conditions for testimonial knowledge: '*S* comes to know that *h* on *W*'s testimony [if and only if]: *W* knows that *h*, tells *S*, and his telling *S* brings it about that *S* believes that *h* and *h* is evident for *S*' (Ross 1975: 53). Welbourne – who aims to drive a wedge between justified belief and knowledge by claiming that knowledge, unlike belief, is 'commonable' (see discussion in Chapter 2) – likewise demands that knowledge can only travel along uninterrupted chains of knowers:

> I take testimony to be essentially concerned with communicating knowledge, so I hold that it is necessary, if there is to be a successful

process of testimonial transmission, that the speaker have knowledge to communicate. Thus I stipulate that the speaker knows that *p*. (Welbourne 1994: 302)

Lackey likens the strong transmission model to a view according to which 'the picture we have of testimonial knowledge is like a chain of people passing buckets of water to put out a fire': 'Each person must have a bucket of water in order to pass it to the next person, and moreover there must be at least one person who is ultimately acquiring the water from another source' (Lackey 1999: 471). Similarly, in the case of a chain of interlocutors, each previous testifier must have had knowledge that *p* if the final recipient of the testimony is to gain testimonial knowledge that *p*. The demand that the first instance of knowledge must originate 'from another source' reflects the strong view's commitment that testimony can be a source of knowledge *only* in virtue of transmitting already existing knowledge; it also illustrates why reductionist theories of testimonial justification are especially well-aligned with the transmission model.

Not every adherent of the transmission model is a proponent of its strong version. Sometimes, when presenting the gist of the model in condensed form, authors have elided some of the finer differences between the strong and the weak versions of transmission; when taken out of context, such passages can easily overstate the extent to which an author is committed to one or the other version. For example, Burge has been regarded as an adherent of strong transmission (Lackey 1999: 471–2), but upon closer inspection can be seen to hold a more nuanced position. Although he writes that '[i]f the recipient depends on interlocution for knowledge, the recipient's knowledge depends on the source's having knowledge as well', he immediately goes on to qualify this claim:

> In requiring that the source have knowledge if the recipient is to have knowledge based on interlocution, I oversimplify. Some chains with more than two links seem to violate this condition. But there must be knowledge in the chain if the recipient is to have knowledge based on interlocution. (Burge 1993: 486)

What Burge is suggesting is that 'knowledge gaps' in the chain of transmission may be permissible – that is, there may be some interlocutors who merely pass on the information that *p* without themselves knowing that *p* – so long as *someone* in the chain possesses the requisite knowledge. Graham makes this point nicely when he writes that the mainstream view of the transmission model holds that 'what is essential is not whether *the particular speaker* on whom the hearer relies knows of what he speaks, but rather whether *the chain* "knows", in a *non-testimonial* manner, the proposition the speaker asserts' (Graham 2006b: 109). An important task, then, lies in determining which 'knowledge gaps' are harmless and which threaten to undermine the transmission of testimonial knowledge.

Audi, in his discussion of the transmission model, raises the possibility that transmission may work differently for knowledge and justification. According to Audi, 'if I do not know that *p*, my testimony that *p* cannot transmit to you testimonially based knowledge that *p*; but even if I am not justified in believing *p*, my testimony can give you testimonially based justification for believing it, through providing the main materials for your becoming justified in believing it' (Audi 1997: 410). You may become justified in believing what I say, even when I lack justification myself, by combining 'the way I attest to the proposition, together with your background justification regarding me and the circumstances' (ibid.). My act of testifying may be an ineliminable ingredient in your chain of reasoning that issues in your being justified, and in this sense your accepting what I say would generate justification for you. Under favourable conditions, such newly generated justification may well suffice for knowledge on your part, but your knowledge would no longer be knowledge you had received from me; instead, it would be knowledge in virtue of justification that was generated – not transmitted – in the process of testifying. Contrasting the 'normal' case of transmission of knowledge from a knowledgeable testifier to the recipient with the case of testimonially generated justification, Audi suggests that it would be 'natural to say that in the first case you would gain knowledge *through* my testimony, whereas in the second you would gain justification *from* my testimony, but not through it' (ibid.).

However, it may not be possible to keep the transmission of knowledge and justification as neatly apart as Audi would like. After all, if circumstances in your social environment reliably conspire in such a way as to result in your knowing that *p* whenever you accept my say-so that *p* – even in cases where I lack knowledge or justification that *p* – it may perhaps be a moot point to insist on a demarcation between (proper) 'testimonial knowledge' and (mere) 'knowledge from testimony'. At the very least, one can expect to find cases of the latter in which testimony, for all intents and purposes, may be considered a generative source of knowledge.

2. Testimonial knowledge from non-knowledge

In Chapter 4, we briefly considered a scenario discussed by Ross (1975: 42) who invites the reader to imagine a 'situation where an authority intends to assert (for some pedagogical reason) something he believes false', but which is in fact true: 'Suppose a student "taking him at his word" finds the statement evidently true, though the student had never given thought to the matter before; may not the assertion become evident to the student?' (Recall that, for Ross, the status of 'being evident' is an essential feature of knowledge.) At the same time, as we saw in the previous section, Ross is committed to the strong transmission model, according to which a hearer can only acquire genuine testimonial knowledge if the speaker, too, has the knowledge in question. As a result, the ability of a speaker to make a potential piece of knowledge evident to the hearer 'even if he neither knows nor believes it', Ross argues, gives rise to 'an irresolvable doubt as to whether we have merely a justified true belief or knowledge about something that we have been told' (Ross 1975: 43). Such doubts reflect the strong internalist commitments of his position, which lacks the resources to adjudicate between true cases of knowledge transmission and 'spurious' cases of the sort envisaged in Ross's hypothetical scenario. However, in the years since Ross's paper, epistemological externalism – particularly in the form of reliabilism – has gained considerable ground, warranting a reconsideration of prospective cases of gaining testimonial knowledge from non-knowledge.

In her important and influential 1999 paper 'Testimonial Knowledge and Transmission', Lackey offers just such a reassessment and identifies several pathways by which a hearer can acquire testimonial knowledge from a speaker who herself lacks knowledge – either because she does not believe what she asserts or because her justification is insufficient for knowledge. The latter may occur when the speaker holds a false belief which, if true, would defeat the testimonial claim, but which she keeps to herself. Both scenarios are best discussed by way of example. The first example, which has become known under the heading of the 'creationist teacher', is introduced by Lackey as follows:

> [CREATIONIST TEACHER.] Suppose that a Catholic elementary school requires that all teachers include sections on evolutionary theory in their science classes and that the teachers conceal their own personal beliefs regarding this subject-matter. Mrs Smith, a teacher at the school in question, goes to the library, researches this literature from reliable sources, and on this basis develops a set of reliable lecture notes from which she will teach the material to her students. Despite this, however, Mrs Smith is herself a devout creationist and hence does not believe that evolutionary theory is true, but she none the less follows the requirement to teach the theory to her students. Now assuming that evolutionary theory is true, in this case it seems reasonable to assume that Mrs Smith's students can come to have knowledge via her testimony, despite the fact

that she fails [to have the requisite belief] and hence does not have the knowledge in question herself. (Lackey 1999: 477)

As Lackey sees it, the conclusion that Mrs Smith's students acquire testimonial knowledge of evolution on the basis of their teacher's testimony is quite independent of whether one is committed to a reductionist or anti-reductionist epistemology of testimony. As discussed in previous chapters, anti-reductionists typically demand only that the recipient of testimony have no defeaters – such as evidence to the contrary of what is being asserted, or doubts about the reliability of the speaker – yet, as the example has been constructed, Mrs Smith gives her students no reason to doubt her sincerity or competence. (Note that one could strengthen the example further by stipulating that Mrs Smith takes special care to finetune her teaching to the best available scientific evidence, out of a nagging worry that her personal beliefs might otherwise lead her to neglect her professional duties.) From a reductionist perspective, the example likewise seems unassailable, since one can easily stipulate that the students have ample (first-hand) evidence, both of Mrs Smith's past reliability – her reports typically reflect the facts, where these can be checked first-hand – and of her professionalism and commitment to being a good teacher. Hybrid views of testimony, too, are compatible with the claim that Mrs Smith is able to impart knowledge to her students that she herself lacks. On the hybrid model favoured at the end of Chapter 6 (which posits that background knowledge justifies default acceptance, except when the best explanation of the telling makes it improbable that what we are told is unreliable), the best explanation of Mrs Smith's classroom testimony would likely appeal to her professional role and impeccable track record as a teacher – which, *ex hypothesi*, is indeed what makes Mrs Smith teach the best available scientific knowledge to her students, even if she herself misses out on the knowledge in question. (For a fuller discussion of this response to the 'creationist teacher' case, see Gelfert 2010b: 393.)

Why might one nonetheless insist that Lackey's intuition is mistaken and that Mrs Smith's students do not acquire knowledge based on their teacher's testimony? One line of criticism takes its lead from the fact that, as the case is described, the teacher is intentionally telling her students what she considers to be a falsehood. By her own lights, she is deliberately deceiving the students under her tutelage. This, one might argue, would raise doubts about the stability of the – on this occasion, accurate – information she disseminates. Would she perhaps be equally likely to teach manifest falsehoods if told to do so? As Audi has argued, 'given [her] willingness to deceive the students regarding *p*, there are relevantly similar cases in which

[she] does so without even believing the evidence supports *p* and where it is false' (Audi 2006: 30). The suggestion is that one cannot acquire testimonial knowledge from a habitual deceiver, even when the information presented is reliably true. But even if one were to agree that Mrs Smith's behaviour indicates a character flaw of sorts, or some other deficiency – perhaps a blameworthy disconnect between her beliefs and her actions – why should this suffice to invalidate her (by stipulation, objectively reliable) testimony as a source of knowledge for her students? After all, as Lackey notes, '*ex hypothesi* Mrs Smith consulted reliable books in the library to develop her reliable lecture notes, and hence it is unclear how there could be any unacceptable degree of accidentality' (Lackey 1999: 480) in her telling the truth in the case at hand.

To strengthen her case, Lackey considers the hypothetical case of Bertha, the 'consistent liar' (Lackey 2008: 54). At a certain point in her life, following a trauma, Bertha became prone to telling lies – not just any random lies, but systematic lies pertaining to her experiences of wild animals. In order to cure Bertha of her pathology, it was decided to perform a radical neurosurgical procedure on her, which rewired her belief-forming processes in such a way as to reliably compensate for her attempts to lie. Thus, nearly every time Bertha looks at a giraffe, she now believes that it is a horse, but – as an effect of her pathological tendency to lie – will report that it is a giraffe (and so forth for other animals). As a result, the people around her will reliably gain true wildlife-related information from Bertha. Indeed, thanks to the efforts of her neurosurgeon, Bertha is *hardwired* to speak the truth, even if she does not speak *from knowledge*. Bertha, we might say, is an excellent 'wildlife-detector'. Denying that hearers can acquire testimonial knowledge from Bertha's testimony, Lackey argues, 'conflates *reliable knowers* with *reliable testifiers*, that is, it conflates subjects reliably forming beliefs themselves with speakers reliably communicating information to others' (Lackey 1999: 481). So long as our interlocutor's *statements* are reliable, it does not matter for the purpose of knowledge acquisition, whether they privately believe or disbelieve what they are attesting to – provided they reliably attest to the truth.

Whereas in the 'creationist teacher' and 'consistent liar' examples, it was the lack of belief that posed a challenge to the transmission model, in another class of cases it is the presence of doxastic defeaters on the part of the speaker that prevents her – but not, so the argument goes, the hearer – from acquiring knowledge. A doxastic defeater, here, refers to a belief *d* held by the speaker *S*, which, if true, would undermine whatever justification *S* might have for believing another proposition *p*. Since *S* takes *d* to be true, she lacks justified true belief – and therefore knowledge – that *p*. On the strong transmission model, *S* would thus not be in a position to impart testimonial knowledge that *p* to her audience. Yet it is not clear that the mere possession of a doxastic defeater on the part of the speaker must necessarily stop the hearer from acquiring testimonial knowledge on the basis of her testimony that *p*. This can be made plausible by considering cases where the speaker's original belief (that *p*) is true and reliably formed – as in the case of a simple perceptual belief ('there is a tree in front of me') – whereas the defeater, *d*, is false and is believed only as the result of deception, manipulation or confusion. In Lackey's example, Jim asks Jane for directions to a nearby café, which Jane gladly points out to him. However, unbeknownst to Jim, Jane is momentarily plagued by severe sceptical doubts – so much so 'that she can scarcely be said to know anything at all' (ibid.: 484), including whether or not there is an external world (let alone a café in the vicinity). Although Jane's occurrent sceptical worries function as a defeater of her own knowledge, it seems implausible that this should affect Jim's ability to acquire knowledge on the basis of her testimony, given that her original beliefs about the geography of her environment were reliably formed and she does not communicate her nagging sceptical doubts to him. In this second class of cases of testimonial knowledge from non-knowledge, it is because of the non-transmission of doxastic defeaters that we can credit the hearer, but not the speaker, with knowledge that *p*.

Lackey takes these and similar examples to show that the transmission model places undue emphasis on the epistemic properties *of beliefs*, focusing on whether properties such as the justificatory standing of a given belief are successfully being transmitted from the speaker to the hearer. This, it is claimed, gets the epistemology of testimonial interactions backwards, since what is given to us as recipients of testimony is never a belief *simpliciter*, but a (written or verbal) statement expressing a propositional content. Thus, 'in order to have a *fully general* epistemology of testimony, the epistemic conditions for testimonial beliefs need to be imposed on the statements of speakers, not on their beliefs' (Lackey 2008: 58–9). Rather than contrasting 'testimonial knowledge' and 'knowledge from testimony', we acquire testimonial knowledge from others *by way of* learning from their words.

3. Defending the transmission model

The 'creationist teacher' and 'consistent liar' cases discussed in the previous section are meant to drive a wedge between the speaker's justification for belief and the hearer's ability to acquire knowledge on the basis of the speaker's testimony. In particular, a speaker need not be a reliable believer in order to function as a reliable testifier. From a reliabilist perspective, it then follows almost as a corollary that a hearer can acquire testimonial knowledge that *p* from a speaker who fails to know that *p*, if only the latter reliably attests to the fact that *p*. The conclusion that has been drawn from this observation is two-fold: First, the transmission model has been claimed to be inadequate, insofar as it rules out acquiring testimonial knowledge from non-knowers. The burden of proof is on defenders of the transmission model to show why, in the above cases, Mrs Smith's students do not acquire knowledge, whereas those of her (non-creationist) colleague – who teaches the exact same content, using the same teaching methodologies – do. Second, by making testimonial knowledge a matter of how reliable the information conveyed by the speaker's statements is, the suggestion is that other epistemic properties that may potentially be transmitted – such as the 'extended warrant' a claim might enjoy – play no determining role in whether or not the hearer does, in fact, acquire knowledge. Both of these partial conclusions have met with opposition from critics of Lackey's generative account; let us consider each criticism in turn.

Regarding the alleged inadequacy of the transmission model, one line of criticism has been that, although Lackey's counterexamples are effective against its strong version, more moderate versions of transmission remain unaffected by them. As Graham notes, the 'orthodox view' of transmission that dominates much of the epistemological literature on testimony does not demand that, for the hearer *H* to be in a position to acquire testimonial knowledge, the speaker *S* must have knowledge at the point of testifying, but merely that *someone* in the chain of communication leading up to the present encounter, must have had non-testimonial knowledge. (See Graham 2006b: 106.) As Dummett puts it, in order for the hearer to acquire testimonial knowledge that *p*, 'the original purveyor of the information – the first link in the chain of transmission – must himself have known it, and therefore have been in a position to know it, or it cannot be knowledge for any of those who derived it ultimately from him' (Dummett 1993: 422). Similarly Fricker: 'If *H* knows that *p* through being told that *p* and trusting the teller, there is or was someone who knows that *p* in some other way – *not* in virtue of having been told that *p* and trusting the teller' (Fricker 2006: 240). 'Knowledge gaps' in the chain of transmission – whether due to the non-transmission of doxastic defeaters, or because of non-belief on the part of one of the intermediaries – may thus be acceptable on the standard interpretation of the transmission model, so long as, to borrow Burge's phrase, there is 'knowledge in the chain'.

Another strategy of defending the transmission model against the challenge from purported examples of generative testimony would be to argue that transmission is, in fact, what underlies knowledge acquisition in the examples given. That is, rather than retreat to a weaker version of the transmission model by accepting that transmission *of the speaker's belief and its epistemic characteristics* is not always required if the hearer is to acquire testimonial knowledge, this response would address the purported counterexamples head-on, by claiming that some form of transmission of epistemic properties is necessarily involved. A hint as to how this might work is contained in the phrase 'knowledge in the chain', which suggests that justification-conferring grounds may exist outside the psychology of an individual reasoner. This can be made vivid for the case of the 'creationist teacher': as Lackey notes, the teacher, *ex hypothesi*, acquired her information from reliable books that document the scientific consensus. When Mrs Smith presents arguments and findings in support of evolutionary theory to her students, she is articulating the scientific consensus which is itself the result of an objectively justification-conferring body of evidence. Whether or not she privately believes in the fact of evolution is immaterial, insofar as her assertions are backed by relevant and conclusive scientific evidence. Unlike the previous argument, the main point here is not that 'someone else in the chain' possesses knowledge, but rather that there exists a species of epistemic justification that is independent of the doxastic state of any one individual.

The relevant distinction in this context is that between *doxastic* and *propositional* justification. Whereas doxastic justification operates at the level of the beliefs of individuals, propositional justification attaches to propositional claims, whether or not they are believed by the individual in question – or indeed by anyone. (Doxastic justification is often thought to presuppose propositional justification, in that it requires that an individual base her belief on that which propositionally justifies it; for a critique of this view, see Turri 2010.) For example, a student might succeed in proving a mathematical theorem, reasoning successfully from true premises to the correct conclusion, but due to pathological self-doubt about his mathematical abilities might not believe that his proof is, in fact, correct. Although the conclusion is propositionally justified – it is based on a correct proof, after all – and although the student has in-principle access to all the 'ingredients' required for knowledge, he lacks doxastic justification, since he fails to appreciate the probative force of the proof he has come up with. A similar disconnect between propositional and doxastic justification, one might argue, exists in the case of the 'creationist teacher' who passes on all the correct information to her students, but herself fails to form the appropriate doxastic response to the body of evidence she has amassed. Yet, although the teacher lacks doxastic justification, and hence cannot directly transmit *her* knowledge to the students, it does not follow that there is no transmission of justification involved at all: given the fact that the teacher's testimony is based on an extensive review of the relevant scientific literature, she may very well succeed in transmitting sufficient propositional justification for knowledge to her students. Since the students, *ex hypothesi*, have every reason to believe their teacher, they would then base their beliefs on the information made available to them through testimony, thereby acquiring testimonial knowledge as the result of the transmission of (propositional) justification.

4. Knowledge from unsafe testimony?

A very different route by which testimony has been claimed to be a generative source of knowledge is *unsafe* testimony in an appropriately responsive environment. The notion of safety requires some explication. A number of recent epistemologists have claimed that, if someone knows that p, then their belief that p must be 'safe' – that is, it could not easily have been false in a similar situation (Williamson 2000: 147). This so-called safety condition on knowledge has been the subject of much recent debate, and competing notions of safety have been proposed. (For a review, see Pritchard 2008.) For our purposes, a good qualitative way of thinking about the safety of beliefs is in terms of the proximity or distance of possibilities – where the measure of how close two scenarios ('possible worlds') are is their overall similarity. A subject S's belief (that p) is then considered safe, if in all close possible worlds where S believes that p, p is true. Which possible worlds are 'close enough' to merit inclusion in this set is itself a matter of how relevantly similar they are; in particular, it often makes sense to restrict one's attention to scenarios that involve the same basis of belief, for example perception or testimony. For example, your perceptual belief that you, here and now, are reading this book is safe, since it could not have easily been the case that you formed this belief when in fact you were not doing so.

The notion of 'safe testimony' may be defined in direct analogy with the notion of safe belief: 'Where one testifies that p on basis B, one's testimony is safe just if there is no close possibility in which one falsely testifies that p on B' (Pelling 2013: 209). In the case where B refers to perception, and the testifier is sincerely expressing a belief he holds, safe testimony depends on the speaker's having a safe belief. Unsafe testimony may be the result of the speaker's having an unsafe belief or her being caused by other factors to make assertions that could have easily been wrong. From the hearer's perspective, reliance on unsafe testimony would be a very risky way of forming beliefs and, given the safety condition on knowledge, could hardly be expected to result in testimonial knowledge. And yet, as Sandy Goldberg (2005) has argued, there may be cases where an appropriately responsive environment 'cooperates' with the recipient of testimony in such a way as to allow for the acquisition of testimonial knowledge even from unsafe testimony. Again, the basic mechanism is best illustrated by way of example:

[MILK CARTON.] Frank is a writer who spends his mornings in the kitchen, where he follows a mildly eccentric ritual. Every day after finishing his bowl of cereal at around dawn, he discards whatever milk is left, but places the empty carton back in the fridge, where it remains until noon, when he takes out the trash. Today, his sister Mary and nephew Sonny are visiting. Having had a tiring journey, they sleep in and join Frank in the kitchen in the late morning. Mary sees the milk carton in the fridge, assumes it is full, and on that basis tells Sonny that there is milk in the fridge. As it happens, there is indeed milk in the carton this morning, since Frank forgot to perform his ritual. Upon overhearing Mary's testimony, Frank is reminded of his blunder and realizes that he forgot to discard of the milk this morning; at the same moment, Sonny, on the basis of his mother's testimony, forms the belief that there is milk in the fridge. Had Frank performed his ritual, he would have immediately corrected Mary and would have informed his visitors that the carton was empty. (Paraphrased after Goldberg 2005: 302)

As the case is described, Mary's testimony is unsafe: although her statement that there is milk in the fridge happens to be true on this occasion, it might easily have been false. Indeed, on any other morning – when Frank would have followed his ritual – it would have been false, yet Mary would have formed the same belief, on the same perceptual basis (plus inference from background assumptions). And yet, although Mary's testimony is unsafe, Sonny nonetheless acquires testimonial knowledge that there is milk on the fridge on the basis of his mother's say-so. This, Goldberg argues, is because, although his mother's testimony would have been false in most nearby possible worlds, in all of these scenarios his uncle would have immediately interrupted and corrected her, thereby preventing Sonny from acquiring a false belief. In turn, all those nearby possible worlds where Sonny forms the belief that there is milk in the fridge, are at the same time cases in which Frank would have remained silent – that is, cases where he would have forgotten to discard the milk. Frank's continued presence in the kitchen, along with his readiness to speak up in order to prevent Sonny from acquiring a false testimonial belief – what Goldberg calls Frank's 'silent monitoring' (Goldberg 2005: 304) of the testimonial exchange – ensures that any belief Sonny forms on the basis of his mother's testimony is safe and, thus, qualifies as testimonial knowledge.

Goldberg's conclusion that unsafe testimony, given an appropriately responsive environment, can result in testimonial knowledge has been met with some criticism. In particular it has been argued that, if Sonny's belief is indeed testimonial (in the sense discussed earlier), then it cannot be considered safe (and vice versa). As Lackey points out (2008: 82), the temporal order of events is important: Sonny plausibly forms his *testimonial* belief immediately upon receiving his mother's testimony, before Frank has had a chance to either speak up or let Mary's testimony pass silently. If Frank speaks up to correct Mary, Sonny will of course abandon his belief immediately, whereas, if his uncle remains silent, he will retain the belief he initially formed before Frank's (silent or vocal) assessment could take place. Yet this means that, to the extent that Sonny's belief is still the same and is held on the same – exclusively testimonial – basis, it remains as unsafe as it was initially, at the point of belief formation. Alternatively, if one wishes to argue that Sonny's belief 'gains' safety as the result of Frank's silent monitoring, then one can no longer plausibly regard it as exclusively *testimonial* in character. As Lackey puts it, 'though Mary's testimony is *causally responsible* for Sonny's acquiring the belief that there is milk in the refrigerator, Frank's silent monitoring is what *confers on the belief its positive epistemic status*' (Lackey 2008: 84). Goldberg is aware of the objection that, as the case is described, 'it is not Mary's testimony alone, so much as Mary's-testimony-together-with-Frank's-monitoring that generates Sonny's knowledge' (Goldberg 2005: 304–5). However, as he sees it, this objection is premised on the view that we can neatly keep apart reliance on testimony from reliance on our epistemic environment in general – a view that itself is problematic.

Consider a slight modification of the 'milk carton' scenario, such that Sonny is aware of the silent monitoring going on. Clearly, then, Sonny would treat Frank's silence much like he would treat, say, the absence of signs of insincerity or incompetence on the part of his mother – that is, 'as a factor indicating the trustworthiness of [her] testimony' (ibid.: 305). However, from within a reliabilist framework, there is nothing outlandish about the idea that we can gain knowledge in situations where we depend on the *de facto* satisfaction of certain background conditions, without our being aware of them – so long as the combination of processes involved is, in fact, reliable. Given that Frank's silent monitoring is a stable – though, admittedly, entirely contingent – feature of Sonny's epistemic environment, which ensures that any stable beliefs Sonny forms about whether or not there is milk in the fridge are in fact reliable, it would seem gratuitous to demand that Sonny must be aware of this particular reliability-enhancing feature in his environment. For Sonny to acquire testimonial knowledge from the unsafe testimony of his mother, it is sufficient that he finds himself in an appropriately responsive environment – in this case, in the presence of his uncle Frank. (For further criticisms and variations of Goldberg's example, see Pelling 2013.)

5. Generativity of testimony in communitarian epistemology

The examples so far aim to show that testimony can, on occasion, function as a generative source of knowledge. But even if one finds cases like Lackey's 'creationist teacher' and Goldberg's 'milk carton' compelling, there remains a strong sense that generativity of testimony as a source of knowledge is seen as the exception rather than the rule. A natural response for adherents of the transmission model – and indeed a line that most critics have taken – would be to either deny that testimonial knowledge can be acquired in those rare and contrived scenarios, or insist that such cases can in fact be accommodated by the transmission model. Either way, one would be dealing with only a small proportion of cases – too small, perhaps, to pose a serious challenge to the prevailing view that, for the most part, testimony transmits (rather than generates) knowledge.

By contrast, communitarian epistemologists have argued that, far from being the exception, generative testimony is in fact the rule. This claim, if adopted as true, would require a far more radical departure from the transmission model than is entailed by the previous counterexamples. In order to see why, it is worth taking a step back and reflecting on some of the assumptions of communitarian epistemology. In Chapter 2, we considered in some detail Welbourne's suggestion that 'commonability' is the defining feature of knowledge, whereas belief plays at best an auxiliary or derivative role – either as a way of coming to share knowledge by 'believing the speaker', or as the (more or less accidental) mental by-product of an individual joining a community of knowledge. A 'community of knowledge', for Welbourne, is constituted by the mutual recognition of its members, who acknowledge each other as partaking in the same knowledge: 'A primitive community [of knowledge] consists of two people knowing the same thing and recognising each other as sharers in that knowledge; so each can act on the assumption of knowledge in the other and they will be able to act co-operatively' (Welbourne 1986: 25). Whether or not an individual knower can be credited with knowledge thus depends, at least in part, on whether others can potentially come to share in that knowledge and, equally importantly, on whether they can recognize him, and each other, as members of a community of knowledge that is held together by the requisite commitments and entitlements.

How does generativity of testimony enter into this communitarian picture of knowledge? For one, to the extent that testimony is a way of sharing knowledge by making it accessible to others, testimony is involved in constituting communities of knowledge. Whereas epistemological individualism typically regards the giving of testimony as an act of transmitting knowledge from one person to another, communitarian epistemology sees it as a step in the process of enlarging the community of knowledge (provided the testimony is received in the spirit in which it is given). As Kusch has argued, this suggests a strong parallel with how social statuses and institutions – such as marriage or money – are constituted through mutual recognition and performative speech acts. (See Kusch 2002a: 346.) Traditionally, epistemologists have drawn a clear line between constative testimony (such as 'the cat is on the mat') and performative speech (such as the registrar's utterance 'I hereby declare you husband and wife'). One difference lies in the 'direction of fit': for constative testimony to be successful, it must 'fit' the world – that is, it must correctly represent an independent state of affairs in the world. By contrast, performative speech demands that the world 'fit' the content of the utterance and, as in the registrar's pronouncing a couple 'husband and wife', may even bring about the very state of affairs in the (social) world it refers to. Yet if, as communitarian epistemology claims, knowledge itself is socially constituted – through mutual recognition of membership in a community of knowledge – this asymmetry between constative and performative speech acts can no longer be upheld.

The way communities of knowledge are 'performatively enacted', however, is rarely as explicit as in the case of the registrar's marrying a couple. A better analogy, Kusch suggests, would be social institutions like the convention of greeting people. Such institutions are neither brought about by the actions of a single individual, nor are they explicitly agreed upon at the collective level; as Kusch notes, 'we do not create social institutions by speaking in chorus' (Kusch 2002b: 67). At the same time, it is clear that the sum-total of individual actions – of greetings and non-greetings – determines the shared norms and standards of when it is appropriate to greet someone (or not) and which types of behaviours and utterances are fit for the purpose. In other words, in such cases

> the communal institution-creating performative testimony is typically *fragmented and widely distributed over other speech-acts*. The communal performative is never explicitly made; it is only made implicitly or indirectly. (Ibid.)

The relation between constative and performative speech acts, thus, is not one of strict opposition. Just as performative speech depends on shared (and, on this occasion, non-negotiable) understandings of contexts, meanings, and actions, so constative testimony almost always carries with it a performative element – if only because it reinforces and entrenches existing concepts, categorizations or taxonomies:

> Every constative testimony about elephants carries part of the communal performative speech-act which constitutes the category of elephants, and in doing so, re-enforces the conventional ways of delimiting this category, and helps to entrench the conventional exemplars. (Kusch 2002b: 69)

Generativity of testimony, on Kusch's communitarian account of knowledge, is simply a ubiquitous by-product of the performative character of all communication:

> Testimony, even past-tense constative say-so, is always in part performative. All testimony carries parts of widely distributed communal performatives. The 'always' is important here. I am not concerned with a special case; I am concerned with *all* testimony. All testimony is *in part* performative; thus all testimony is generative of knowledge [. . .]. (Kusch 2002a: 349)

As mentioned earlier, these conclusions constitute a significant departure from traditional epistemology. In its most radical form, communitarian epistemology aims at nothing short of the displacement of our traditional notion of knowledge in favour of an account of knowledge as a social status. (See Kusch 2002b.) One potential objection against this project arises from the worry that, by emphasizing what knowledge has in common with *other* social statuses, one might end up neglecting any distinctive features that set knowledge – and the communication of knowledge – apart from other social statuses. After all, as Kusch himself is well aware, while we might 'get by without the social institutions of money and marriage', it is much harder 'to imagine what life would be like without telling how things are' (ibid.: 75).

Study questions

1 One possible objection to the CREATIONIST TEACHER case (Section 2) is that, although Mrs Smith lacks knowledge, she reliably reports something that is known by others. In this sense, her testimony may still be considered transmissive, not generative. How might one modify the case in order to avoid this objection? (One such modification is discussed in Graham 2006b: 112–13.)

2   Lackey (2008: 79–97) has argued that Goldberg's MILK CARTON case (Section 4) is not, in fact, an instance of safe testimonial knowledge from unsafe testimony: Sonny's belief is either *unsafe* (immediately before Frank's act of monitoring) or *no longer testimonial* (once Frank has concluded his monitoring and/or has spoken up). Try to reconstruct the temporal sequence of events in the interaction between Mary, Sonny, and Frank in the different (actual and counterfactual) scenarios, and evaluate whether Lackey's criticism is valid.

3   Give an example of how, on Kusch's communitarian account, an instance of constative say-so may contribute to a communal performative.

Further reading

The transmission model of testimony is closely associated with the thought that when we assert that *p*, we *express* our belief that *p* (rather than merely indicate its presence by other means, or offer the audience our assurance that *p* is true); on this *belief expression model*, linguistic communication affords a way of sharing (the contents of) our beliefs with others. Owens (2006) defends such a belief expression model of testimony. By contrast, Buenting (2006) rejects the idea that, for a testimonial exchange to be successful, what is required is the 'duplication' of the speaker's belief in the hearer. Goldberg (2009), in considering the merits of the (normative) view that a speaker ought only speak from knowledge, also considers which conditions need to be in place (including, which features of assertion a hearer must be sensitive to), in order for a hearer to acquire knowledge on the basis of the speaker's say-so.

8

Trust and assurance

Trust is a fundamental element of human sociality and is central to human flourishing. Overstating only slightly, Sissela Bok notes: '*Whatever* matters to human beings, trust is the atmosphere in which it thrives' (Bok 1999: 31). Much research on trust has focused on its social aspects, yet early sociologists were also among the first to recognize the complexity of our concept of trust. Here is Georg Simmel, commenting in 1900 on what is involved in placing trust in another person by believing him:

> To 'believe in someone', without adding or even conceiving what it is that one believes about him, is to employ a very subtle and profound idiom. It expresses the feeling that there exists between our idea of a being and the being itself a definite connection and unity, a certain consistency in our conception of it, an assurance and lack of resistance in the surrender of the Ego to this conception, which may rest upon particular reasons, but is not explained by them. (Simmel 2011: 191)

Philosophy has been slow – and epistemology even slower – to catch up with the empirically and conceptually rich discussions of trust emerging from the social sciences. This is in spite of the obvious significance of trust in our epistemic dealings with others. Indeed, in the past few chapters we have often appealed, both implicitly and explicitly, to trust as a factor in our acceptance of other people's testimony ('simple trusted acceptance'). It is therefore time to analyse the concept of trust in greater detail, and the present chapter aims to do just that. After contrasting trust with other forms of reliance in the first section, we will encounter two recent trust-based accounts of testimony, both of which emphasize the second-personal nature of trusting others for knowledge, before finally turning to the thorny topic of generalized public (or institutional) trust in one's social-epistemic environment at large.

1. Trust and other varieties of reliance

In order to appreciate the specific role of trust in our epistemic lives it is important to understand it as one among a range of different ways in which we rely on others. For example, in modern, highly differentiated societies, we rely on various forms of infrastructure and sociotechnical systems for the provision of necessary goods and services, and we causally depend for our survival and well-being on all those individuals involved in the production and provision of such services. In this sense, I may be said to rely on my phone company to provide me with a connection, given that I regularly pay my bills. Yet such weak predictive reliance seems different in character than trust in a specific person. As Govier notes, 'trust is paradigmatically a relation between individual persons'. Though a person 'can be said to trust or distrust God, an ancient author, the forces of nature, himself, his senses, the brakes on his car, a bank machine, or the family dog' (Govier 1993b: 157), this usage of the idiom of trust and distrust is perhaps best understood in a metaphorical sense. This does not mean that we can only trust individuals we know well, such as friends and family. As Annette Baier reminds us:

> We sometimes let ourselves fall asleep on trains or planes, trusting neighboring strangers not to take advantage of our defenselessness. We put our bodily safety into the hand of pilots, drivers, doctors, with scarcely any sense of recklessness. (Baier 1986: 234)

In these cases, where specific individuals can be identified – either because they occupy positions of authority (such as the pilot or doctor) or because we directly encounter them, for example as fellow passengers – talk of 'trust' seems entirely permissible. The same goes for trusting other people for knowledge:

> We often trust total strangers, such as those from whom we ask directions in foreign cities, to direct rather than misdirect us, or to tell us so if they do not know what we want to know; and we think we should do the same for those who ask the same help from us. (Ibid.)

Trust, thus, is not so much a matter of prior acquaintance between truster and trusted, but instead is an attitude that we adopt towards other people, placing ourselves in a position of dependency on their good will.

As Baier sees it, the main difference between trusting others and merely relying on them, is 'reliance on their good will toward one, as distinct from their dependable habits, or [reliance] on their dependably exhibited fear, anger, or other motives compatible with ill will toward one, or on motives not directed on one at all' (ibid.). Whereas in the latter cases, one would merely be predicting the other party's future behaviour, based on reliably exhibited character traits or probable motives, in the case of trusting others one is implicitly acknowledging that one's dependency on the other person runs deeper than this. This is because, as Govier puts it, there is 'an interpretive and inductive gap, between our information about the other's behavior and our overall sense of his or her motivation and character' (Govier 1993: 166). In the case of trusting others for knowledge, this is especially pertinent, since the testimony of others can easily – and often does – involve contexts, encounters and subject matters of which we have no extensive prior experience. As Edward Hinchman notes with respect to trusting the testimony of others, the problem of trust is 'that *for all you know* the speaker not only does not care about not misleading you but could not be brought to care' (Hinchman 2012: 59). Trusting someone – whether in practical matters or for knowledge – thus entails, in a phrase due to Gloria Origgi, 'an accepted vulnerability to another's possible, but not expected, ill will' (Origgi 2004: 64). As these authors argue, trust is neither reducible to mere predictive (or inductive) reliance, nor is it merely a matter of psychological expectation – perhaps infused with an affective-emotional component (even though all of these may accompany instances of trust). Instead, it is an attitude which acknowledges an irreducible interpersonal element and which – once it is acknowledged by the trusted – may both play a motivating role and act as a normative constraint on the other party's behaviour.

What matters most for the purposes of the epistemology of testimony, is 'epistemic' trust – where the attribute 'epistemic' indicates that it 'somehow furthers the goal of acquiring true beliefs and avoiding false ones' (Lackey 2008: 226). Before turning to this aspect in more detail, however, it will be instructive to briefly sketch some of the other ways trust has been theorized in philosophy. In moral philosophy, both the role of trust as a prerequisite for morality and the ethical status of trust relationships has been discussed. Regarding the former, Baier notes that 'morality, as anything more than a law within, itself requires trust in order to thrive', but immediately goes on to say that, of course, 'immorality too thrives on some forms of trust' (Baier 1986: 232). While the presence or absence of trust alone does not settle substantive moral questions, it is nonetheless possible, Baier argues, to devise a 'moral test' to determine the ethical status of trust relationships. The crucial question is whether 'knowledge of what the other party is relying on for the continuance of the trust relationship would [. . .] itself destabilize the relation' (ibid.: 255). If, say, the other party is relying on threats, manipulation, or deception (e.g. by misrepresenting factors relevant to its perceived trustworthiness), the relation would likely fail the test. A related point concerns the virtuous nature of trust relationships: Just as one may view trustworthiness as an individual virtue, so trust itself may be viewed as a social virtue that cannot be reduced to the narrow pursuit of self-interest. In political philosophy, trust is seen both as the basis of (peaceful) transfer of power to those in authority and as that which holds together modern liberal civil societies. (Consequently, the perceived erosion of trust in political institutions and mechanisms has given rise to critical analyses of the ways in which liberal democracies 'perform' relationships of trust; see, for example, O'Neill 2002.) In social theory, trust is often regarded as a form of 'social glue' that holds together relationships at various levels of complexity. Exactly how this social function of trust should be theoretically analysed is itself a matter of controversy. Some authors have emphasized the role of 'unreflective pre-logical, or pre-judgmental acceptance and confidence' (Govier 1993: 156). Others claim that, though trust relationships (e.g. between strangers) may often look like spontaneous acts of good will, they are in fact a form of rational choice, based on expectations about the self-interested behaviour of both parties.

Several strands of this debate converge in interesting ways in the domain of science, considered both as a system of knowledge and as a social enterprise. Hardwig, in a series of papers, has argued that scientific knowledge presents a challenge to the traditional ideal of epistemic independence (see also the discussion in Chapter 1). This is because the amount of data produced and the degree of specialization required in most disciplines far exceeds what a single knower could ever hope to master. As a result, researchers must collaborate – as indicated by the long lists of co-authors of many scientific papers – and must trust one another for knowledge: 'In most disciplines, those who do not trust cannot know; those who do not trust cannot have the best evidence for their beliefs' (Hardwig 1991: 693–4). Far from this being a shortcoming of scientific knowledge, it is the inevitable result of the extraordinary success of science as an institution that produces knowledge – too much knowledge for a single individual to grasp. For this reason, scientists routinely engage in the sharing of information, results, methods, and materials, and they trust one another's 'epistemic character' (ibid.: 700) – where the latter reflects such individual character traits as truthfulness, conscientious work and self-criticism. Even competence, though not strictly a character trait, 'standardly depends on character', given that it requires 'habits of self-discipline, focus, and persistence' (ibid.). The epistemic interdependence that characterizes science and other knowledge-producing institutions thus calls for moral trust – that is, 'trust in the character of the testifiers' (ibid.: 702).

Others have resisted Hardwig's conclusion, arguing instead that trust and trustworthiness in science can be accounted for in entirely prudential terms, as an essentially self-interested strategy. As Michel Blais argues, while trust is indeed essential to science – since, without cooperation, no single scientist could hope to further his standing in the profession – what motivates trustworthiness is not a moral sense of obligation or an acknowledgement of the interpersonal dimension of the relationship between truster and trusted, but instead is the recognition that one would forego future benefits by defecting from the 'knowledge game'. Such defection might take the form of cheating, fabricating results, failing to share results and so forth – all of which hold the promise of short-term rewards, such as getting ahead of the competition, securing a competitive research grant or publishing an otherwise unpublishable paper. Blais explicitly endorses a parallel between rational choice theory and accounts of trust in science: 'Only cooperation, as defined [. . .] in game theory and as illustrated in the Prisoner's Dilemma, is necessary for the justification of vicarious knowledge' (Blais 1987: 370). In the case of science, however, unlike in the Prisoner's Dilemma, the short-term gains from defection pale by comparison with the punishment that is meted out by the scientific community against offenders: permanent exclusion from the game. If scientists are found to be cooperating, then this is not because they are motivated by good will or altruism, but because they fear the threat of future exclusion were they to defect – or so the story goes.

Blais's proposal is a good example of how rational choice theorists have aimed to redescribe social phenomena in terms of self-interest and individual choice. Yet there are good reasons to be sceptical about the merits of this project, both in general and in relation to the case of trust in science. Hardwig, in his rebuttal, points out that Blais is overstating the threat to scientific 'defectors', given that permanent exclusion is, in fact, quite rare and tends to be reserved to severe cases of scientific misconduct. By contrast, 'other sloppy, careless, or deceptive research practices that may be even more damaging to the reliability of scientific testimony' (Hardwig 1991: 703), but do not fall under the categories enshrined in official 'codes of conduct', may go unpunished. Scientists trust each other in many more subtle ways than is captured by the 'tit for tat' strategy favoured by Blais. Even if one grants that the game-theoretical account of trust has some initial plausibility in the case of scientific testimony, given the iterative nature of how scientists share and generate results, it is questionable whether such an approach generalizes to other forms of testimony. As Origgi observes:

> In particular, a tit for tat strategy makes sense if basically the same game with similar pay-offs is played again and again and if, in this game, defection is advantageous unless it is sanctioned. In personal relationships, however, the goals of communication are extremely varied. (Origgi 2004: 64)

Our overall testimonial practices are diverse, both in terms of their content and their goals, and they are subject to a range of moral, psychological and contextual factors. We can hardly expect a simplistic model of what it means to trust another's testimony to do justice to this diversity. Rather than opting for a simplistic model, it may be more fruitful to provisionally take talk of the 'moral' or 'interpersonal' dimension of trust at face value and attempt to *explicate* its meaning rather than eliminate it in its entirety.

2. Inviting and deciding to trust

An important strand in the philosophical literature on trust concerns the relation between trust and our voluntary abilities. Can we simply decide to trust? Or, failing that, how can we bring about conditions that make it easier for us to enter into relationships of justified trust? The answers to this question mirror the debate about doxastic voluntarism and the ethics of belief. On the one hand are those who argue that it is sometimes rational – and psychologically possible – to believe *at will*, for example when practical interests would make it desirable to hold the belief in question. For example, parents might choose to believe that their imprisoned son is innocent, even though there is strong evidence that he did, in fact, commit the crime. A moderate version of such direct doxastic voluntarism would hold that we have direct voluntary control only over believing (or disbelieving) propositions for which the evidence is inconclusive; a strong version would go further by arguing that, in certain situations, we can believe against the evidence. Those who, on the other hand, reject direct doxastic voluntarism need not claim that we have no control whatsoever about what we believe. Belief is not merely something that happens to us passively, but is the result of various belief-forming mechanisms that operate in different situations, and we have considerable – though admittedly imperfect – control over which situations to expose ourselves to. While I may not be able to ignore undesirable evidence that stares me in the face, I may choose to avoid situations where I would be likely to encounter such evidence. Similarly, while I may not be able to trust a random interlocutor at will, I have some control over whom to consult for information: thus, I may seek out sources whom I already trust on the relevant issues, or I may engage in activities that are conducive towards building trust.

The fragility of trust, and the difficulty (or impossibility) of forcing trust where it is absent, is widely acknowledged in everyday language. We speak of 'building' trust and of 'winning' someone's trust (where 'winning' has the connotations of good fortune rather than of winning a battle). Assurances of one's trustworthiness – in an attempt to win someone over – can be outright suspicious and, even when genuine, are often futile:

> 'Trust me!' is for most of us an invitation which we cannot accept at will – either we do already trust the one who says it, in which case it serves at best as reassurance, or it is properly responded to with, 'Why should and how can I, until I have cause to?' (Baier 1986: 244)

Only children, Baier argues, are 'able to trust simply because of encouragement to trust' (ibid.). Does this mean that children have voluntary control over when (and whom) to trust, whereas adults lack such a capacity? This would be as remarkable as it is improbable. A more plausible interpretation is that children, by and large, are more trusting and thus respond to direct encouragement ('Trust me!') more easily. Adults, by contrast, have learned to distinguish between contexts that justify a trusting attitude and those that do not and, presumably, have also learned from experiences where their trust was misplaced. This, however, does not entail that adults have no influence whatsoever on when, and whom, to trust. As Baier argues, her account 'has been designed to allow for unconscious trust, for conscious but unchosen trust, as well as for conscious trust the truster has chosen to endorse and cultivate' (Baier 1986: 245). The notion of 'cultivation' is important, since it emphasizes that acquiring responsible habits of trusting takes time and requires practice. Only by seeking out situations that are conducive to trusting relationships with others, can 'we come to trust ourselves as trusters' (ibid.); theoretical reflection alone cannot achieve this. (Richard Holton, in spite of claiming to distance himself from Baier, echoes this when he notes that 'a trusting relationship makes a greater range of trust available to me'; Holton 1994: 71.) I may be able to favourably assess the trustworthiness of someone with whom I have no dealings, on the basis of information about his reliability, competence, and overall sincerity, without thereby coming to trust the person: whether or not to *trust* the person is not a live question, until one has specific cause to do so in a concrete setting.

As this discussion makes plain, there is no guarantee that the invitation to trust will be accepted. But even if it may not always sway the recipient – since, as discussed, in order for the invitation to be effective, it may already require a modicum of trust on his part – the fact of its issuance may nonetheless be significant. In the case of testimony, the act of telling may itself be a reason to trust, since it amounts to an assumption of responsibility on the part of the speaker. More precisely, since we often act on testimony-based beliefs, and thus may suffer negative consequences if it turns out that our interlocutor was wrong (whether due to deception or carelessness), we need a way of deferring the burden of responsibility for some of the testimonial beliefs we have acquired. This is where the act of telling is significant. As Edward Hinchman puts it, 'a speaker takes on this burden by addressing her hearer in the way distinctive of telling' (Hinchman 2005: 563). In performing the speech act of telling, the speaker is not merely making evidence available in a neutral, non-committal manner, for her hearer to assess and weigh against competing considerations; instead, she is inviting her hearer to trust her. In telling her hearer that p, she is at the same time pledging to be in a position of knowledge and is presenting herself as a direct source of epistemic warrant:

> When a speaker tells her hearer that p [. . .] she acts on an intention to give him an entitlement to believe that p that derives not from evidence of the truth of 'p' but from his mere understanding of the act she thereby performs. (Ibid.: 564)

The hearer may, of course, refuse the invitation, but in doing so he is depriving himself of the possibility of delegating responsibility to the speaker. From the perspective of the speaker, 'if you take my word on the basis of accepting a thesis for which you don't simply take my word, it would seem I'm off the hook: the sense in which I may get you into trouble is merely causal, not epistemic' (ibid.: 563). If the hearer refuses to accept the speaker's testimony in the spirit in which it is given – namely, as an invitation to trust – and instead treats it merely as evidence, to be assessed by himself independently, he cannot later hold the speaker accountable for what she said (except, perhaps, in cases of deliberate deception). You can only hold me to my word, if you accepted my word in the first place. Recognizing S's intention to vouch for the truth of her testimony, yet ignoring it as a reason for belief, as Hinchman sees it, constitutes an abuse on the part of the hearer, A, since 'in declining S's invitation A treats S's telling as a telling he merely hears, or overhears, and not as a telling addressed to him' (ibid.: 566).

Where Hinchman sees a clear asymmetry between being the addressee of the speaker's testimony, as opposed to merely overhearing what she is asserting, others have argued that such a distinction is, in fact, irrelevant. Consider Lackey's case of an 'eavesdropper' overhearing a conversation:

> [EAVESDROPPER.] Ben and Kate, thinking they are alone in the office, engage in a private conversation, in the course of which Ben tells Kate that their boss John is having an affair with a new intern, Irene. Their co-worker Earl who, unbeknownst to Ben and Kate, has been eavesdropping on their conversation, likewise comes to believe, solely on the basis of Ben's truthful and reliable testimony, that his boss is having an affair. (Modified after Lackey 2008: 233)

Assuming that Earl and Kate are epistemic peers – they share the same background knowledge, both about Ben as a testifier and about the target of the gossip, John and Irene, and they are equally competent and attentive recipients of testimony – 'then what could distinguish their beliefs epistemically?' (Lackey 2008: 234). From a reliabilist perspective, it may indeed seem puzzling why Earl and Kate should not enjoy the same epistemic status – given that, as the case is described, Ben's testimony is, in fact, reliable. The difference that is invoked by Hinchman – that, in the case at hand, Ben would have reason to feel slighted if Kate refused to trust him, but not if Earl did – appears to have no bearing on the reliability of the information exchange: 'Ben's inviting Kate but not Earl to trust him does not make it more likely that the testimonial belief in question is true for Kate but not for Earl – they are both receiving testimony with the same degree of reliability, the same kind of truth-tracking, the same amount of proper functioning, and so on' (ibid.: 235). While this criticism is legitimate, insofar as it shows that, given favourable conditions, an eavesdropper is not always epistemically worse off than the addressee of the testimony, it does not show that awareness of (and invitations to) trust are '*epistemically superfluous*' (ibid.: 233). This is because it overlooks an important aspect of trusting relationships: their mutual responsiveness. In addressing Kate (rather than Earl), Ben is able to adjust various aspects of his testimony to the fact that it is *Kate* who trusts him; by contrast, 'Earl's trust makes no difference to Ben's performance, while Kate's trust does' (Nickel 2012: 306). (Philip Nickel has called this aspect of testimonial relationships 'dependence-responsiveness'; Nickel 2012.) Although an eavesdropper may be able to acquire the same (potentially high-quality) information from overhearing a speaker's assertions, the addressee of her testimony – assuming the relationship of trust is genuinely reciprocal – enjoys an additional specific reason to believe the speaker, insofar as her invitation to him carries with it the assurance that she is trustworthy *when addressing him*.

3. The assurance view of testimony

Another trust-based account of testimony – closely related to the 'invitation to trust' view, but with some notable differences in emphasis – has recently become known as the *assurance view* of testimony. (See Moran 2005.) It aims to make explicit what it is about the speaker's act of telling that constitutes a special reason for belief for the addressee. In the previous section, we saw that a plausible case can be made that being the addressee of testimony puts one in an epistemically privileged position, insofar as it gives one reason to assume that the speaker is appropriately responsive to the fact of one's dependence to her. By contrast, an eavesdropper who merely overhears what the speaker tells another person cannot assume that, in asserting what she does, she is appropriately responsive to him – since he is not the addressee of her testimony. In issuing an invitation to trust, the speaker is offering to assume responsibility for the hearer's belief formed on the basis of her testimony; the rejection of this invitation is therefore likely to be equated with having been rebuffed by the hearer. The assurance view of testimony can be thought of as an attempt to give a more precise characterization of both of these aspects of the testimonial exchange – that is, of the speaker's specific responsiveness to the hearer, and of her offer of assuming responsibility for any of the hearer's beliefs that are directly based on her testimony.

Regarding the first point, Moran's assurance view locates the specificity of the testifier-addressee relationship in the testifier's intentions and their successful recognition by the addressee. In this regard, the assurance view is indebted to Paul Grice's account of meaning and communication. (See Grice 1957, 1969.) On this account, the mechanism that enables communication is as follows. The testifier S aims to get her addressee H to believe a proposition, p, by getting him to recognize that this is what she is trying to do. More specifically, H is intended to arrive at his belief that p by considering S's act of telling (e.g. her utterance of certain sounds) to be evidence of her intention to get H to believe that p. In successful cases of trusted communication, recognition by H of this intention on S's part will suffice both as H's reason for attributing to S the belief that p, and as the reason for his own testimony-based belief that p. Recognition of the speaker's intention thus plays a crucial role within the Gricean framework. Originally proposed as an account of non-natural meaning, which Grice thought to be wholly derived from speaker intention in the way described, the 'Gricean mechanism' easily carries over to the domain of epistemology. Importantly, recognition of the speaker's intention should not be thought of as an optional or auxiliary feature of the communicative act, but as essential to it. As Moran describes Grice's view, 'nothing can count as a case of nonnatural meaning if the relevant belief could be expected to be produced whether or not the intention behind the action were recognized' (Moran 2005: 14). By extension, there is an unbridgeable difference between letting another person know by telling him that p and by confronting them with evidence that p. What makes an utterance an instance of *telling* – quite apart from its informational content – is S's successful presentation of herself as assuming responsibility for it (on the basis of her intending to communicate to H that p):

[By contrast,] any phenomenon with some independent evidential import will naturally be one which might well be expected to induce belief without the recognition of anyone's intention. That's just what it is for a phenomenon to be ordinary evidence for something else. If his utterance is to count as an instance of telling someone something, however, the speaker must present his action as being without epistemic significance apart from his explicit assumption of responsibility for that significance. (Ibid.)

Telling someone that *p*, on this account, is precisely *not* another form of offering evidence in support of *p*. Recall that, as discussed in Chapter 4, Moran recommends we should be more sceptical of empirical findings that someone else intended to be perceived by us as evidence, as this would suggest that what may look like evidence is in fact not genuine, but is the result of manipulation or tampering. By contrast, when a speaker performs the act of telling that *p* – counting on her intention to be recognized – she freely assumes responsibility for her utterance as a reason for belief, and it is this which gives the hearer a positive reason to believe that *p*. This explains the specific role of recognition of the speaker's intention and, Moran argues,

> it is *only* such a role that accounts for how, in the case of speech, the recognition of intention *enhances* rather than detracts from the epistemic status of the phenomenon (utterance), reveals it to be something other than doctored evidence. (Ibid.: 18)

In a counterpoint to reliabilist views, the assurance view holds that the epistemic status of testimony is not solely a matter of the brute reliability of what is being asserted, but depends crucially on the speaker's intentions (and, except in special cases, on their successful recognition by the hearer). As Moran puts it, in the most basic case of testimony 'it is the speaker who is believed, and belief in the proposition asserted follows from this' (Moran 2005: 2).

In the previous section, we discussed the situation of a speaker feeling slighted because her invitation to trust was rejected without compelling reason. What about the corresponding scenario of a hearer who finds that his trust in the speaker was misplaced? According to the assurance view, the very structure of the testimonial exchange – the fact that, in telling, the speaker freely chose to assure her addressee that *p* – entails that the addressee acquires a *right of complaint*. As in the case of a broken promise, the party that has been let down has legitimate cause for complaint – whereas no such cause would exist for someone who had rejected the promise when it was offered or who had merely counted on the relevant course of action to be completed, without having been promised it. (Benjamin McMyler has recently argued, along similar lines, that the addressee of testimony acquires a more specific 'epistemic right of deferral' – that is, the right 'to defer relevant challenges back to the original speaker'; McMyler 2011: 62.)

This way of looking at testimony also sheds light on the asymmetry that trust-based accounts claim exists between the addressee of testimony and someone who merely overhears the speaker making an assertion: while the overhearer may, on occasion, stand to profit epistemically from what he hears, he – unlike the hearer – does not acquire a right of complaint in case the speaker's assertions turn out to be wrong. Whatever epistemic benefits accrue to the overhearer are entirely derivative: '[W]hile the overhearer may get a reason to believe without having the right to complain that is conferred on the addressee, the fact that the overhearer of the assertion acquires any reason to believe from listening to these words is dependent on their being addressed to someone, with the force of assuming responsibility and thereby conferring a right of complaint' (Moran 2005: 22). The overhearer is not party to the normative relationship that binds the speaker and the addressee; whereas their relationship is reciprocal, insofar as the addressee's right of complaint is matched by the speaker's right to feel slighted if her offer to assume responsibility is rejected without good reason, the overhearer can at best adopt an external ('third-person') perspective on what is, at heart, a second-personal relation between the speaker and her addressee.

4. Public and institutional trust

Any discussion of the role of trust in testimonial knowledge would be incomplete without considering, at least in brief outline, the significance of public or institutional trust. The idea that trust is as much an individual attitude towards specific others as it is a medium that pervades all aspects of social and public life, is expressed aptly by Baier who observes that we 'inhabit a climate of trust as we inhabit an atmosphere and notice it as we notice air, only when it becomes scarce or polluted' (Baier 1987: 234). Just as breathing comes naturally and is necessary to our physical survival, so trusting is something that is second nature to us and is essential to our successfully navigating the social world. But just as we need to stop breathing when the air around us is polluted, we also need to suspend trust when our social environment turns untrustworthy. How do we calibrate the granting and suspension of trust to the trustworthiness of the social world around us? Clearly, the extent of our default acceptance of the testimony of others needs to be pegged to the level of trustworthiness of our social environment. For an assessment of the latter, we rely on what Govier calls *general social knowledge* – 'a person's overall sense of how society works and how people of various types (in various contexts and social roles) are likely to act towards him or her' (Govier 1993b: 158). The information we receive from our various sources 'is ultimately interpreted and evaluated by an individual according to an inchoate but fundamental sense of how the social world works' (ibid.: 159). As we saw earlier, such an assessment need not (and, for the reasons discussed in Chapter 5, likely could not) take the form of reductionism, but instead draws on a wide range of (inductive or abductive) evidence, personal experiences, already trusted testimony, social background knowledge and various situation-specific factors. Individual instances of accepting or rejecting testimony, thus, take place against the backdrop of (and are partly determined by) the level of general trust the recipient places in his or her social-epistemic environment.

In the social sciences, trust is typically discussed in functional or descriptive terms, and is defined in a way that accounts for certain forms of individual or collective behaviour, such as individual risk-taking and social cooperation. The significance of generalized trust as the basis for cooperation, and the collective or economic benefits that accrue from this, is sometimes couched in the language of 'social capital'. Thus understood, the concept of trust itself becomes a 'conceptual tool' (Coleman 1988: S96) for bridging two divergent streams within the social sciences: methodological individualism, which holds that social phenomena can be fully explained in terms of the motivations and actions of individual agents, and holism, according to which social phenomena need to be understood in their own (irreducible) terms. Trust, on this view, provides a link between individual purposive action and the emergence of social organization, since it shows how individuals can be responsive to the social contexts they find themselves in. Other authors have emphasized the functional role of trust as a way of reducing complexity, since, as Niklas Luhmann argues, trust is a strategy to 'overcome an ever-present threshold of anxiety', thereby allowing us to 'rely on unsure premises and by doing so increase their [subjective] certainty value' (Luhmann 1995: 128). As sociologists J. David Lewis and Andrew Weigert put it:

> Trust is a functional alternative to rational prediction for the reduction of complexity. Indeed, trust succeeds where rational prediction alone would fail, because to trust is to live as if certain rationally possible futures will not occur. [. . . In] the absence of trust, the monstrous complexity posed by contingent futures would again return to paralyze action. (Lewis and Weigert 1985: 969)

As this brief outline makes clear, public or institutional trust, although characterizable in functional terms, has a psychosocial component, which manifests itself in recognizable ways at the individual phenomenological level. When Luhmann speaks of 'anxiety', which takes hold in the absence of trust, or when Simmel conceives of trust as containing an 'element of social-psychological quasi-religious faith' (Simmel 2011: 192), it is this aspect of generalized trust in one's social environment they have in mind.

One might worry that talk of trust as a pervasive 'substrate' of social life (or as a form of 'faith') renders it unanalysable and quasi-mysterious. But this would overlook the fact that we often have good reasons for placing trust in the social world around us, or at least for trusting many subsystems within our social environment. This is because our practices of trusting (and, on occasion, distrusting) the various institutions, groups of people, media, etc. we encounter are themselves responsive to changes in our social environment. We learn from past mistakes where our trust in certain institutions or people was misplaced as well as from past successes, and we rely extensively on background knowledge we possess in virtue of our being competent members of society. Such background knowledge is not limited to our first-hand experiences as participants in trusting relationships, but extends to our awareness of normative relationships, social conventions, legal arrangements and regulatory frameworks in society – knowledge of which is itself to a large extent acquired through testimony and reliance on trusted sources. Furthermore, as I argued in Chapter 6, some of the most compelling reasons we have for believing testimony to be a dependable source of knowledge are, in fact, abductive: they are based on the thought that, if testimony were by and large unreliable, or if those to whom we turn for knowledge were usually untrustworthy, the overall success of such collective projects as science, history and education would be a miracle. Given that all of these endeavours are manifestly testimony-dependent, their overall success is best explained by the overall reliability of our testimonial practices – where 'success' includes the ability to reliably filter out erroneous information before it reaches us. It is on the basis of such implicit and explicit background knowledge that each of us constructs a model of the social world, which can then be evaluated individually whenever necessary. Epistemic trust in the social world around us, on this account, is not 'free-floating', but is intimately tied – in phenomenologically salient ways – to our experiences of the social world, and our mental model of it.

While it would be impossible to do justice to all aspects of institutional trust in the limited space permitted here, two further points merit mention. Whereas the first point relates to the project of cultivating trust – specifically, trust in social institutions – the second point concerns a challenge posed by the problem of institutional trust to interpersonal accounts of the kind discussed in the previous section. From the outline presented here, it is clear that the cultivation of public or institutional trust is a long-term project, as merely improving the objective reliability of the various social processes involved in the production and communication of knowledge is not enough: individuals also need time to adjust their expectations and their internal representations of social reality accordingly. Furthermore, any procedures and mechanisms aimed at improving overall trustworthiness and reliability need to be themselves trusted. For example, as Cynthia Townley and Jay Garfield rightly note, any mechanisms to improve accountability or transparency must themselves 'be grounded in further networks of trust if our society is not to degenerate into a complex of coercive practices' (Townley and Garfield 2013: 106). Second, it is worth pondering whether second-personal accounts of epistemic trust can accommodate the notion of institutional trust explored in this section. Consider the specificity of the relationship between testifier and addressee, which earlier in this chapter proved to be important in drawing a distinction between the epistemic status of the addressee and that of an eavesdropper. Second-personal accounts posit that the addressee can reasonably expect the speaker to be motivated to tell him the truth by her recognition of his dependence on her. Yet for many cases of institutional trust this picture seems overcomplex. As Hinchman argues by way of example:

> I trust the bank teller to give me prompt and competent service concerning my banking needs, and in doing so I expect her to be moved by my dependence on her but not solely or even primarily by my *particular* dependence on her. I merely trust her to do her job. (Hinchman 2012: 61)

One response to this challenge might be to claim that institutional trust, and public trust more generally, are really a species of mere (predictive) reliance and should be deemed instances of 'trust' only in a metaphorical sense. Such a response, however, would ignore both the psychosocial dimension of trust in one's social-epistemic environment and the specific form of dependence involved when we trust someone in their capacity as a bank teller or as the representative of another social institution. As these considerations show, the problem of public or institutional trust still has much in store for epistemologists willing to seriously engage with social reality in its many facets.

Study questions

1. Does inferentialism about testimonial justification, for example of the kind defended by local reductionists, preclude any right of complaint on the part of the hearer? What does this tell us about the assurance view of testimony?

2 Is it possible to *decide* to trust someone?

3 How might one evaluate the trustworthiness of institutions?

Further reading

The literature on trust research is vast and varied, ranging from empirical studies to sociological analyses and conceptual investigations. An important and influential, though by now slightly dated, anthology is Gambetta (1988). For a recent edited collection of new essays on the philosophy of trust, see Mäkelä and Townley (2013). Foley (2001) offers a book-length account of intellectual trust as the basis of inquiry and argues that self-trust is prior to trust in others; as Foley sees it, self-trust 'radiates outward' and grounds our (epistemological and other) inquiry. O'Neill (2002) discusses the fragility of social trust, and of trust in public institutions in particular. Govier (1993b), in an interesting combination of experimental and conceptual work, builds up an epistemology of trust on the basis of interviewees' responses to hypothetical stories involving trusting relationships. Faulkner (2007), a precursor to his 2011 book, argues that it is an audience's attitude of affective trust that provides it with a trust-based reason for accepting the speaker's testimony.

9
Expert testimony

Having discussed various general theories of testimony in the past few chapters, in the next two chapters we will be looking in detail at specific kinds of testimony, drawn from different ends of the spectrum in terms of the perceived authoritativeness and reliability of its source. Whereas the next chapter will analyse *prima facie* dubious forms of testimony (such as gossip and rumour), the present chapter will look at the testimony of those who are widely credited with specialist expertise. The role of expert testimony – in law, policy, medicine and other areas of (public and private) life – has been steadily on the rise and has recently begun to receive increased attention from epistemologists interested in applying our general theories of knowledge to concrete social forms of reliance on the epistemic authority of others. In addition to the overarching question of who is an expert, other important problems that will need to be addressed concern the need to adjudicate between conflicting expert testimony and the problematic status of laypersons' appeals to expert opinion.

1. Expertise and epistemic dependence

Reliance on the expertise of others is a pervasive feature of modern life. We routinely trust the pronouncements of those with specialist knowledge, both for the purpose of collective decision-making and in the choices we make as individuals: When a patient accepts his doctor's advice to start taking statins on a daily basis, so as to lower his cholesterol levels, he implicitly trusts her judgement as a medical expert that this is what his condition calls for. The doctor, in turn, relies on the expertise of the medical community when she reasons on the assumption that elevated cholesterol levels pose a health risk, as well as on the expertise of pharmaceutical researchers and various regulatory bodies when she prescribes a drug that she is told is effective in bringing about the desired outcome. Government agencies routinely rely on expert advice from scientists, economists and other experts – increasingly so, if one believes critics who fear that, as a result of overreliance on technical experts, democracy will gradually evolve into technocracy. (For a historical take on the rise of technical and scientific expert advisers, see Smith 1992.) The need for, and growth of, specialist expertise is further underscored by the increasing differentiation and division of labour in contemporary technologically advanced societies. Whereas reliance on the testimony of others has, arguably, been part of the human epistemic predicament for as long as humans have had language, the rise of experts as a distinct class of properly credentialed knowers is a fairly recent phenomenon. As Stephen Turner describes it, the modern ideal type of the 'expert' – where the term refers to individuals 'who are subsidized to speak as experts and claim expertise in the hope that the views they advance will convince a wider public and thus impel them into some sort of political action or choice' – appears in its present form only 'at the end of the 19th century in the United States, and developed hand-in-hand with the development of philanthropic and charitable foundations' (Turner 2001: 133).

Given this prominent role of expertise in virtually all aspects of contemporary life, one natural way to approach its epistemology is through the notion of 'epistemic dependence', which we encountered in Chapter 1 (Section 1). Hardwig, who introduced the term into the philosophical debate in the sense intended here, argues that many areas of knowledge – notably science – have reached a level of complexity that is incompatible with epistemic individualism. If we wish to credit ourselves with knowledge of any reasonably advanced scientific fact, we must accept that the evidence in favour of the corresponding claims is typically unavailable to us – and that, were we to have access to some of the evidence, we would typically lack the expertise to assess the relevant evidentiary relationships. What justifies my beliefs, then, is a matter of other people's reasons for belief, authoritative judgements and expertise. As Hardwig puts it, '[a]ppeals to the authority of experts often provide justification for claims to know, as well as grounding rational belief' (Hardwig 1985: 336). What holds for the layperson also applies to the experts themselves, at least outside their immediate area of expertise. Their knowledge, too, depends in various ways on the results, information and training they have received from others: 'Thus, if scientists, researchers, and scholars are knowers, the layman-expert relationship is also present *within* the structure of knowledge, and the expert is an expert partially because he so often takes the role of the layman *within his own field*' (ibid.: 345–6).

An important, though not the only, manifestation of our dependence on expertise is the acceptance of expert testimony. It is no surprise, then, that epistemological discussions of expertise have largely focused on when to accept what putative experts tell us. Nothing reflects the identification of the issue of expertise with the question of when to accept expert testimony better than the title of an influential paper by Alvin Goldman: 'Experts: which ones should you trust?' (Goldman 2001). Goldman's account will be discussed in detail in Section 3 below; it is worth noting, however, that in public debate we encounter expertise not just directly, in the form of expert testimony, but also indirectly, whenever an interlocutor makes an appeal to expert opinion in order to sway us. In Section 4, we shall therefore compare and contrast the cases of (direct) expert testimony and (indirect) appeal to expert opinion. For the moment, however, let us focus on the paradigmatic case of direct testimony by putative experts. Why, one might ask, does expert testimony deserve special *epistemological* attention? To be sure, the topic may hold special significance for sociologists, policymakers and, given the aforementioned worries about technocracy, perhaps even some political philosophers, but what is in it for epistemologists? There are, I suggest, several reasons why social epistemologists should be interested in appeals to expert opinion, and in direct expert testimony in particular. For one, in spite of its 'formal origins' (see Chapter 1, Section 2), much of contemporary epistemology of testimony has focused on informal testimony as a source of knowledge. By contrast, expert testimony often occurs in formal contexts which, although more constraining, can help to refocus attention on some key aspects of testimonial dependence. A similar observation is made by Kauffeld and Fields who argue that formal testimony,

> as a form of testimony [. . .] that makes explicit much that is assumed or goes unremarked upon in ordinary conversational settings, [. . .] can give us guidance as to where we should be looking in these less formal contexts to find the element that we need. (Kauffeld and Fields 2003: 3)

While 'formal testimony' is here understood as 'that which is delivered before courts of law and commissions of inquiry' (ibid.), the general point can be easily extended to other forms of consulting experts, for example in medicine or policymaking.

Another distinctive feature of expert testimony concerns the nature of the epistemic asymmetry between speaker and hearer. In the standard cases of 'ordinary' testimony typically discussed in the literature – for example, asking a stranger for the time, being told by a friend that he had a minor car accident and so forth – what confers epistemic authority on the speaker is the 'purely positional advantage' (Williams 2002: 42) he enjoys over the hearer: the speaker was simply in the right place at the right time, whereas the hearer was not. If the recipient of the testimony had access to a reliable watch, or could travel back in time and switch places with the testifier, he could have acquired the desired knowledge just as directly as the speaker. In the case of reliance on another's expertise, the epistemic asymmetry runs deeper than mere difference in spatio-temporal location. An expert has at his disposal an extensive and integrated body of specialist knowledge, relating both to facts and to relevant methodologies; importantly, an expert should also possess 'a set of skills or methods for apt and successful deployment of this knowledge to new questions' (Goldman 2001: 92) in his domain of expertise. The layperson lacks these skills and competencies; it is precisely this asymmetry which confers epistemic authority on the expert's testimony. For the layperson confronted with a piece of putative expert testimony, this creates a new epistemological challenge. Given that the recipient would need to know all sorts of things of which he is ignorant before he could hope to assess the speaker's claims directly, he needs to trust the speaker. But he also needs to trust that the speaker is, in fact, an expert. For, as Hardwig notes:

> If I do not know these things, I am also in no position to determine whether the person really is an expert. [. . .] For example, I may suspect that my doctor is incompetent, but generally I would have to know what doctors know in order to confirm or dispel my suspicion. (Hardwig 1985: 340)

One of the goals of an epistemology of expert testimony, then, must be to inquire into how a layperson can hope to assess the speaker's putative status as an expert, without having to become an expert himself.

2. The expert as witness

The role of the expert as a source of testimony finds perhaps its clearest expression in the archetypal figure of the *expert witness* before a court of law. Many of the more general epistemological problems of expert testimony manifest themselves in a stark and exaggerated form in the legal context. This applies especially to legal proceedings that involve a jury of the defendant's peers, as is the case for many criminal cases in the United States and elsewhere. In an adversarial system, where the defendant's lawyers and the prosecution each build their case with an eye towards the jury's final verdict, the choice of expert witnesses – such as forensic scientists or child psychologists – is of crucial importance. For the lay members of the jury this means not only that they will often be confronted with *conflicting* expert testimony, given that the defence will usually wish to rebut the opinions of the prosecution's experts (and vice versa), but that they also need to be alert to the various pressures and biases that emerge from experts being turned into, as one legal commentator puts it, 'commodities that are bought and sold in the market for effective testimony' (Gross 1991: 1134). As legal practitioners are well aware – and, one assumes, many jurors suspect – experts are often nominated for strategic reasons, and not because of their superior epistemic reliability: 'The confident expert witness is less likely to have been chosen because she is right, than to have been chosen because she is confident whether or not she is right.' (Ibid.)

Focusing on the dysfunctional aspects of legal expert testimony, however, should not obscure the fact that relying on expert testimony in many cases is an excellent – and, for a layperson, often the only readily available – source of knowledge. As Hardwig rightly emphasizes, 'even if a layman, because of his relative inability to discriminate among the experts, ends up appealing to a lesser instead of a greater expert, the lesser expert's opinion will still be better than the layman's' (Hardwig 1985: 341). One should also not be too quick to dismiss as insignificant seemingly superficial aspects such as smoothness of presentation, general persuasiveness and rhetorical skill on the part of the expert witness. While such characteristics may not be relevant to the question of whether or not the witness is an expert, they nonetheless have a role to play in determining whether he can function successfully as a source of knowledge for others. It is certainly easy to feel cynical about the criteria of expert selection used by some legal practitioners: for example, Scott Brewer quotes a litigator as saying 'I like my expert to be around 50 years old, have some grey in his hair, wear a tweedy jacket and smoke a pipe.' But the converse point certainly holds: 'Some people may be geniuses, but because they lack training in speech and theater, they have great difficulty conveying their message to the jury.' (Both quotes from Brewer 1998: 1623.) If, as Goldman argues, '[e]xpertise is not all a matter of possessing accurate information' (Goldman 2001: 91), the same could be said, even more emphatically, about the status of being a (good) expert witness.

How do we usually encounter expert witnesses? In most formal or institutional contexts, expert testimony is something that is solicited rather than volunteered: The patient sees his doctor to seek advice on a medical condition he is experiencing. The government appoints a panel of experts to report on the environmental effects of a proposed piece of legislation. Both would be well-advised to be extra cautious when it comes to freely volunteered opinions by self-appointed 'experts', such as miracle healers offering their services and political think tanks offering 'bipartisan' advice. Unlike in the standard case of testimony discussed in the epistemological literature, we do not typically – at least not in the paradigmatic cases that demarcate reliance on experts as a distinct class of epistemic dependence – come across a piece of testimony and then ask ourselves whether the testifier is knowledgeable or not. Rather, we first identify putative experts and then solicit their testimony. (We may, of course, subsequently come to question their standing as experts, but we typically require special reasons for doing so.) Much effort, both implicit and explicit, goes into the selection of experts, in terms of background assumptions as well as institutional organization. Indeed, contemporary societies have developed elaborate systems of accreditation and credentialing, which provide 'markers' such as academic degrees, elected memberships (e.g. in academic societies), and professional certifications, all of which can serve as proxies for specialist expertise.

The presence of reliable, and widely recognized, credentials offers a partial solution to what Goldman calls the 'novice/expert problem': that is, the paradigmatic case of a layperson ('novice') being confronted with testimony by a putative expert, whose testimony he must either accept or reject. The novice will typically lack the expertise to assess the truth or falsity of the testifier's claims, or her objective epistemic standing, directly, but through relying on proper credentials, he can at least acquire good reasons for believing that she is regarded by other experts as their epistemic peer. There are, however, obvious limitations to this approach: often, what is needed is expertise of a more specialized kind than the 'coarse-grained' qualifications indicated by degree certificates, accreditations and professional affiliations. Individual experts may also 'go rogue' and use their professional credentials to actively spread misinformation. (For an epistemological case study in connection with fraudulent expert testimony concerning vaccine safety, see John 2011.) Even when a layperson has managed to distinguish between real and fake experts, as long as there is no broad consensus within the community of experts itself, the layperson will often have to adjudicate between conflicting expert opinions. This 'novice/2-expert problem' may seem even more daunting, since it appears to demand *of the layperson* greater insight into the relative merits of each opinion than even the experts possess.

Experts, too, are faced with the challenge of continuously evaluating each other's standing as epistemic peers. Goldman refers to this predicament, 'in which experts seek to appraise the authority or credibility of other experts', as the 'expert-expert' problem (Goldman 2001: 90). What causes disagreement among experts? In addition to factual disputes – for example, about whether a purported empirical finding is true or not – there may be differences in methodological outlook, background assumptions, and disciplinary training, all of which influence the interpretation and explanation of empirical data and their significance. For many complex problems, it is far from clear what should count as reliable evidence in the first place. This is obvious in the novice/

expert case, for example when a patient consults his family doctor precisely in the hope of gaining greater clarity as to whether a certain minor ailment is evidence of a more serious underlying disease; however, it also applies to the expert/expert scenario. Thus, experts may rationally disagree, on the basis of incomplete evidence, about whether certain empirical findings (e.g. geographical clusters of cancer cases) are evidence of a particular hypothesis (e.g. that mobile phone towers pose a health risk), especially when the causal relationships governing complex processes are not well-understood.

3. Goldman's account of expert testimony

As a layperson, what stance should I adopt with respect to putative expert testimony? Given that I lack access to (or understanding of) the expert's reasons for belief, one might argue that, as Hardwig puts it, 'I am also in no position to determine whether the person really is an expert':

> By asking the right questions, I might be able to spot a few quacks, phonies, or incompetents, but only the more obvious ones. (Hardwig 1985: 340)

But recall that, in many contexts, expert testimony is not just volunteered in a 'take it or leave it' fashion, but is solicited by those in need of information and evidence-based advice. This gives the audience considerable leverage, in that the audience can actively engage an expert, ask for clarification and pose questions. The point is not that the audience should adopt the mantle of a 'rival expert', but that it should make use of the opportunity to come to a more well-rounded assessment of the expert's views, as well as of their factual and theoretical basis. This becomes even more important in the 'novice/2-expert' problem, when the audience must decide which of the two conflicting experts to trust (or whether to withhold judgement altogether).

Goldman has identified 'five sources of evidence that a novice might have, in a novice/2-experts situation, for trusting one putative expert more than another' (Goldman 2001: 93):

A   Arguments supporting the expert's views, or rebutting rival opinions.

B   Agreement from other (putative) experts.

C   'Appraisals by "meta-experts" of the experts' expertise' (including formal accreditations and credentials).

D   Evidence of relevant interests and biases.

E   Evidence of the experts' past performance and their individual track records.

Whereas evidence that falls into categories (A), (D) and (E) can potentially be ascertained by the hearer herself (even though, in most cases, such evidence too will include information gained from others), (B) and (C) explicitly draw on further additional expert testimony. Agreement among different experts – evidence from category (B) – can be an excellent guide to the truth, just as in the case of corroborating testimony from (non-expert) eyewitnesses, provided the testifiers are at least partially independent. As more and more witnesses arrive independently at the same conclusion, the likelihood that such agreement is the result of mere coincidence quickly becomes vanishingly small. Category (C) – appraisals by meta-experts – either involves reliance on specific others, for example well-established experts whom the hearer already trusts, or, perhaps more often, reliance on the institutional testimony of degree-awarding universities, professional organizations or scientific associations that act as a proxy for the scientific community. (On a speculative note, this may be why purveyors of misinformation, such as lobby groups and crackpot scientists, so often take to forming their own credentialing infrastructure in the form of 'academies', 'institutes' or 'think tanks'.)

Of the five sources of evidence distinguished by Goldman, only category (A) is immediately available whenever an expert argues her case, and does not require additional background research on the part of the hearer. For, as Goldman puts it, it consists precisely in the '[a]rguments presented by the contending experts to support their own views and critique their rivals' views' (Goldman 2001: 93). Depending on the precise form and shape in which the lay recipient encounters each expert's arguments and her opponent's rebuttal, different scenarios of how he might go about assessing each speaker's performance are conceivable. If, for example, the layperson consults published expert opinions on a topic of known controversy (say, the economic cost of adapting to rising sea levels), he might look for argumentative strategies of rebutting opposing views in the documents he consults. In the course of doing so, he might consider questions such as the following: 'Do rebuttals rely on the same evidence as the positive thesis defended by the respective authors?' 'Is the factual characterization of the opposing view charitable in that defenders of that view could accept it?' Finding answers to these questions will of course not be without difficulties. In the case of scientific controversies, arguments directed at other experts may not be accessible to the layperson, either because he lacks familiarity with (or access to) the relevant sources (e.g. academic journals), or because understanding the arguments would itself require a degree of expertise that the layperson cannot reasonably be expected to have.

It is useful to distinguish within the experts' discourse between *esoteric* and *exoteric* claims. Esoteric statements are those that 'belong to the relevant sphere of expertise' and as such are inaccessible – either epistemically or semantically – to the layperson *N*. Exoteric statements, by contrast, lie outside the sphere of expertise; assessing whether they are true or false is well within reach of the layperson's understanding, 'either at the time of their assertion or later' (ibid.: 94). The temporal aspect is important, given that, as Scholz puts it, 'the epistemic status of a given statement may change from one time to another since the epistemic standpoint can change from one time to another' (Scholz 2009: 201) – hence the value and significance of expert predictions. Whether or not there is going to be a lunar eclipse a year from now is presently an epistemically esoteric statement for those of us who are not astronomers, yet when the time comes, the claim can be verified through simple visual inspection (assuming a clear night). The main challenge for the lay recipient of expert testimony consists in extrapolating from the exoteric part of the experts' discourse to judgements concerning the acceptability of the esoteric claims in question. While successful extrapolation of this sort is no mean feat, one should also not exaggerate the divide between the exoteric and esoteric parts of expert discourse. Whereas strong epistemic individualism holds that, as Hardwig summarizes it, unless I have access to the speaker's reasons for belief, 'I am in no position to determine whether the person really is an expert' (Hardwig 1985: 340), a more realistic assessment would recognize that, even if absolute certainty about my interlocutor's expert status is out of reach, I can still gather quite a lot of circumstantial and argumentative evidence in support of judgements concerning her level of expertise.

Experts – for example in legal proceedings or at public hearings – are often asked to translate their opinions and findings into a language that is accessible to a group of non-expert decision-makers, such as the members of a jury or a group of legislators. One might argue that such a process of translation, far from solving the problem of accessibility, should compound worries about what may have been inadvertently 'lost in translation' and what may have been deliberately left out – either in the interest of simplicity or in order to advance a hidden agenda. This is where Goldman's fourth recommendation becomes important – that is, the need on the part of the hearer to be alert to 'evidence of the experts' interests and biases vis-à-vis the question at issue' (Goldman 2001: 93). Some of this assessment may be undertaken by rival experts themselves, especially in the course of public hearings or scholarly debate. For the layperson, this opens up the possibility of coming to an *indirect* assessment of the putative experts, by judging their argumentative performance relative to one another. If one speaker displays 'dialectical superiority' (ibid.: 95) over the other, the lay hearer may take this as a *prima facie* indicator of her greater expertise.

Dialectical superiority, for Goldman, goes beyond simply 'greater debating skill' – the way a defence lawyer addressing a criminal jury might be trained to sway the jurors in her final statement – and includes superiority in engaging the opposing party (in this case: the other expert) on their own terms. As an example, consider a lay hearer, H, who encounters two rival experts E_1 and E_2.

If E_1 manages to offer what appears to be a convincing rebuttal whenever E_2 makes a positive claim, whereas E_2, in similar circumstances, keeps changing the topic instead of rebutting any of E_1's argument, H may regard such dialectical superiority as a *prima facie* indicator of E_1's greater expertise. Note that, in order to make assessments of dialectical performance, it is not always necessary that H be able to assess the content, plausibility or likelihood of either E_1's or E_2's arguments. While H may lack the expertise to assess the esoteric content of the discourse between the two experts, he may very well have sufficient background knowledge and observational skill to recognize an expert's genuine rebuttal and tell it apart from, say, an evasive response or an attempt to change the topic. Whether a rebuttal is 'genuine' depends less on whether the corresponding claim is true or not (which may be an esoteric matter to the layperson), but is a matter of the claim's relevance, in the sense that, *if true*, the claim that is made would undermine the opponent's thesis. It is possible, then, to arrive at judgements of credibility entirely on the basis of dialectical superiority: observed instances of dialectical superiority on the part of an expert are indirect evidence of her superior level of expertise. Importantly, such a fallible 'inference to the better expert' may well be within the reach of the layperson, since indicators of dialectical superiority may be successfully recognized even when one lacks expert knowledge of the subject matter at issue.

It is worth emphasizing that *indirect* assessments of expertise need not be restricted to the hearer's (passively) observing the relative performance of two experts. By engaging a putative expert directly, and requesting arguments from him to support his conclusions, a non-expert may elicit relevant evidence even in the 'layperson/1-expert case'. As Jean Goodwin puts it, 'the layperson may want to monitor the effort the expert is putting in, either by direct observation (where possible), or by asking the expert to recount the process by which he made his judgment':

> Note that in doing so, the layperson is not seeking to second-guess the expert's judgments or review the evidence for herself. Instead, the expert's conspicuous ability to recite in detail the grounds of his judgments can give the layperson some confidence that he took pains to have grounds at all. (Goodwin 2010: 139)

Goodwin's example of monitoring for effort and diligence on the part of the expert shows that the list of relevant characteristics can be extended beyond those given in (A)–(E) above. Other authors have argued for the significance of virtues such as openness to new evidence, patience in dealing with objections and willingness to afford 'more fair opportunity to the conflicting expert to express her opinions' (Matheson 2005: 152). As David Matheson has argued, an expert's dialectical performance manifests itself not only at the rhetorical level, but also has a moral quality, which derives from considerations of fairness, intellectual honesty, and receptivity to other views and new evidence. This suggests, not implausibly, that 'moral superiority' in the way an expert conducts himself in debate with his peers can serve as yet another (fallible) indicator of his overall trustworthiness.

4. Expert testimony versus appeals to expert opinion

We often encounter expert claims not in the form of direct testimony by putative experts, but via *appeals to expert opinion* by non-experts. Let us assume, for the sake of simplicity, that we are dealing with the familiar set-up of two interlocutors engaged in discussion. One of the conversational partners ('the speaker') might, in the course of a conversation or argument, appeal to an expert opinion in an effort to sway his interlocutor (the 'hearer' or 'respondent'). In order for such an appeal to lend the speaker's argument additional weight in the eyes of the hearer, it is important that the speaker advertise his appeal to expert opinion as such. The speaker might of course be tempted to pass himself off as an expert, and might just get away with it, but if the interaction between the two partners is sustained over time, the risk of being found out is high (and the corresponding social sanctions might be severe), especially in cases where the speaker cannot be certain that his interlocutor is less well-informed than he is. A less risky strategy would be for the speaker to advertise the fact that he is himself relying on an expert's epistemic authority. Rather than pretend to be an expert himself, the speaker thus adopts the role of a 'conduit' for an expert's authoritative claims. Indeed, only by making his appeal to (external) expert authority explicit, does the speaker stand any chance of boosting the hearer's confidence in his claims beyond the initial credibility they would have, were they to be presented as the speaker's personal (=non-expert) opinion. Furthermore, from the perspective of the hearer, the bar for warranted trust in the claim in question would be lowered in such a case, since it is no longer the speaker's expertise that is at issue, but his ability to identify relevant expert opinions and his willingness, on this occasion, to report them correctly. The latter may still be uncertain, or even controversial: Is the cited expert indeed a relevant authority? Does the speaker report her views accurately? It is for this reason that, as Douglas Walton puts it, 'it is proper for the respondent to ask critical questions concerning the documentation of the appeal to authority' (Walton 1997: 226).

Walton argues, in a similar vein as Goldman does for the 'novice/2-expert problem', that one can bring to bear a number of general critical questions on laypersons' appeals to expert opinions. Each of these questions – for example, the *expertise* question ('How credible is *E* as an expert source?') or the *trustworthiness* question ('Is *E* personally reliable as a source?') – is to be understood as comprising more specific sub-questions: the expertise question may be explored by inquiring into the cited expert's academic credentials, his professional accreditations, or – in the case of science – his track record of peer-reviewed publications. Likewise, trustworthiness may be evaluated by his track record as a truthful testifier or, where such information is unavailable, by asking the speaker for evidence of *E*'s choice of methods and overall conscientiousness. Eliciting such information about the cited expert *E*, through a series of critical questions – and revisiting such information, if necessary, later on during the dialogue with the speaker – is of obvious value in assessing appeals to expert opinion. However, when we accept such an appeal, we do not rely on the epistemic authority of the putative expert alone – we also rely on the speaker's functioning as a *successful* conduit for the expert's opinions. While merely reporting an expert's claims does not require that the speaker have access to the same reasons of belief as the expert, it does require, minimally, that the speaker is both able and willing to adequately recount the expert's opinions in relevant ways. With respect to competence and sincerity, a speaker's appeal to expert opinion needs to be treated with the same caution as any testimonial report – perhaps with more, given that we know how easy it is for a layperson to misinterpret an expert's pronouncements and how tempting it might be for an interested party to misrepresent what an expert said, if it serves their cause.

The overall picture that emerges from this analysis of expert testimony as an epistemological problem is, in Goldman's words, 'decidedly mixed, a cause for neither elation nor gloom' (Goldman 2001: 109). In today's highly differentiated and technologically mediated societies, reliance on expert testimony is a necessity, and no layperson can feasibly undertake to check first-hand the expertise of all the putative experts she will encounter, either directly (as testifiers) or indirectly (via appeals to expert opinion). At an abstract level, the recognition that there are others with greater expertise should entail a stance of epistemic deference on the part of the layperson:

> The rational layman recognizes that his own judgment, uninformed by training and inquiry as it is, is *rationally inferior* to that of the expert (and the community of experts for whom the expert usually speaks) and consequently can always be *rationally* overruled. (Hardwig 1985: 342)

This recommendation, however, is of little use in cases of genuine disagreement among qualified experts: which of two conflicting expert opinions is the layperson supposed to defer to? In the legal context, where procedures are needed to resolve such impasses, this has occasionally given rise to counterintuitive rules. Thus, in an important ruling by the US Supreme Court (*Daubert v. Merrell Dow Pharmaceuticals, Inc.*, 1993), which interpreted key provisions of the Federal Rules of Evidence, the judges laid down general criteria (such as empirical testability, peer reviews, reliability and acceptance by the scientific community) for what constitutes scientific knowledge. However, in cases of conflicting assessments by scientific expert witnesses, where such assessments meet these minimal criteria, it was determined that 'the decision as to who is *correct* is to be given by the judge to the *least* epistemically competent institutional actors, the nonexpert judge or jury' (Brewer 1998: 1600). From an epistemic standpoint, this is a deeply puzzling recommendation. As Brewer rightly asks: 'How can an epistemically responsible decision emerge from that rule?' (ibid.). While perhaps a case can be made that, in legal proceedings, having an arbitrary decision procedure is better than having none at all, it would certainly be epistemically irresponsible to extend this approach to expert testimony in general. The mere fact that dissenting experts can always be found does not give the layperson licence to adjudicate on matters that are well beyond his grasp.

Study questions

1 Can dialectical superiority serve as an adequate proxy for expertise?

2 Other than predictions of directly observable phenomena, what would be examples of *esoteric* statements that may become *exoteric* over the course of a layperson's investigations?

3 Under what circumstances may institutionally recognized expertise come apart from epistemic authority?

Further reading

An excellent anthology, which includes reprinted versions of Goldman (2001), Brewer (1998), Hardwig (1985), and many other relevant papers, including from neighbouring disciplines such as science studies, is Selinger and Crease (2006). For a useful collection of cutting-edge papers at the intersection of epistemology, argumentation theory and science studies, see Kutrovátz and Zemplén (2011). For insightful discussions of the notion of epistemic authority and its flip side, epistemic deference, see Keren (2007) and Pappas (2000), respectively.

10

Pathologies of testimony

In the previous chapters, we have encountered various theories of how we can hope to acquire knowledge from testifiers of diverse backgrounds and experiences, ranging from epistemic peers of ours, who simply happened to be 'in the right place at the right time', to expert witnesses whose specialist knowledge makes them indispensable sources of information in all sorts of contexts. Yet one might harbour the nagging suspicion that the near-exclusive focus on the communication of knowledge – that is, on discourse which ostensibly, if not always sincerely, aims at conveying truths – masks a lacuna in the epistemology of testimony. Critics of traditional epistemology have sometimes referred to this preeminence of knowledge as the ultimate goal of epistemology – to the exclusion of other considerations – as its 'epistemophilia'. (According to Cynthia Townley, the term is due to Lorraine Code; see Townley 2011: xxi.) As Townley puts it, epistemophilia 'mandates knowledge increase as the only epistemic good', yet in doing so fails to 'encourage a full understanding of epistemic responsibility, of what I should do precisely as an agent concerned with knowledge, in either a personal or professional capacity' (Townley 2011: 25).

Miranda Fricker, whose work on epistemic injustice will be discussed in Section 6 of this chapter, makes a similar point when she notes that philosophers 'are very keen to understand what it is to get things right', but insists that 'we should not stop there if we also want to understand the human practices that may only very patchily approximate the rational ideal' (Fricker 2007: vii). Philosophical insight, so the suggestion goes, is not only a matter of coming to a mutual understanding of what goals and values we should aspire to and promote, but also requires attention to the manifold ways in which we – or our surroundings – fall short of these ideals or frustrate their pursuit. Whereas the former – our treasured goals of knowledge, truth, justice, etc. – have an air of universality, analysis of the latter often requires close attention to highly specific dysfunctions, misfires and failures. (This calls to mind the opening line of Leo Tolstoy's *Anna Karenina*: 'All happy families resemble one another, each unhappy family is unhappy in its own way.') It stands to reason that much can be learned from investigating the various ways in which things may go awry, but it is equally clear that such an investigation will not get very far without a genuine willingness to engage with social reality in its sometimes messy complexity. This is why much of this chapter will be dealing with three specific misfires of the institution of testimony: rumour, urban legends and gossip. It is only after careful consideration of these three cases that a more general account will be developed in the final section.

1. Testimony and its pathologies

In line with epistemology's overall focus on truth (rather than falsehood) and knowledge (rather than ignorance), epistemological accounts of testimony have traditionally taken as their paradigmatic case the trusted acceptance, by the intended audience, of the sincere and reliable testimony of a competent speaker. This general outlook, however, runs into problems as soon as one shifts attention from idealized reconstructions of how testimony is offered and received to the messy realities of everyday communication. If 'testimony proper' consists only of exchanges that are genuinely intended to convey knowledge from the speaker to the hearer, then many communicative practices – such as small talk, moralizing, gossiping, rumour – can hardly be regarded as instances of testimony; at best they share some formal characteristics with true cases of testimony – such as the fact that they involve a source (the speaker) and an audience (the hearer). They do not, however, share the same epistemic goal of imparting knowledge – though, of course, they may serve other goals, such as creating social cohesion or satisfying the speaker's desire to be the centre of attention.

Lying is perhaps the most extreme example of 'mimicking' testimony while directly violating the goal of imparting knowledge; after all, the liar *knows* his pronouncements to be false and intends for the hearer to adopt a false belief. As the clearest contrast case to truthful testimony, lying has received its fair share of philosophical attention. (For a collection of essays, see Martin 2009.) However, comparatively little attention has been paid to those communicative practices which, although not outright deceptive, nonetheless show a significant deviation from the goal of conveying knowledge. What comes to mind are instances of informal, sometimes speculative communication, such as gossiping, rumour-mongering or simple small talk. While some of these – such as small talk – are generally considered harmless, perhaps even polite, others typically invite 'moral or epistemic suspicion' and, adopting the terminology suggested by C. A. J. Coady (2006), may be deemed 'pathologies of testimony'. The view that rumour and gossip are epistemically deficient and/or morally blameworthy has been the majority opinion in philosophy. Thus, Montaigne equates rumour with 'public error' (1958: 786), and Kant argues that 'the intentional *spreading* (*propalatio*) of something that detracts from another's honour – [. . .] *even if what is said is true* – diminishes respect for humanity' (Kant 1996: 212; italics added). However, given the various differences between gossip, rumour, and related speech acts, one cannot simply assume that their perceived shortcomings have a common source; in order to make this case, one first needs to develop a principled taxonomy of testimonial pathologies.

Coady considers three examples of *prima facie* pathologies – gossip, rumour and urban legends – and discusses whether in each case the epistemic and moral suspicion which they are typically placed under is justified. One possible way of settling the question would be by brute stipulation – for example, by *defining* gossip as always malicious (hence, morally blameworthy), rumour as unreliable (and hence epistemically deficient), and urban legends as fictions (i.e. an unreliable guide to reality). Brute stipulation, however, would not only beg the question of precisely what is epistemically, or morally, deficient in these cases, but would also do violence to our ordinary linguistic usage of the terms in question, which is a great deal more flexible and admits of significant continuity with more respectable uses of testimony as well as among the various pathologies: Gossip is not necessarily unreliable – nor, as we shall see, is rumour – and 'something that begins as gossip may well continue as rumour' (Coady 2006: 263). Only with respect to urban legends – recurring stories that are preserved in considerable narrative detail (e.g. 'the dotty grandma who tried to dry her damp poodle in the microwave'), but are variously attributed to different times, places and sources ('the cousin of a friend') – does it appear to be a definitional truth that they should be considered fictions rather than reports of actual events. In general, however, as Coady is correct to point out, 'whether some communication is a degenerate form of testimony cannot simply be read off from the content or form of its telling, though either may give clues to this fact' (ibid.: 269).

While I concur with Coady that the three phenomena he identifies – gossip, rumour and urban legend – are clear *prima facie* cases of pathologies of testimony, I hope to demonstrate that one can move beyond merely giving a list of suspicious forms of testimony, by identifying instead what the various kinds of pathologies have in common. In other words, rather than use the expression 'pathology of testimony' as an umbrella term for a number of independently characterizable communicative practices, it will be worthwhile investigating what renders them 'pathological' in the first place.

This difference in theoretical outlook, however, should not obscure the fact that there is qualitative agreement on the extension of the term, and especially on some of the core cases.

2. Rumour

Merely asserting that rumour, along with the other testimonial pathologies, constitutes a distortion of testimony as a way of conveying knowledge, is not in itself very informative. What is needed is an inquiry into the question of *what a rumour is*. As with any good definition, we are as much interested in finding out about commonalities as in getting clearer about specific differences. For example, while it may be tempting to settle the issue via a stipulative definition, as suggested earlier this would leave a good number of questions unanswered and would risk driving, yet again, a wedge between our epistemological account and the social practices we are interested in. Before venturing our own proprietary definition of what a rumour is, it will therefore be useful to review some tentative characterizations that can be found in the literature on rumour research.

Modern rumour research can be traced back to early empirical studies of the reliability of rumours in situations of natural disaster and war. Thus, in the immediate aftermath of the 1934 Bihar earthquake, Indian psychologist Jamuna Prasad (1935) found that rumours mostly concerned the physical extent of the destruction and loss of life, and the possibility of new impending calamities. A classic study of rumour in wartime is Gordon Allport's and Leo Postman's *The Psychology of Rumor* (1947), which was concerned, to a large part, with the potentially disruptive effects rumours can have in crisis situations. Allport and Postman defined rumour as 'a specific (or topical) proposition for belief, passed along from person to person, usually by word of mouth, without secure standards of evidence being present' (Allport and Postman 1947: ix). On the one hand, this places rumour firmly in the realm of *prima facie* testimonial interactions between individuals, on the other hand it suggests (but does not entail) that the dominant mode of transmission of rumours is strictly linear in character. The latter point is borne out by several of the laboratory studies conducted by Allport and Postman, in which an 'eyewitness' to an event recounted the situation to another, who in turn described it to another, and so forth – until the report reached a research associate who carefully noted the content and analysed any deviations from the original account. Transmission of rumour was thus 'idealized' as a linear series of simple, unidirectional acts of communication; more complex interactions, which might have involved the recipient questioning the speaker's reasons for the telling – similar to the recommended strategies for assessing expert testimony (see Chapter 9) — were abstracted away in the setup of the study.

Allport and Postman formulated what they called 'the basic law of rumors', which held that 'first, the theme of the story must have some *importance* to speaker and listener; second, the true facts must be shrouded in some kind of *ambiguity*' (Allport and Postman 1947: 33). Importance and ambiguity were regarded as 'essential conditions' of the occurrence of rumours, and were thought to contribute in equal measure to the overall transmission and circulation of rumours. Apart from the difficulty of quantifying any of these factors, let alone establish a law-like mathematical relationship between them — as was Allport and Postman's declared goal — other aspects of their account that met with criticism included its narrow focus on linear transmission, which 'ignores the social context within which rumors develop, spread, and gain meaning' (Miller 2006: 507), and its restriction to just two variables — when, so the criticism goes, 'there are variables besides importance and ambiguity that influence the origins and perpetuation of rumors' (Rosnow 1991: 485). Challenges to the idea that 'importance' and 'ambiguity' are the only factors in determining rumour circulation arise from both conceptual and empirical considerations. Regarding the concept of ambiguity, it is important to distinguish between the objective inconclusiveness of available evidence, and a generalized sense of ambiguity that also encompasses subjectively experienced personal anxiety. At the empirical level, several researchers have reported that, under certain conditions, subjects are 'more inclined to rate the rumors they spread as *unimportant* rather than important' (ibid.: 486). Two possible explanations for the latter phenomenon come to mind: First, when the stakes are sufficiently high — for example, when a community's physical survival depends on ascertaining the truth or falsity of a matter — a rumour may tend to elicit *more*, rather than *less*, critical examination before it is passed on. (The nature of such 'filtering' and its contribution to the reliability of rumour will be discussed in Section 5.) Second, insofar as people also engage in rumour-mongering for entertainment or in order to impress, rather than in an attempt to convey knowledge, people may prefer to pass on rumours they regard as by and large inconsequential.

The social function of rumour and its collective nature were emphasized by Tamotsu Shibutani in his 1966 monograph *Improvised News*, which drew on the author's experience as a Japanese-American who was interned in 'relocation centers' in 1941 and who witnessed the role of rumours in resolving ambiguity and psychological tension. In his book, Shibutani characterizes rumours as 'a recurrent form of *communication through which men caught together in an ambiguous situation attempt to construct a meaningful interpretation of it by pooling their intellectual resources*' (Shibutani 1966: 17; italics original). In particular, he analysed the process by which 'improvised news' evolves to fill a gap in a community's collective understanding of problematic situations. Whenever the collective need for understanding is not satisfied by the information available, shared norms of accuracy, objectivity and fact-finding will be relaxed, thereby allowing rumours to emerge as attempts at collective sense-making. This has direct consequences, amongst others, for the individuation of rumours. Rather than treating rumours 'as stand-alone statements' (Miller 2006: 516) which are passed on from one interlocutor to another, undergoing step-by-step modification, a rumour is 'something that is shaped, reshaped, and reinforced in a succession of communicative acts'; it is 'not so much the dissemination of a designated message as the process of forming a definition of a situation' (Shibutani 1966: 8–9). Whereas Allport and Postman questioned the faithfulness of serial transmission to the original statement, Shibutani argues that rumours 'cannot be identified in terms of any particular set of words', but only 'by abstracting from dozens of communicative acts': 'Rumor is not so much distortion of some word combination but what is held in common' (ibid.: 16).

While Allport and Postman build the absence of 'secure standards of evidence' into their definition of rumour, others have been more cautious on this point. For example, David Coady settles for a definition in terms of two necessary (and, he claims, jointly sufficient) conditions on when a communication constitutes a rumour, namely 'that it has passed through many hands (or lips), and that it has unofficial status at the time and place in question' (Coady 2006: 49). The lack of official confirmation is certainly an important point. However, a more fruitful definition, it seems to me, would neither preempt normative judgements concerning the reliability or trustworthiness of rumours (as Allport and Postman do, at least implicitly), nor would it settle for a definition that (like Coady's) makes no reference to the recipient's perspective. Therefore, let us tentatively characterize rumour as hearsay that is ostensibly propagated and presented as informative – whether or not its status as hearsay is made explicit to the recipient – and that cannot presently be verified, or refuted, by the recipient on the basis of independent evidence. Although this characterization does a better job of stressing the 'local' (rather than 'in-principle') unavailability of independent evidence in many rumour contexts, it risks overshooting the mark by being too inclusive. For one, there are many claims that may be presented as informative or factual, yet which no amount of independent evidence could possibly suffice to verify or falsify. (Perhaps certain religious doctrines fall into this category; or the claim that the universe contains a prime number of galaxies.) What rumours typically require is at least the presumption that relevant evidence *can be had* – and, often enough, is in fact enjoyed by epistemically privileged outsiders. What matters, thus, is not the absence of evidence per se, but the absence of independent confirmation by *authoritative sources*. This is nicely captured by Jörg Bergmann's remark that rumour virtually always involves 'unauthorized messages that are always of universal interest and accordingly are disseminated diffusely' (Bergmann 1993: 70). What lies behind this definition is the recognition that we often need to rely on institutional testimony – for example, reference works, experts, encyclopedias, scientific bodies and trusted news sources – for authoritative confirmation. It is only when either (or both) of these – independent first-hand evidence and official sources – are unavailable, contradictory, or widely regarded as untrustworthy, that conditions are conducive to the development and spread of rumour. Rumour, thus, may be described as *the propagation of ostensibly informative hearsay, usually on a topic of broader interest, and typically communicated via informal pathways in the absence of independent corroboration by either first-hand evidence or official (authoritative) sources.* (This definition follows Gelfert 2013a.) Based on this definition of rumour (and by analogy with 'testimony-based belief' as defined in Chapter 1, Section 1), it is then possible to define *rumour-based belief* as any belief that one reasonably and directly forms in response to what one reasonably takes to be a rumour and which is essentially caused and sustained by it. It is worth emphasizing that nothing said so far implies that rumours are *essentially* unreliable. While our definition invariably links rumour to hearsay, lack of first-hand evidence does not entail that a reported claim is necessarily unreliable. This should be considered a strength of the proposed definition, since it would be both unwise and revisionist of normal linguistic usage to build unreliability into the notion of rumour, given that we know from experience that rumours often have a basis in fact and, indeed, are often true.

3. Urban legends

The example of urban legends (also variously known as urban myths, urban tales or contemporary legends) deserves special discussion, not only because it is singled out by Coady as one of the three central classes of pathologies of testimony, but also because it brings into sharp focus the gap that may open up between the (perceived) authoritativeness of the source and the (actual) reliability of a given report. While urban legends take the narrative form of factual reports, and are often reprinted in (even reputable) local newspapers by editors acting in good faith, they are essentially fictional (hence, unreliable) stories that appeal to the reader's curiosity or emotions and have been embellished to reflect local circumstances.

Many authors assimilate urban legends to rumours, either describing them as 'cases of rumors: unofficial information circulating in society' (Kapferer 1990: 9) or even referring to them as 'exemplary' cases of rumour (Merten

2009: 26). One way this connection can be made plausible is by treating urban legends as persistent rumours that have become divorced from their specific origins. As Allport and Postman put it, an urban legend 'may be regarded as a solidified rumor' (Allport and Postman 1947: 162). Shibutani, while reluctant to equate the two entirely, nonetheless suggests they are continuous with one another when he writes that 'some rumors persist and become incorporated into popular lore' (Shibutani 1966: 130). And yet, we typically have no difficulty distinguishing, at least in retrospect, urban legends – for example, the well-known 'case' of unsuspecting supermarket customers getting bitten by snakes hiding among imported bananas – from rumour (such as financial rumours concerning the impending bankruptcy of a major savings bank). One recognizable feature of urban legends is their use of highly stylized narrative elements. As folklorists have pointed out, the term 'legends' is entirely apt, insofar as the stories – much like earlier legends and fairytales – aim at conveying a moral rather than factual knowledge. Typically, as with urban legends concerning dangers to children (such as the legend of LSD-coated 'lick and stick' tattoos), they depict 'conflicts between the apparent conditions of modern society and the traditional values of individuals and families' (Miller 2006: 510).

As fictional stories, urban legends conform to their own (albeit variable) narrative conventions; whatever basis in fact they may have had, has been transformed beyond recognition, via 'a form of collaborative storytelling that is metaphorical in character not bound by time and space limitations'; rumours, by contrast, are 'temporally and locally situated' (ibid.: 508). To the extent that urban legends 'travel' – and, over time, tend to be reported in different news sources as 'recent' occurrences in a 'neighbouring' town – they are often adapted to local circumstances, typically in an attempt to increase their perceived credibility. This is why the details of their spatiotemporal location, as well as information about the alleged source ('a friend of a friend'), are almost always incidental to the story; they matter only to the extent that they keep up the illusion of newsworthiness. The various ingredients of an urban legend – such as locales, protagonists or brands – are constantly being updated to make it superficially indistinguishable from fact-based rumour. For the most part, then – and especially from the epistemic vantage point of a moderately gullible recipient of rumours and urban legends – their similarities in terms of mode of transmission outweigh their dissimilarities in terms of narrative structure:

> Both rumors and urban legends are forms of communication found in networks of informal social relationships. Both are communicative acts in which the content of the stories is imbued with cultural meanings that reside in the communities and social relationships in question. (Ibid.: 510)

Just as '[r]umor is similar to folklore but usually consists of nontraditional material' (Dundes 1965: 247), so it is also the case that 'some legends become rumors and some rumors become legends' (Mullen 1972: 98).

4. Gossip

Gossip, at first sight, might appear to be little else than a subspecies of rumour. Both are usually received 'through the grapevine', even if the content of gossip is more specific than that of rumour, in that the former is mostly about the personal, private and moral aspects of individuals and their actions, whereas the latter also serves as a medium for claims about impersonal states of affairs (e.g. natural disasters) and large-scale developments that cannot easily be attributed to specific individuals (e.g. a financial collapse). But gossip also tends to be more restrictive with respect to its intended audience. Not only does ordinary gossip typically occur only between acquaintances, but it also excludes the target of the gossip from the conversation and, in doing so, is by necessity directed at a restricted audience. This is why gossip is sometimes characterized as informal speech 'between acquaintances', typically 'one-to-one' (and almost always 'face-to-face'), which may or may not be 'unscheduled' (Emler 1994: 135). In Bergmann's fortuitous turn of phrase, gossip consists in 'discreet indiscretions'. Whereas gossip 'possesses relevance only for a specific group' and – *pace* the existence of celebrity gossip – 'is disseminated in a highly selective manner within a fixed social network', no such in-principle restriction exists for the audience of rumours, which spread as 'unauthorized messages that are always of universal interest and accordingly are disseminated diffusely' (Bergmann 1993: 70).

These observations have led some authors to seek a more principled distinction between gossip and rumour. If one's goal is a definition of gossip in its own right, then such a definition should reflect the various ways in which it differs from rumour. According to Klaus Merten, gossip can be distinguished from rumour by 'four precise conditions' (Merten 2009: 16): gossip (1) occurs only among acquaintances, (2) is always about a particular individual, who (3) is known to – and, in turn, knows – everyone in the group, but (4) is not present at the time. To this one might add that, whereas the gossiper may on occasion present himself as privy to first-hand evidence, rumours tend to be reported in a non-committal, second-hand way ('I have heard that . . .'). As Rosnow and Fine mention in passing, 'the basis of gossip may or may not be a known fact, but the basis of rumour is always unsubstantiated' (Rosnow and Fine 1976: 11). The suggestion seems to be that certain instances of first-hand testimony may well count as gossip, whereas rumour, by necessity, is based on hearsay that cannot – at least not momentarily – be confirmed by independent evidence. Thus, if James truthfully reports to his colleagues that he saw John from IT and Jane from HR passionately kissing in the office one evening, this might make for a juicy piece of workplace gossip, but it would not constitute rumour – at least not yet. Only when others chime in, perhaps embellishing the story by adding further supporting details about John and Jane's alleged affair, and the claim begins to circulate – without any longer being attributable to James – then what started off as a piece of (first-hand) gossip would have matured into a full-blown rumour (much to John and Jane's dismay, one assumes).

What, in this context, are we to make of so-called celebrity gossip, which fills the pages of the yellow press and is widely disseminated via the internet? While the content of celebrity gossip covers much the same ground as its less illustrious cousin, in that it deals mainly with – real or fictitious – romantic relationships (and their inevitable break-ups), pregnancies, rivalries, health issues, minor misdemeanours and so forth, its dissemination is not restricted to specific social networks. There is also no pretence that the target of the gossip should be shielded from the fact that (s)he is being gossiped about. Whereas everyday gossip is received 'through the grapevine' – via informal networks of communication – celebrity gossip is typically communicated via specialized outlets that lack the informality associated with gossiping among acquaintances and, at the same time, are often known to be unreliable purveyors of unauthorized information. Rather than attempting to accommodate it within a definition of gossip in general, celebrity gossip is perhaps best understood as simply a form of entertainment. (This, admittedly, is cold comfort to any celebrity who feels that a gossip magazine has violated their right to privacy.) Similarly, when gossip spreads beyond a given network of acquaintances, for example because it becomes pervasive in an organization or society, or when its perceived significance transcends narrow concerns of individual conduct – for example because it is seen in the light of larger social or organizational concerns – it may well become indistinguishable from rumour *simpliciter*. As Ralph Rosnow puts it in the form of a rhetorical question: 'When, according to unattributed hearsay, a female executive is alleged to have "slept her way to the top", is this rumor or gossip?' (Rosnow 1988: 14).

Traditionally, philosophy has paid little attention to gossip, and to the extent that it has, it has viewed it in a negative light, placing gossip – and those who engage in it – under moral suspicion. Interestingly, both the person who spreads gossip and the one who believes it, have typically been regarded as sharing the blame. On one construal of the traditional view, the gossiper 'shows a lack of respect for persons' (Taylor 1994: 43), in that he treats the private life of the gossipee as fair game for the amusement and delectation of others. In this sense, the gossipee is being treated as a 'mere means', even if the gossip itself need not be intended as an instrument of manipulation. However, unlike lying, gossip is often truthful and sincere, and in this sense need not directly violate existing epistemic norms. Yet some philosophers have argued that, in spite of its potential function as a source of knowledge, gossip should not be believed *as a matter of principle*. According to Kant, malicious gossip, *even when true*, ought to be dismissed. In his *Anthropology from a Pragmatic Point of View*, Kant makes clear that it is not only the speaker who spreads the information that is at fault, but also the gullible hearer who believes what is manifestly an instance of gossip. Thus Kant issues this forceful demand: 'Not to pay attention to gossip [*Nachrede*] derived from the shallow and malicious judgments of others; for paying attention to it already indicates weakness [of character]' (Kant 2006: 194). In the more recent philosophical literature on gossip, there has been a trend towards rehabilitating gossip, both as a legitimate activity and as a source of knowledge. This development appears to be motivated by three distinct general points, which may be referred to as 1) the grooming analogy, 2) the argument from empowerment and 3) the challenge to hypocrisy. Each of these indicates, in some way or another, a break with the received view of gossip as morally and epistemically blameworthy.

Let us first turn to the grooming analogy. According to this view, the primary function of gossip is not to convey knowledge about the gossipee, but to establish and re-inforce friendships among the gossipers. While some gossip may titillate in virtue of what it is about, it is the frisson of being part of an intimate group of gossipers that makes gossip enjoyable. As Max Gluckman puts it, 'the right to gossip about certain people is a privilege which is only extended to a person when he or she is accepted as a member of a group or set' (Gluckman 1963: 313). Gossiping as a social activity requiring language, one might say, is to humans what grooming is to other social primates. As Gabriele Taylor puts it, 'good personal relationships are an important value in our lives, and the circumstances of gossiping clearly foster such relationships' (Taylor 1994: 41). Gossip thus provides *social glue*, in addition to 'the pleasure of recognition' (ibid.) that comes with being able to empathize with the experiences of others. Given such beneficial effects of the practice of gossiping, it is perhaps no surprise that defenders of the grooming analogy have come to a very different assessment of the moral permissibility of gossip. Taylor in particular claims that 'the Kantian objection need [. . .] not be taken seriously', since 'it is absurd to put so much weight on attitudes [on the part of the gossiper] that may have no practical effect, particularly when we consider the concrete social benefits of gossiping in the form of generating comfortable relationships' (Taylor 1994: 44).

A second, more ambitious defence of gossip is based on recent feminist epistemology and takes its cue from the historical connotations of the term 'gossip': in the English language, the term 'gossips' historically referred to a woman's circle of female friends. As Louise Collins notes, 'the association of gossip with the feminine and a negative evaluation have a long history' (Collins 1994: 114). Historically, the casual and informal character of 'female' gossiping has been contrasted with the 'serious' business of men. As Nicholas Emler caricatures this view (without endorsing it, obviously): whereas 'women chatter, tattle, gab, rabbit, prattle, nag, whine, and bitch', men open their mouths only in order 'to accomplish something of consequence – to discourse, debate, philosophize, exchange ideas, conduct business, or engage in politics' (Emler 1994: 118). That such a 'feminization' of gossip does not reflect social reality, but instead expresses sexist prejudice, goes without saying. It also severely overstates any real existing contrasts between informal ways of knowing – such as knowledge gained from casual, everyday conversation, which may or may not include gossip – and official pathways of learning, such as formal education and scientific inquiry, where the latter have historically been male-dominated. One strategy of defending gossip would be to think of 'gossip as inquiry' (Ayim 1994: 85) – that is, as itself on a par with more traditionally respected sources of knowledge. An alternative, and perhaps more plausible, strategy would be to start from the observation that gossip may exhibit certain positive epistemic qualities – for example by being more egalitarian, nuanced and imaginative that traditional forms of knowledge production and communication are lacking. This might be of special significance in such areas as ethics, politics and knowledge of the social world at large. The very 'unruliness of gossip' (Code 1994: 104) may expose some official 'knowledge' as mere prejudice, while bringing to the fore previously overlooked interests and injustices. Gossip, thus, may have an empowering effect, at the epistemic level as well as, ultimately, in the political domain.

The claim that gossip can disrupt entrenched hierarchies can be given a more radical interpretation, and has given rise to a defence of gossip as a way of challenging hypocrisy. Thus, Ronald de Sousa argues for a fundamental re-thinking of the public/private distinction. In an argumentative move that may seem prescient, given that it foreshadows some of the challenges to privacy in connection with electronic social networks such as Facebook, de Sousa argues for an extension of the principle of 'freedom of information' to the private realm. Since that part of our life which is usually considered private may, 'in terms of the actual quality of our lives [. . . ,] well be the most important one, accurate knowledge about it is crucial' (de Sousa 1994: 30).

In some cases, gossip may be society's best shot at exposing hypocrisy or uncovering cases of abuse and discrimination. As de Sousa puts it:

> La Rochefoucauld taught us that hypocrisy is the tribute that vice pays to virtue. But what is discretion but hypocrisy in the third person? [. . .] I suggest that the indiscretion of gossip is, in a small way, a saintly virtue. (Ibid.: 31)

Rehabilitating gossip as a source of knowledge and legitimate social activity is, of course, one thing, praising it as a 'saintly virtue' is quite another. It is perhaps worth noting that gossip itself has also a potentially oppressive aspect – not so much for its intrusion into privacy as such, but because it provides an effective tool for disciplining those who challenge, or violate, the existing social order. As the nineteenth-century liberal philosopher John Stuart Mill – himself the target of much gossip over his relationship with Harriet Taylor (who was then living in separation from her husband John) – noted in his *On Liberty*, society, through the judgements of others,

> practises a social tyranny more formidable than many kinds of political oppression, since, though not usually upheld by such extreme penalties, it leaves fewer means of escape, penetrating much more deeply into the details of life, and enslaving the soul itself. (Mill 1989: 8).

At best, then, gossip is a double-edged sword, to be used – if at all – with great care.

5. Can rumour-based belief be reliable?

For the recipient of a rumour – whether it is reported *as* rumour ('I have heard that . . .'), or simply presented as true – what matters epistemically is its reliability. Given that, in the case of rumour, we are dealing explicitly with extended chains of transmission – so much so, that the term 'rumour' is sometimes understood as referring to the collective phenomenon, rather than to the individual speech act – it is important to be clear what is meant by 'reliability'. On the one hand, there is the reliability of the process of transmission from one interlocutor to the next; understood in this way, reliability is a matter of the faithful reproduction of a rumour as it is being passed along a chain of interlocutors. On the other hand, there is the reliability of a particular speaker's statement as (at least potentially) a source of knowledge; on this understanding, a rumour is reliable if, by accepting it, a hearer would be acquiring a potential piece of knowledge.

Keeping in mind that the reliability of the *transmission* and the reliability of the *information* (as ultimately received by the hearer) are conceptually distinct considerations, we can now explore possible relationships between them. While it is obvious that much depends on the chain of transmission by which a given claim has reached the recipient, it is far from obvious exactly how the trustworthiness of a particular claim should be affected by the fact that it was passed on as rumour. Indeed, there are prima facie equally plausible considerations that pull in different directions. On the one hand, as with every case of testimony, there is the possibility of deliberate or accidental distortion at every intermediate step in the chain of transmission, so that over time one should expect the initial information to become corrupted. On this view, a piece of testimony can only be as accurate as the knowledge possessed by the initial source and will likely deteriorate as it is being passed along a chain of interlocutors. On the other hand, one could emphasize the active role of interlocutors in selecting information they regard as sufficiently trustworthy to merit being passed on to others. On this alternative view, interlocutors act as safeguards of reliability, by passing on information they themselves regard as trustworthy and by speaking up against claims they regard as erroneous or unreliable. (The latter would be reminiscent of Goldberg's 'silent monitoring' of a speaker by a third party; see the discussion in Chapter 7, Section 4.) Both considerations – the danger that information will degrade as it is being passed on, and the possibility of interlocutors acting as 'filters' – have a certain prima facie plausibility, and both have been highlighted by different authors.

Shibutani notes that, as rumours travel, some individuals 'may purposely exaggerate or invent for effectiveness', thereby giving rise to a 'cumulative process' of growth, whereby 'details are added', along with 'names and specific references to places' (Shibutani 1966: 84–5). This suggests that one cannot assume that, in informal communication, rumours are faithfully and reliably reproduced. However, it is not only the mode of transmission that is relevant here; just how reliable a rumour will be as a source of information also depends crucially on the conditions of its emergence. In situations where 'collective excitement is mild' and 'unsatisfied demand for news is moderate', rumour construction 'occurs through critical deliberation', which may involve close examination of available information, the collective appraisal of the plausibility of claims, and the placing of 'a premium upon facts' (ibid.: 70–1). By contrast, in situations where an identifiable dynamic of events is already unfolding, rumours may *extrapolate from* the facts, rather than *contribute to* a reliable representation of reality; as a result 'a total picture may be constructed that is quite inaccurate, but highly plausible' (ibid.: 77). When extrapolation from the facts is coupled with a general sense that nothing can be done to influence the unfolding dynamic – that is, when ego-involvement is low – the accuracy of information inevitably suffers: 'Where action is impossible or not seriously contemplated, accuracy of definition is not decisive, and people may say things that please them' (ibid.: 91).

Drawing on the idea that individuals in a chain of communication can function as 'filters', David Coady has recently argued that rumour does not deserve its bad reputation as an intrinsically unreliable source of knowledge. On the contrary, the fact that a rumour has passed 'through many hands (or lips)' (Coady 2006: 49) should count in favour of its reliability:

> [I]f you hear a rumour, it is not only *prima facie* evidence that it has been thought plausible by a large number of people, it is also *prima facie* evidence that it has been thought plausible by a large number of reliable people. And that really is *prima facie* evidence that it is true. (Ibid.: 47)

As Coady sees it, 'the "distance" of rumours from an original eyewitness account is not a general reason for scepticism about them', but, on the contrary, 'may make belief in rumours more warranted' (ibid.: 48). It would seem, then, that passing information along a chain of interlocutors need not diminish its reliability, but may in fact increase it. For empirical support of this thesis, Coady turns to anti-rumour campaigns carried out by the US Army during the Second World War, which aimed at 'dispersing the normal channels along which rumours passed' (ibid.). Ironically, by inhibiting the flow of information, thereby effectively reducing the number of pathways by which rumours were transmitted, the campaigns had the opposite effect of making rumours even less reliable (and therefore more misleading). Theodore Caplow explains why the break-up of stable networks of transmission led to a decrease in the reliability of rumours:

> Distortion in terms of wishes and avoidance seems to be an individual rather than a group characteristic. As channels solidified, this phenomenon became comparatively rare, because of the exclusion of persons associated with previous invalidity. When they were broken up [in the course of the anti-rumour campaigns], wish fulfillment again became conspicuous. (Caplow 1947: 301)

Coady interprets this as a compelling evidence that 'the survival and reproductive success' of rumours is 'partly dependent on their being disseminated by people widely known to be reliable sources' (Coady 2006: 47). Reliable interlocutors, thus, act as 'filters' of sorts, removing unsubstantiated rumours from circulation. Matthew Dentith makes a similar point, when he argues that '[a]s a rumor spreads it will inevitably encounter more in the way of interested hearers who will not pass on the proposition unless they consider it to be plausible' (Dentith 2013: 51). Chances are that, by the time we encounter a rumour, it will have gone through various stages of 'filtering', thus making it more likely to merit belief, or so the argument goes.

Which of these counteracting considerations will prevail depends crucially on the dynamics of communication within a social network. For example, while it may be true that less reliable rumour-mongers are less likely to be believed, they may also be more likely to spread rumours, in which case their loquaciousness might offset any 'filtering' by the extended social environment. The actual reliability of rumours is therefore a function of contingent factors that reflect specific social arrangements and dynamics within a population. It is perhaps not surprising, then, that empirical estimates of the general reliability of rumours vary widely. Whereas some empirical studies have found that only a negligible number of rumours were reliable (Weinberg and Eich 1978), others have put the figure of reliable rumours at more than 80 per cent (Rudolph 1973), with rumours in some organizations being 'nearly 100% true' (DiFonzo and Bordia 2006: 262). The prospects of relying on rumour for information are thus decidedly mixed: whereas in some contexts, rumour appears to reliably communicate accurate information, in other situations it is disastrously off the mark. One might very well ask whether the recipient of a rumour can ever be justified in relying on rumour for information.

In order to see why one might consider trusting (at least some) rumours, in spite of the highly variable *overall* reliability of rumour as a source of information, it is worth taking a step back to reflect on some of the less obvious ways in which we depend epistemically on our environment. When we base a particular belief of ours on someone's testimony, this is an instance of direct dependence. But we also depend on our epistemic environment in more indirect ways. For example, we all depend, to a varying degree, on our social environment for keeping us abreast of important events and developments in the ever-changing world around us. In normal everyday encounters, others often volunteer information they think we ought to know about, and many of us have epistemic routines – such as following the news – that naturally expose us to a broad range of factual and timely information. Clearly, someone who reads a newspaper for general knowledge about, say, domestic politics has the reasonable expectation that what he reads is not only truthful and accurate, but is also comprehensive in that it does not leave out important information. Even if we cannot expect completeness from one source alone, we trust that other sources – formal and informal, official and unofficial – will fill us in on any important news we might have missed. In other words, we depend on our social environment not only for individual pieces of information, but for *coverage*. Goldberg, who has highlighted this (indirect) form of epistemic dependence, speaks of reliance on the '*coverage-reliability* of one's community' (2010: 154). Importantly, it is not only new beliefs for which we rely on our epistemic environment; many of our extant beliefs, too, depend for their justification on our not having heard anything to the contrary. This echoes an observation by McDowell who notes that many of our knowledge claims are about 'impermanent states of affairs to whose continued obtaining we have only intermittent epistemic access' (McDowell 1994: 201). If we wish to credit ourselves with continuous and robust knowledge of such facts (e.g. knowledge that p), we need to appeal to what Goldberg calls the '*truth-to-testimony* conditional' (Goldberg 2010: 157): 'If $\sim p$ were true I would have heard it by now.'

We are now in a position to see why a policy of outright dismissal of rumours, on the basis of their variable reliability, might be too short-sighted. Assuming that one does not have defeating beliefs, or other prior reasons for suspecting the rumour to be false, the decision to reject the corresponding claim – for example, that p – would presumably be based on the following heuristic: *If p were true, I would have heard it by now (via official channels of communication)*. (The specification 'via official channels of communication' is necessary in order to establish the requisite contrast between rumours and official communication, without which it would not make sense to argue for the rejection of a claim solely on the basis of its having been received *as rumour*.) But this heuristic is simply a version of the truth-to-testimony conditional, restricted to official channels of communication. In order to be able to deploy it, we must assume that our 'official' information environment is coverage-reliable. This raises the obvious question: What if official channels of communication are not open (e.g. during wartime, or in disaster situations when official information channels are disrupted), or are unreliable (e.g. in countries with heavy censorship)? In information-deprived social environments with little coverage-reliability, rumours may transmit information that could not otherwise be had. (For an extended argument to this effect, see Gelfert 2013a.) While this argument renders rumours neither intrinsically reliable nor essentially unreliable, it does show that rumours may on occasion be an indispensable source of information.

6. Epistemic injustice

Our discussion so far has focused on pathological uses of the speech acts of reporting and asserting performed by the speaker. Much of the epistemic and moral suspicion in these cases will be directed at the speaker, who, in spreading gossip or passing on a rumour, may be behaving in a blameworthy way. But what about the moral and epistemic responsibilities on the part of the hearer? Receiving testimony may not be an entirely passive act and may incur responsibilities, not only because the hearer may learn something that entails an obligation to act in certain ways, but also in terms of how the hearer conducts himself in relation to the speaker's act of testifying. Miranda Fricker, in her work on epistemic injustice, has explored this latter kind of responsibility in the way we individually and collectively conduct ourselves – that is, as (active) *hearers* rather than (merely passive) *recipients* of testimony.

Fricker distinguishes between two ways in which a speaker may be wronged epistemically. The first of these, which Fricker dubs a *testimonial injustice*, wrongs the speaker specifically in her capacity as a testifier and can be traced to the audience's failure to grant her the credibility she deserves. Given the fallibility of judgements of credibility, minor mismatches between a testifier's perceived credibility and her actual reliability may often be unavoidable and, although unfortunate, may be non-blameworthy. But in many cases, speakers – through no fault of their own – suffer a systematic credibility deficit, for example because of prejudice on the part of their audience. The paradigm case would be the one described in Harper Lee's novel *To Kill a Mockingbird*: an all-white jury in an Alabama courtroom in the 1930s whose members cannot bring themselves – and do not even attempt – to entertain the idea that the testimony of a black man might be more trustworthy than the (as it turns out, fabricated) accusations of a white girl. In this case – and similar ones, which are a dime a dozen – the prejudicial credibility deficit assigned to the speaker does epistemic as well as moral damage. At an epistemic level, the hearer is depriving himself of the possibility of acquiring knowledge. In many cases, the hearer may not even *want* to know, in which case the damage is less to the individual hearer, but to the institution of testimony itself – which, as discussed in Chapter 2, is based on the reciprocal giving and receiving of knowledge.

Testimonial injustice may be directed at specific individuals and can be highly localized. (As a humorous example, consider the case of Bernard Black, the misanthropic protagonist of British TV comedy series *Black Books*, 'Grapes of Wrath', who dismisses the testimony of a contractor on the grounds that 'I don't trust him – he has no nasal hair!') However, when prejudice is *systematic*, in that it is bound up with an individual's social identity – for example, because it targets a person's race, gender, sexual orientation or socio-economic background – the corresponding testimonial injustices will likewise be far-reaching. What makes identity-based prejudice so pernicious is that it 'renders one susceptible not only to testimonial injustice but to a gamut of different injustices, and so is systematically connected with other kinds of actual or potential injustice' (Fricker 2007: 27). Being denied a fair hearing as the result of testimonial injustice, the victims of identity prejudice – typically members of minorities – often suffer persistent exclusion and unfair treatment at the hands of a biased majority.

The second type of epistemic injustice, although equally detrimental to the enterprise of knowledge and perhaps even more debilitating to the individual, is somewhat more elusive. In instances of what Fricker calls *hermeneutical injustice*, a speaker is effectively condemned to silence by a collective lack of appropriate conceptual resources that would allow her to express her experiences, concerns and grievances in a manner that would make them intelligible to others – and, in many cases, to herself. That there is often a gap between one's own phenomenologically salient first-hand experiences and what one can successfully communicate of them to others, is of course a common human experience. An injustice arises, however, when 'the cognitive disadvantage created by this gap impinges unequally on different social groups' (ibid.: 6). As an example, consider the case of women who experienced sexual harassment at the workplace prior to the time that this concept became widely known. One can easily imagine the questions and self-doubts that a victim in this context might be pondering: Were the male co-worker's unwanted advances perhaps to be understood as a clumsy, but innocent 'compliment' of sorts? Was she perhaps overreacting by being upset at the persistent sexual innuendo of his remarks? Etc. In such a scenario, although the moral responsibility for the sexual harassment lies squarely with the co-worker, the victim's sense of confusion and her inability to adequately conceptualize her experiences cannot be blamed on any one person or group in particular, but rather on a failure of society at large. Yet the lack of an identifiable culprit does not render the lack of adequate hermeneutical resources any less unjust – especially so, given that various modes of social organization according to power, privilege or class

> can skew shared hermeneutical resources so that the powerful tend to have appropriate understandings of their experiences [. . .] whereas the powerless are more likely to find themselves having [. . .] at best ill-fitting meanings to draw on in the effort to render [their social experiences] intelligible. (Ibid.: 148)

As this discussion of the two-fold concept of 'epistemic injustice' shows, pathological distortions of testimony – whether at the level of individual speech acts or at the collective level of testimony as a social practice – are not always due to moral or epistemic failures on the part of the speaker, but can also result whenever an audience or community fails to live up to its responsibilities towards a (prospective) *bona fide* testifier.

7. A Kantian perspective

In our earlier discussion of gossip (Section 4), as well as in Section 1, we have already encountered several remarks by Kant concerning the moral blameworthiness of rumour and gossip. The intentional spreading of rumour and gossip, we were told, 'diminishes respect for humanity' and is a sign of 'weakness of character'. It might be tempting to dismiss such rhetoric as simply an instance of philosophical moralizing, as indeed Taylor appears to do when she insists that the Kantian objection is 'absurd' and therefore 'need not be taken seriously', especially when not all instances of testimonial pathologies do *actual* harm. In the present section, I wish to argue that such a dismissal is a little too facile and that a Kantian perspective may, in fact, be helpful in arriving at a more unified account of the various testimonial pathologies. Extrapolating from some of Kant's remarks, I shall propose a definition of the term 'pathology of testimony' that not only subsumes Coady's somewhat eclectic list of speech acts (rumour, gossip, urban legends), but also forges a link with Fricker's notion of epistemic injustice.

Although his primary concern in the *Metaphysics of Morals* is neither with epistemology nor with testimony, Kant, in the second part of the book ('Doctrine of Virtue'), offers what may be considered a taxonomy of testimonial pathologies. He is especially scornful of defamation (i.e. gossip with malign intent), which he considers to be 'contrary to the respect owed to humanity as such'. The intentional dissemination of gossip and scandalous rumours casts 'a shadow of worthlessness over our race itself', makes 'misanthropy' and contempt for others 'the prevalent cast of mind', and dulls our 'moral feeling'. As Kant sees it, it is 'a duty of virtue not to take malicious pleasure in exposing the faults of others' (Kant 1996: 212), or to hold them up to the ridicule of others. Ridiculing someone 'in order to deprive him of the respect he deserves' is deemed 'an even more serious violation of one's duty of respect for other human beings' (ibid.: 213). (The only exception Kant allows is the 'defensive' use of ridicule against someone else's mockery – but even then, Kant argues, it will often be 'more befitting the dignity of the object and respect for humanity either to put up no defense against the attack or to conduct it with dignity and seriousness'.) As mentioned earlier, speech acts such as spreading malicious gossip are blameworthy even when they turn out to be truthful. Defamation, understood as a pathology of testimony in the broad sense, thus goes beyond the legal category of *slander*, which – as a case of 'a *false* defamation' – may be brought before a court of law (ibid.). The obligation not to defame, gossip about or mock another person derives not from any legal consideration, nor is it simply a corollary of the imperative not to lie, but instead is a direct consequence of our duty of respect for other human beings.

Generalizing from Kant's discussion of gossip, defamation and mockery, perhaps then it is possible to *define* the term 'pathology of testimony' as simply *any type of overtly informative speech act that disrespects another person in their capacity as a rational being*. (This definition, and the subsequent discussion, follows Gelfert 2013b.) In many cases, the disrespect is directed at the person *about* whom claims are made: for example, the gossipee, or the person who is subjected to mockery. But one can also conceive of cases where the testimony is not about other people, yet there is nonetheless something about the testimonial interaction that is disrespectful to specific others. Thus, the speech act may be carried out with the goal of impairing the hearer in his capacity as a rational being – for example, by manipulating the hearer's emotional state, framing (factually correct) information in misleading ways and distracting the speaker with irrelevant detail. These and other strategies of manipulation are, of course, common in such areas as advertising, public relations, political propaganda, and corporate communication, but their widespread use should not obscure their morally problematic status. Misusing communication in order to persuade another person *in a way that does not respect their autonomy as a rational being* stands alongside malicious gossip, defamation and mockery as one kind of testimonial pathology among others.

The speaker, too, can suffer disrespect in her capacity as a rational being – for example, when her audience refuses to grant her the credibility she rationally deserves. Our proposed definition of what constitutes a 'pathology of testimony' thus includes within its scope testimonial injustices of the kind discussed in the previous section. It also accommodates cases of more subtle failures to respect others as rational beings: a case in point would be Coady's example of 'urban myths' – which, interestingly, are also mentioned by Kant in the form of 'fairy tales that have been passed on by word of mouth' (AA, VIII, 394). In such cases, although the claims in question are not about other people (except perhaps incidentally), and even though the specific act of propagating them need not disrespect either the speaker or the hearer, their intentional spreading – as Kant sees it – is nonetheless contrary to reason. Those who engage in the promulgation of urban legends, conspiracy theories, pseudo-science, etc. are often immune to criticism and, as Kant puts it, are driven by a desire 'to make imperceptible the blatantly obvious nonequivalence between loquacious ignorance and thorough science' (AA, XI, 141). Such careless broadcasting of unsubstantiated claims, be they fabrications or urban legends, may be considered a pathology of testimony in its own right, inasmuch as it disrespects the very standards of evidence and rationality that form the basis of testimony as a source of knowledge. Although such communications do not inflict a wrong upon *specific* others, they nonetheless do damage to our shared testimonial practices and, in Kant's language, may well be regarded as being 'contrary to the respect owed to humanity as such'.

Study questions

1 What explains the high degree of variation in the empirically measured reliability of rumours (cf. the empirical studies cited in Section 5)? Which social or institutional circumstances may be conducive to the empirical reliability of rumours?

2 The proposed definition, in Section 7, of 'pathology of testimony' as referring to any overtly informative speech that disrespects others as rational beings, is broader than the list of specific pathologies discussed in this chapter. What are some other examples?

3 How can *hermeneutical injustices* be ameliorated?

Further reading

A useful introductory text on questions of applied social epistemology, which includes chapters on rumour and conspiracy theories, is Coady (2012). Gossip is discussed from various angles by the contributors to Goodman and Ben-Ze'ev (1994); the conceptual foundations and social impact of rumour and legend are explored in the essays contained in Fine, Campion-Vincent and Heath (2005). Some of the material in Sections 2–4 above has been discussed more fully in Gelfert (2013c); the account of rumour as a form of epistemic dependence is spelled out in detail in Gelfert (2013a), while the account of Kant's views on rumour, gossip, urban legends, and pseudo-science draws on (Gelfert 2010c; 2013b). The idea of *epistemic coverage*, which is invoked in Section 5, is developed in detail by Goldberg (2010). Fricker's concept of *epistemic injustice* has spawned a growing literature; for a special issue exclusively devoted to the topic, see Bohman (2012).

11

Testimony and the value of knowledge

The past ten chapters have surveyed a wide variety of theoretical positions with respect to the epistemic standing of testimony as a source of knowledge. We have explored the role of testimony in a number of different settings, ranging from the testimony of experts and eyewitnesses in the legal context to mundane practices of asking and telling, all the way to borderline cases such as gossip and rumour. In the present chapter, we will take a step back and reflect on the question of the value of knowledge itself. Why do we even need the concept of 'knowledge' when, for all practical intents and purposes, true belief is all we need in order to be assured of the success of our plans and projects. As we shall see, the case can be made that it is our need for good informants – that is, our dependence on the testimony of others – which motivates the concept of knowledge in the first place. More specifically, our contemporary concept of *knowledge* may be thought of as deriving from the (genealogically prior) concept of a 'good informant'. We shall analyse two such genealogical accounts of the concept of knowledge in the first two sections, before discussing how a genealogical approach may be able to shed light on the question of why knowledge should be thought of as more valuable than (mere) true belief. The final section adds a postscript, which reflects on the question of how our increasingly technologically mediated ways of communication may affect the future shape and direction of social epistemology.

1. The genealogy of concepts

In recent years, a strand of epistemology has gained currency that attempts to address questions about knowledge not primarily by way of conceptual analysis (i.e. by attempting to define knowledge in terms of necessary and sufficient conditions), but by explicating the function of our concept of knowledge through an exploration of its *genealogy*. What is a 'genealogy'? As far as family resemblances between philosophical concepts go, one can consider 'genealogy' a close, but somewhat more rebellious, cousin to the concept of 'critique'. Where the latter, in its Kantian sense, refers to the self-examination of reason, by which we may hope to find out about the limits of reason, while at the same time asserting its preeminence within its proper domain of application, genealogy is not concerned with establishing rules and norms, let alone with policing them. Instead, as Raymond Geuss puts it, 'it is a summons to develop an empirically informed kind of theoretical imagination' and 'intrinsically serves to destroy the semblance of self-evidence and immediate givenness' that attaches to a given social institution, value system or concept (Geuss 2002: 212–13). While Geuss's main concern is with the moral and political domain, his general point extends also to genealogical approaches in epistemology. What are some of the aspects of traditional epistemology that one might suspect of having merely the 'semblance of self-evidence', without in fact being self-evident? Two widely shared assumptions about the concept of knowledge come to mind. First, the assumption that knowledge must lend itself to an analysis in terms of necessary and sufficient conditions; second, the commitment to the idea that knowledge is a species of belief. (For criticism of the latter presupposition, see also the discussion of Welbourne in Chapter 2, Section 1.) Taken in conjunction, these two fundamental tenets add up to a commitment to the familiar epistemological project of searching for necessary and sufficient conditions that determine which of our true beliefs should count as knowledge. This search only accelerated when Edmund Gettier, in 1963, showed that the three conditions implicit in the notion of 'justified true belief' were alone insufficient for knowledge: for example one might have a true belief (e.g. 'it is 9:30 a.m') on the basis of a justified method of belief acquisition (e.g. by looking at one's watch), yet the belief is only accidentally true (say, because one's watch stopped at 9:30 p.m. the night before). Such Gettier cases led to the collective, yet unsuccessful, search for what has been called the 'missing fourth condition' – a condition that, if added to the 'justified true belief' requirement, would conclusively render a belief an instance of knowledge. (See text box 'Is justified true belief knowledge?', pp. 45–6.)

One of the genealogical approaches to be discussed in the next section, Craig's project of a 'conceptual synthesis' with respect to knowledge and its value, explicitly takes aim at the necessary and sufficient conditions approach in epistemology:

> Here we see starkly a major disadvantage of the approach which takes its sole target to be the listing of logically necessary and sufficient conditions. If it can be argued that belief is not a necessary condition of knowledge, then belief will make no appearance on the final balance sheet. [. . .] Of all its deep centrality nothing whatever remains – it could be as incidental as the fact that nearly all knowers are less than 150 years old. (Craig 1990: 14)

Craig's point is this: if one regards necessary and sufficient conditions as exhausting the meaning and significance of concepts such as 'knowledge', one unduly restricts the scope of philosophical inquiry. There is more to our concepts than their conditions of proper application; in particular, in order to gain a deeper understanding of our *present* conceptual practices, one needs to pay attention to the 'marks' left by *previous* (i.e. genealogically prior) uses of a concept and its predecessors. Such marks may fall short of being either necessary or sufficient conditions, but they often speak to the value of our having the corresponding concept in the first place.

At its most general level, a genealogy may be defined as a narrative that tries to explain an institution, value, or concept 'by describing a way in which it came about, or could have come about, or might be imagined to have come about' (Williams 2002: 20). As such, a genealogy may be based on empirical findings as much as on imagination; thus, most genealogical narratives will be located somewhere along the spectrum between real history and fiction. An important device for the construction of imaginary genealogies is the idea of the *State of Nature*. This idea invites us to consider a 'simplified, imaginary, environment', which is inhabited by 'a group of human beings who co-operate but are not kin' (ibid.: 21). The (fictional) inhabitants of the State of Nature, though severely limited in the range of behaviours and options available to them, are nonetheless imagined as continuous with human beings as we know them, insofar as they are equipped with 'certain kinds of human interests and capacities, which, relative to the story, are taken as given' (ibid.). Exactly which conceptual capacities are included in a particular State of Nature story, will, of course, make all the difference and, therefore, needs to be specified well in advance of any conclusions that may be drawn from it. A typical basic characterization might, for example, refer to 'a small society of human beings, sharing a common language, with no elaborate technology and no form of writing' (Williams 2002: 41).

A State of Nature, thus, may be understood as an abstraction from real societies, which have 'many more cultural practices, more determinate and, no doubt, locally peculiar'; by contrast, the account of the fictional protagonists of the State of Nature story will be 'stripped down to certain functional ideas implicit in their use of language for basic human purposes' (ibid.). The idea, then, is to include just enough detail in a State of Nature story to allow one to draw inferences regarding the point of a conceptual practice, given plausible conditions under which it may be expected to arise. One might wonder why one should prefer such a method over the traditional 'necessary and sufficient conditions' approach to conceptual analysis. In response to such worries, the following remark by Kusch comes to mind: 'One of the most valuable aspects of genealogy is its systematic use of the idea that the evolution of concepts and the development of social relations are inseparable' (Kusch 2009: 70). Indeed, as Bernard Williams argues, the genealogical method, properly understood, allows us to steer a middle path between naïve reductionism with respect to present concepts and practices – whereby one imposes functional categories on what is essentially a contingent historical-evolutionary phenomenon – and a simplistic view of the past which mistakes functional characterizations of the origins of a conceptual practice for 'actual hominid prehistory'. According to Williams, genealogy 'keeps historical facts and functionalist abstraction in their places' (Williams 2002: 35).

2. Knowledge and the State of Nature

The title of this section is taken from Craig's influential 1990 book *Knowledge and the State of Nature: An Essay in Conceptual Synthesis*, in which he builds on earlier work on 'the practical explication of knowledge' (1986). Craig takes as his starting point a claim about our epistemic needs and argues that any comprehensive investigation into the concept of knowledge had better be able to account not only for the value of knowledge, but also for how our corresponding conceptual practice – our various ways and criteria of ascribing knowledge to ourselves and others – might have come about:

> We take some prima facie plausible hypothesis about what the concept of knowledge does for us, what its role in our life might be, and then ask what a concept having that role would be like, what conditions would govern its application. (Craig 1990: 2)

The conceptual need that is filled by our (current) concept of knowledge is, in a sense, more basic than that concept itself, and would manifest itself even among the inhabitants of the State of Nature, in the form of simple requests for information from others. Indeed,

> the members of any society will be interested in obtaining information from their fellows, and to this end they will develop a concept very like our concept of a good informant – one who (predictably) believes the truth on a given matter, and is prepared, and available, to pass his opinion on comprehensibly and without dissembling. (Ibid.: 96)

Having a concept of knowledge, or something very much like it, is useful in order 'to flag approved sources of information' (ibid.: 11) – that is, in order to pick out reliable and sincere informants – since, even in the imaginary State of Nature, some people will be in a better epistemic position than others when it comes to certain relevant facts. *Ex hypothesi*, in the State of Nature, there exists no social differentiation into, say, experts and laypersons – in this sense, all members are epistemically on a par with one another (barring, perhaps, some natural variation in individual epistemic capacities). Nonetheless, some people will simply have been in the right position, at the right time, to acquire a certain desired piece of information, whereas others may not have been. In other words, while the imaginary State of Nature does not allow for any strong asymmetry in terms of *expertise*, it does allow for what Williams calls 'purely positional advantage' (Williams 2002: 42).

The mere existence of purely positional advantages already creates an incentive for developing a concept that allows one to pick out good informants. Following a suggestion by Kusch, let us call the concept involved in identifying good informants *protoknowledge* (Kusch 2009: 65), so as to indicate that it is a precursor notion to our (current) concept of knowledge. In order for the concept of protoknowledge to fulfil its proper function, it must be assumed that there are certain (possibly variable) 'indicator-properties' that determine the limits of its proper application. Which properties of an informant are relevant, of course, depends on the context and aim of inquiry. 'Being 6 ft tall' may be a relevant indicator property when the object of one's epistemic desire is surrounded by a wall that is 5 ft high, but in other contexts may be entirely irrelevant. In more general terms, when we credit someone with protoknowledge, what we are looking for are several desirable properties in our potential informant, such as (1) being 'likely enough in the context to be right about whether *p*', (2) being 'communicatively available and open (including sincere)', (3) bearing indicator properties so that one can 'reliably recognize that (1) and (2) are satisfied' (Fricker 2008: 39–40). It is worth noting that these are not strict necessary and sufficient conditions on the concept of protoknowledge, but are desiderata associated with it, which may only be imperfectly realized.

As the name suggests, *protoknowledge* is not identical to *knowledge*, and we still need to give an account of how the concept of knowledge – knowledge 'as we know it', so to speak – arises from the need for picking out good informants. What connects the two, according to Craig, is a process of *objectivization*. As collectives of individuals evolve from the State of Nature into more complex societies, it becomes more difficult for them to keep track of which indicator properties are relevant to which question, and who possesses them. Sometimes – for example, when I become involved in group action – 'circumstances will arise in which it is important to me that someone in the group holds a true belief as to whether p, and quite unimportant whether the route by which they have acquired it would have been open to me or not' (Craig 1990: 92). In other words, our appraisals of others as good informants gradually become detached, both from our own practical needs and epistemic capacities and from the context of specific testimonial encounters. At the same time, novel applications of the concept become possible: inquirers begin to question whether they themselves have the requisite indicator-properties – and, if they do, may start crediting themselves with knowledge. Furthermore, they may rely on others for their recommendations of good informants – making first-hand protoknowledge an ever more elusive quantity. At the end of this process of objectivization, one arrives at 'the idea of someone who is a good informant as to whether p whatever the particular circumstances of the inquirer, [. . .] someone with a very high degree of reliability, someone who is very likely to be right' (ibid.: 91). Objectivization thus turns out to be a driving force in the evolution from the epistemic State of Nature, with its ascriptions of protoknowledge to others, to actual societies with their high degree of division of epistemic labour and their collective (as opposed to agent-specific) standards of what constitutes knowledge.

In his book *Truth and Truthfulness* (2002), Williams builds on this examination of the concept of knowledge and extends it in several significant ways. For one, Williams supplements Craig's State of Nature narrative with 'real genealogy' – where the latter means shifting our attention 'to cultural contingencies and history' (Williams 2002: 39). At the same time, he distinguishes between two important dimensions of the practice of seeking out good informants, which are not always kept apart in Craig's account, namely our twin concerns for accuracy of our interlocutors' information and for sincerity on the part of our informant. Whereas Craig's imaginary State of Nature story only allows for a relatively 'thin' conception of accuracy and sincerity – he takes accuracy to refer to the speaker's disposition to believe truths, and sincerity to his disposition to say what he believes – Williams argues that we must understand them in a 'thick' sense, as core virtues of truthfulness. (In order to indicate this shift, Williams uses uppercase spelling – 'Accuracy' and 'Sincerity' – to refer to the 'thick' concepts.) This is necessary because, like many institutionally valuable goods that depend for their usefulness on (possibly costly) individual contributions, the sharing of information is subject to a free-rider problem. It may be to my advantage to keep some of my knowledge to myself, or even to make misleading assertions to others – even though I myself may have acquired the very same knowledge thanks to others' being Accurate and Sincere.

A highly complex society, in which individuals cannot easily be penalized for violating the twin demands of Accuracy and Sincerity – for example, by excluding them from the practice of sharing information (as, let us assume, might happen among inhabitants of the State of Nature) – requires more than an acknowledgement of their status as instrumental goods; Accuracy and Sincerity must eventually be recognized as intrinsic goods. As Kusch puts it, for members of a community to trust each other's reports, 'they must be convinced that accuracy and sincerity are non-negotiable' (Kusch 2009: 74). For Williams, this can only be achieved if the 'thin' conception of accuracy and sincerity gives way to a 'thick' version that makes more substantive demands on the informant than merely insisting that he form reliable beliefs and truthfully express them. In particular, this 'thicker' understanding of what it takes to be Accurate and Sincere must be psychologically salient to the informant himself, and other interlocutors like him, in the sense that 'it must be possible for them to relate trustworthiness to other things that they value, and to their ethical emotions' (Williams 2002: 91–2). Elgin puts this point nicely, when she argues that, on Williams's account, the virtue of Sincerity, 'although grounded in asserting what one believes to be true, is not simply a matter of asserting what one believes to be true', but additionally 'requires sensitivity to contextual factors, such as the expectations and intentions of the parties to the exchange, to determine whether and to what extent truth-telling is called for' (Elgin 2005: 347).

3. The value of knowledge

The genealogical approach sketched in the previous two sections has direct implications for another core debate which has recently moved to the forefront of contemporary epistemology and which concerns the question of the *value of knowledge*. What lies at the heart of this debate is a puzzle concerning the (alleged) surplus value of knowledge as compared with true belief. Why, one might ask, should we value knowledge more than mere true belief? To be sure, when it turns out that something we thought we knew was true (and believed by us) merely as a matter of luck, we might feel uncomfortable realizing how easily we might have been wrong. But on the plausible assumption that whatever epistemic value accrues to our beliefs is ultimately derived from their utility in contexts of practical decision-making, it is not obvious that anything is gained from relying on a belief that qualifies as knowledge, as opposed to relying on a belief that is 'merely' true. What matters to the empirical success of an individual's plans and actions is whether they are based on beliefs that are *true*, not on whether they are based on beliefs that qualify as knowledge. Jonathan Kvanvig has recently referred to this problem as the 'Swamping Problem', which takes its name from the idea that the truth of a belief *swamps* whatever other redeeming features (e.g. reliability, likelihood, etc.) it might possess.

At first sight, the Swamping Problem appears to also pose a problem for the genealogical approach, since it appears to remove any rationale for individual epistemic agents to value protoknowledge over mere true belief. (See also Kusch 2009: 67–8.) Consider Fricker's explication, discussed in Section 2, of Craig's concept of protoknowledge in terms of three conditions: its being likely enough to be true in the given context, its being communicatively available, and its being identifiable as such in virtue of certain 'indicator-properties'. Let us assume an epistemic agent S has acquired a true belief that p from protoknower K – that is, from someone whom he has identified as a good informant. While it is statistically true that beliefs acquired from K are more 'likely to be true in the given context' than those acquired from a random individual who lacks the status of protoknower, according to the Swamping Problem this statistical fact should add nothing to the value of S's belief that p, *given that p is true*. From a genealogical point of view, this raises the legitimate question of why knowledge is ubiquitous in human social and cognitive life, and almost universally valued by all – in other words, why humans have evolved to be *knowers* (rather than *true believers*) – when the Swamping Problem would suggest that having knowledge confers no practical advantage over holding a true belief.

Even if one grants the importance of the Swamping Problem for the individual epistemic agent – a claim that has itself been the subject of much philosophical debate (for a criticism of the Swamping Thesis see, for example, Carter and Jarvis 2012) – its merits as a challenge to the genealogical approach are far from clear. Here I shall mention only two possible responses to the claim that the (individual) Swamping Problem undermines a genealogical explanation of how our collective concept of knowledge might have emerged. Both responses are based on the thought that certain aspects of our talk of knowledge are best explained, not by individual epistemic goals (e.g. the goal of acquiring true beliefs), but by collective goals of a population of epistemically interdependent social beings. The first suggestion, which is inspired by a theoretical proposal due to Steven Reynolds (who, remarkably, does not link his theory to that of

Craig), contends that the primary, though not the only, purpose of saying that people know is 'to encourage good testimony' – where the criteria of what constitutes 'good testimony' must, of course, 'be characterized in a way that avoids presupposing that such testimony expresses knowledge' (Reynolds 2002: 143). For example, people might notice 'circumstances that tended to make a person's testimony helpful in their projects, practical or intellectual, and subsequently they would praise a person's testimony' (ibid.: 147); over time, they might come to apply the evaluative concept of protoknowledge to all interlocutors in similar circumstances who enjoy similar exposure to the facts and who comply with generally accepted testimonial norms. In the first instance, however, the concept would be applied only to *exemplary* cases of testimony – which, in turn, means that 'one standard way of urging improvement in the norms would be to deny' an instance of testimony this evaluative status (ibid.: 148). The genealogical point of the concept of knowledge, then, consists not in any direct practical value for the individual epistemic agent, but in its indirect function of encouraging good testimonial practices at the communal level.

The second suggestion, due to Markus Werning, adds an evolutionary twist to such considerations of the collective, as opposed to individual, value of knowledge. With respect to the Swamping Problem's assimilation of the value of knowledge to that of (mere) true belief, Werning points out that, from an evolutionary perspective, being 'merely a truthful believer is not an evolutionary trait at all because it cannot be passed on' (Werning 2009: 152). What is being selected for in evolutionary processes is not individual beliefs – that is, *synchronous representations* of the world by an individual – but *the capacity to generate such beliefs* in ways that increase overall fitness. In an ever-changing environment, it would be neither feasible nor prudent to transmit belief systems in a wholesale fashion, since 'what can be transmitted isn't synchrony, but mechanisms of synchronization' between an organism's mental representations and the external environment. Or, put more succinctly, 'the trait of being a truthful believer can only be inherited *as* the trait of being a knower' (ibid: 2009: 151–2; italics added). An evolutionary perspective on the emergence of our concept of knowledge both broadens and modifies the genealogical picture developed in the previous two sections. For one, it requires taking seriously empirical results from the study of human evolution – rather than shielding genealogies from scientific evidence, as Williams appears to do when he insists that 'The State of Nature is Not the Pleistocene' (Williams 2002: 27). (For a more fully developed critique of both Craig and Williams on this point, see Gelfert 2011c.) A suitably broadened, scientifically informed inquiry into the origins of our concepts, however, also holds the promise of vindicating some of the core insights of the genealogical approach – by showing how our concept of knowledge might have arisen from a constellation of social and evolutionary pressures which includes, but is not limited to, the need for 'tagging' good informants and for cultivating good testimonial practices.

Let us conclude this section by highlighting another such collective desideratum: the need for a way of indicating collective agreement that, in a given case, inquiry has been taken far enough. After all, knowing when to stop is itself an important element of responsible inquiry and is a skill that needs to be acquired and passed on. Klemens Kappel, in a recent paper, has referred to this role of the concept of knowledge in the process of inquiry as the need for an *inquiry-stopper* (Kappel 2010: 74). As Kappel sees it, this need is the result of a trade-off between, on the one hand, the possible gains in certainty that may be expected from further inquiry and, on the other hand, the associated expenditures in terms of time and effort:

> At any given point in enquiry we face a decision task, which consists in weighing the risk of being wrong about p against the risk of wasting time and resources on further enquiry whether p in the event that p is true. [. . .] In addition, there will be a point where even beginning to calculate in this way risks being a waste of time and energy, though for obvious reasons it may be even more difficult to decide when this point has been reached. (Ibid.: 76)

From the genealogical perspective, which places collective needs at the heart of its account of the concept of knowledge, the decision task faced by an individual epistemic agent is but one side of the coin; the other side of the coin is the collective problem of how to allocate limited shared resources. It seems plausible, then, that a population of epistemically interdependent beings would experience a conceptual need for designating instances where inquiry has, for all intents and purposes, been taken far enough. The concept of knowledge may thus be thought of as, at least in part, also a response to the epistemic coordination problem of indicating collective agreement on when inquiry has reached closure.

4. The future of testimony in an age of technological mediation: A postscript

More so than ever before, we live in highly differentiated, technologically mediated, and increasingly globalized societies. Our ancestors, whether in the real world's distant past or in the fictional worlds conjured up by genealogies of knowledge, could not have dreamt of the speed and reach of our communication technologies, nor could they have fathomed the degree of mobility that characterizes contemporary developed societies. Equally unimaginable would have been the rapid growth of specialist knowledge across so many branches of science, technology, society and culture. (Least of all, one imagines, could they have foreseen that an ever-growing list of specialized disciplines of inquiry would one day include a philosophical subdiscipline called 'the epistemology of testimony'!) Our entrenched epistemic concepts of belief, knowledge, justification, etc. have so far served us well and have proved remarkably robust – notwithstanding the significant shifts that have occurred within epistemology itself over the past century or so. Yet, if there is one thing that a genealogical perspective teaches us, it is that concepts that now are 'second nature' to us, would likely cease to seem natural, were conditions and circumstances to change radically.

As we look around us today, we see fundamental shifts in the way we receive, filter and process social information. Much communication takes place electronically, via email and social networking sites, and requests for information are increasingly fulfilled by relying on internet search engines whose algorithms, in turn, take into account information about the user – either because it was freely volunteered by the user upon registration or because it was extracted from his search history and other electronic traces. How do we assess such sources of information, given that they often lack attributability to specific epistemic agents (see Chapter 1, Section 3.4)? Since we can expect the line between (recognizably human) testimony and electronic information to become increasingly blurred, finding ways of accommodating such new forms of communication and learning within our philosophical theories of knowledge is an important task for social epistemology. To adapt a phrase from Reid, the 'social operations of mind' are liable to become increasingly *technologically mediated operations of mind*. It would, of course, be naïve to expect changes in our preferred communication technologies to suddenly give rise to radical changes in our conceptions of justification, knowledge and testimony; however, it would be equally naïve to think that the dominant form of testimony will forever remain of the interpersonal, face-to-face variety that currently serves as an 'intuition pump' for many of our best-developed epistemological theories of testimony. At the very least, social epistemology as a philosophical discipline would be well-advised to continue to broaden its horizon and remain attuned to our ever-changing epistemic practices. Whatever the future of testimony, and whatever its future social forms, it is to be hoped that the various theoretical approaches discussed in this book will help us make sense of the social fabric of knowledge and our place within it.

Study questions

1. Both Craig (1990) and Williams (2002) insist that the fictional inhabitants of the State of Nature must be thought of as having largely the same cognitive apparatus as we have today. What is the rationale for this *constancy assumption*, and how might one challenge it?
2. What other epistemic values, in addition to truth, are there?
3. How might online communication and search engines be modified to address the need for identifying good informants?

Further reading

Craig (1990) and Williams (2002) are the central texts for any discussion of the genealogical approach in epistemology and will reward the reader, in equal measure, with insight and inspiration. A number of papers that expand on the genealogical approach are gathered in Gerken, Kallestrup, Kappel and Pritchard (2011). Essays on the value of knowledge, ranging from discussions of the Swamping Problem to a consideration of the role of practical contexts in knowledge attributions, have been collected in Haddock, Millar and Pritchard (2009). A good illustration of what a social-epistemological engagement with contemporary technological developments might look like is Miller and Record (2013).

Glossary

a priori/a posteriori distinction – Whereas a priori knowledge can be gained without recourse to experience, a posteriori knowledge requires empirical investigation of the world (and hence is also called 'empirical knowledge').

abduction – often used as a synonym for INFERENCE TO THE BEST EXPLANATION; sometimes used specifically to refer to the process of hypothesis generation in science.

Acceptance Principle – An anti-reductionist principle proposed by Burge as a default rule for accepting testimony: 'A person is entitled to accept as true something that is presented as true and that is intelligible to him unless there are stronger reasons not to do so' (Burge 1993: 467). See also ANTI-REDUCTIONISM.

analytic – A statement or proposition is analytic if it is true entirely in virtue of the meanings of its constituents, for example: 'All bachelors are unmarried.' See also SYNTHETIC.

anti-reductionism – Anti-reductionism about testimony rejects the idea that, for a TESTIMONY-BASED BELIEF to be justified, it needs to be supported by beliefs originating from non-testimonial sources; instead, testimony is regarded as a *sui generis* source of knowledge and justification.

assurance view – The assurance view (proposed by Moran 2005) regards the speaker's testimony that p as a way of assuming responsibility for the truth of p; this is intended to give the audience a non-evidential reason for belief that p, namely by believing the speaker.

Bayes's theorem – Bayes's theorem is a direct consequence of the axioms of probability theory and the definition of conditional probability: $P(h|e) = P(e|h)P(h)/P(e)$. Its epistemological significance derives from the fact that it points to a consistent way of revising one's degree of belief in a hypothesis h in the light of incoming evidence e.

coherentism – Coherentism holds that the justification of a belief is a matter of its coherence with other beliefs, where coherence is understood to comprise not only logical consistency, but also explanatory, abductive and inductive considerations. Coherentists reject the existence of a privileged class of (foundational) 'basic beliefs'. (See also FOUNDATIONALISM.)

community of knowledge – According to Welbourne, a community of knowledge is constituted by the mutual recognition of its members, who acknowledge each other as sharing in that knowledge, 'so each can act on the assumption of knowledge in the other and they will be able to act co-operatively' (Welbourne 1993: 25).

contingent – A contingent proposition is one that is not necessary, and whose negation is also not necessary; its truth thus is contingent on circumstances that might very well not have been. (See also NECESSARY.)

coverage – a property of one's social and epistemic environment. According to Goldberg (2010), an environment is coverage-reliable if, across a wide range of beliefs and given certain background conditions, it supports the following *truth-to-testimony conditional*: 'If ~p were true, I would have heard about it by now.'

credibility – often used interchangeably with TRUSTWORTHINESS. In the legal domain, the term 'credible witness' is the preferred expression to refer to witnesses who the court has reason to believe are more than likely to be truthful, in view of their EXPERTISE, knowledge, training, and apparent character traits such as honesty, sincerity and forthrightness.

deduction – refers to the process of reasoning from one or more premises to conclusions, using only the rules of deductive logic.

defeater – belief or evidence that undermines the justification of another belief.

dialectical superiority – refers to the relative performance of conflicting expert witnesses on such measures as quality of delivery (including demeanour), responsiveness to challenges, ability to rebut arguments and so forth.

doxastic voluntarism – Doxastic voluntarism holds that we have voluntary control over our beliefs.

empiricism – Empiricists hold that all knowledge is eventually derived from sensory experience. Historically, empiricists have been suspicious of (alleged) a priori knowledge (e.g. knowledge of logical truths); they also reject the thought that there could be innate knowledge. (See also A PRIORI/A POSTERIORI DISTINCTION; RATIONALISM.)

entitlement – introduced by Burge (1993) as the externalist analogue of the internalist notion of justification. Entitlements derive from our legitimate reliance on *bona fide* sources of knowledge, such as memory, perception and testimony. (See also JUSTIFICATION; EXTERNALISM; WARRANT.)

epistemic dependence – refers to any situation or condition in which a subject's belief depends for its formation, sustainment or reliability on the knowledge (or beliefs, or other cognitive states and processes) of other epistemic agents.

epistemic injustice – Coined by Miranda Fricker (2007), this term describes cases of injustice where someone is wronged specifically in their capacity as a knower. This may occur when an audience systematically (i.e. not by accident) denies a speaker the credibility she deserves, for example as the result of prejudice. In addition to such *testimonial injustice*, there is also *hermeneutical injustice*, which describes a situation where someone is handicapped in their ability to make sense of – and communicate to others – their social experience, due to the collective lack of conceptual resources. (See also PATHOLOGY OF TESTIMONY.)

epistemic peer – Two epistemic agents are epistemic peers with respect to a particular question or domain of knowledge when they possess relevantly similar epistemic virtues, and are equally familiar with evidence and arguments bearing on the topic in question. In recent *epistemology* *of disagreement*, a more technical definition is sometimes used, according to which epistemic peers are antecedently equally likely to give the right answers on a given question. (See also VIRTUES, EPISTEMIC.)

evidentialism – Evidentialism holds that an epistemic subject is justified in believing that *p* at a given time if and only if her evidence for *p* at the time supports her belief that *p*. Historically, in connection with the ethics of belief, evidentialism has been associated with Clifford's remark that 'it is wrong always, everywhere, and for anyone to believe anything upon insufficient evidence' (1879: 183).

expertise – Expertise is typically a matter of possessing comprehensive specialist knowledge in a particular domain, combined with an ability to deploy this knowledge in order to successfully investigate new questions. (See also DIALECTICAL SUPERIORITY.)

externalism – Externalism in epistemology holds that whether or not a subject's belief enjoys a positive epistemic status depends, in part, on objective factors and conditions that are external to the subject and will often be cognitively unavailable to her. According to externalism, if conditions are right, a subject need not have cognitive access to reasons for belief, in order for her to be rightly credited with knowledge. (See also INTERNALISM; RELIABILISM.)

fallibilism – the thesis that no belief, claim, theory, etc. can ever possess conclusive justification or certainty. Fallibilism may be restricted to certain domains of knowledge (e.g. empirical knowledge), while exempting others (e.g. logic and mathematics). (See also JUSTIFICATION.)

folk psychology – our commonsense attributions of beliefs, desires, motivations, and other mental states to other people, on the basis of which we explain, predict, and justify their behaviour and actions.

foundationalism – Foundationalism is the view that a body of knowledge is hierarchically structured, in that there is much indirect knowledge which (at least in part) depends for its justification on direct (foundational) knowledge, which is not so dependent. (See also COHERENTISM.)

genealogy – A genealogical account constructs a (typically fictional) developmental story of how a concept might have arisen from a hypothesized STATE OF NATURE. The plausibility of such an account derives either from its making minimal empirical assumptions or, in the case of *real genealogies*, from its attentiveness to genuine historical, cultural and, in some cases, evolutionary findings.

Gettier case – see TRIPARTITE DEFINITION OF KNOWLEDGE.

global reductionism – Global reductionism rejects the claim that testimony is a distinct *sui generis* source of knowledge and justification: whatever epistemic justification a TESTIMONY-BASED BELIEF may possess must ultimately be derived from more basic sources of justification (perception, memory and inference). Testimony as a source of knowledge can thus be assimilated, in a wholesale manner, to these more basic sources. (See also LOCAL REDUCTIONISM.)

gossip – Gossip consists of informal communication among acquaintances, about matters (typically of a personal nature) concerning another individual who is not co-present at the time, but is known to those in the group. Unlike RUMOUR, gossip may include instances of first-hand testimony. (See also RUMOUR; URBAN LEGEND; PATHOLOGY OF TESTIMONY.)

hearsay – any second-hand report of another person's testimony. In the legal context, any statement made out of court that is reported in court and offered as evidence in support of another claim. (See also RUMOUR.)

hermeneutical injustice – see EPISTEMIC INJUSTICE.

induction – Induction refers to the (fallible) process of reasoning from observed cases to future cases of the same kind (*enumerative induction*), or to a (fallible) generalization on the basis of observed evidence. (See also INFERENCE TO THE BEST EXPLANATION; ABDUCTION.) In a more generic way, 'induction' is sometimes used as an umbrella for any non-deductive form of inference. (See also DEDUCTION.)

inference to the best explanation – an inference from the fact that a particular hypothesis would explain the EVIDENCE to the truth of that hypothesis. Given that evidence is usually compatible with a range of potential explanations, there has been considerable philosophical debate about what makes one explanation 'better' than another. Possible criteria include simplicity, scope, unification, and overall likelihood, among others. (See also INDUCTION; ABDUCTION.)

inferentialism – Inferentialism in the epistemology of testimony is the position that a TESTIMONY-BASED BELIEF depends for its JUSTIFICATION on other (non-testimonial) beliefs. More specifically, in the context of LOCAL REDUCTIONISM, inferentialism refers to the demand that, for a hearer to be justified in forming a testimony-based belief, he must have successfully discharged his epistemic responsibility to monitor the speaker for possible signs of insincerity or incompetence. (See also LOCAL REDUCTIONISM.)

institutional testimony – testimony that is underwritten by a social institution and may be communicated by a spokesperson; examples include press releases, official gazettes, bus timetables, degree certificates, financial data, etc.

internalism – Internalism in epistemology holds that whether a belief is justified depends on the subject's having formed her belief responsibly, on the basis of considerations that were cognitively accessible to her at the time. (See also EXTERNALISM.)

justification – The concept of justification is central to the project of epistemology; as a result, its precise meaning tends to vary from one epistemological theory to another. Broadly speaking, 'justification' refers to any consideration that, from a perspective that aims at truth and/or the fulfilment of one's epistemic responsibilities, would count in favour of a belief. In a narrower (internalist) sense of the word, 'justification' is sometimes reserved for those (argument-like) considerations that are in principle cognitively available to the subject who holds the belief in question. (See also WARRANT; ENTITLEMENT.)

justified true belief – see TRIPARTITE DEFINITION OF KNOWLEDGE.

local reductionism – Local reductionism acknowledges that any attempt to reduce the justification of testimony-based beliefs to more basic epistemic sources must proceed on a case-by-case basis.

While it insists that, for a *mature reasoner*'s TESTIMONY-BASED BELIEF to be justified, it must have been evaluated on the basis of (some) non-testimonial evidence, it concedes that in performing such evaluations it is necessary to rely on some conceptual, linguistic and other background knowledge that was acquired during an earlier *developmental phase*, on the basis of uncritical acceptance of testimony from parents and teachers, among others. (See also GLOBAL REDUCTIONISM.)

mundane testimony – testimony concerning matters that we can reasonably expect any interlocutor to be competent and sincere about, for example concerning who they are, where they live, what time it is and so forth.

necessary – A necessary truth is a proposition that could not have been false under any circumstances. This is sometimes expressed by saying that a necessary truth is a proposition that is true in all possible worlds. (See also CONTINGENT.)

pathology of testimony – Initially introduced by C. A. J. Coady (2006) as an umbrella term for the phenomena of gossip, rumour and urban legend; according to our definition, developed in Chapter 10, any type of overtly informative speech act that disrespects another person in their capacity as a rational being.

PR thesis – The 'presumptive right' (or PR) thesis holds that, even in the absence of specific evidence of the speaker's TRUSTWORTHINESS, the hearer has the epistemic right to believe what the speaker says merely on the ground that it has been asserted. Commitment to the PR thesis entails ANTI-REDUCTIONISM about testimony.

principle of charity – requires that, in a situation where we need to interpret an interlocutor's verbal behaviour, we attribute to him beliefs (and assign meanings to his words) in whatever way would maximize the truth of his beliefs and utterances.

rationalism – Rationalists hold that some propositions are knowable through rational intuition alone; often this is coupled with the view that rationally intuited propositions should form the basis of our knowledge, for example because they include innate principles. (See also A PRIORI/A POSTERIORI DISTINCTION; EMPIRICISM.)

reductionism – According to reductionism about testimony, the mere fact that a belief is based on the say-so of others does not by itself confer epistemic justification on it; whatever justification a TESTIMONY-BASED BELIEF has must ultimately be derived from more basic epistemic sources (such as perception, memory and reasoning).

reference class problem – In order to make valid inductive generalizations or statistical predictions, it is important to determine which class of relevantly similar cases the particular case at hand belongs to. The reference class problem arises from the fact that, in many cases, the choice of reference class is underdetermined.

reliabilism – Reliabilism is a species of EXTERNALISM about epistemic justification, in that it considers the justification of a belief to be a matter of the truth-conduciveness of the way in which it was formed. *Process reliabilism*, in its simplest form, amounts to the thesis that an epistemic agent S knows that p if and only if S believes that p, p is true, and S's belief that p is the result of a reliable process. (See also EXTERNALISM.)

routine, epistemic – a procedure of belief formation which an epistemic agent has elected to follow, even if doing so might lead him to acquire beliefs that contradict, or are in tension with, some of his prior beliefs.

rumour – an instance of ostensibly informative HEARSAY, usually on a topic of broader interest, and typically communicated via informal pathways in the absence of independent corroboration by either first-hand evidence or official (authoritative) sources. (See also GOSSIP; URBAN LEGEND; PATHOLOGY OF TESTIMONY.)

safety – A subject S's belief that p is *safe* if, in all nearby possible worlds (scenarios) where S believes that p, p is not false. (See also SENSITIVITY.)

sense data – Sense data are the mental items of which we have direct awareness in perception and which, on the traditional sense-datum theory, 'mediate' our perceptions of external objects.

sensitivity – A subject S's belief that p is *sensitive* if and only if the following conditional holds: If p were false, then S would not believe that p. (See also SAFETY.)

speech act – A speech act is an instance of communication, typically an utterance, that is produced by the speaker either with the intention that it be recognized as such by the hearer (*illocutionary act*), or in order to bring about a specific (extra-linguistic) effect, for example an action or feeling on the part of the hearer (*perlocutionary act*). For example, an assertion is the illocutionary act of saying what the world is like, whereas boring someone by stating the obvious is a perlocutionary act. Beyond such taxonomies, a speech act is any utterance that serves a communicative function.

State of Nature – An imaginary community of epistemic agents who share our basic cognitive capacities, but lack our high degree of social differentiations and, importantly, lack our concept of knowledge – though they may have substitute criteria to single out interlocutors they perceive to be good informants ('protoknowers'). (See also GENEALOGY.)

synthetic – a proposition is synthetic if it is not ANALYTIC; that is, the truth of such a proposition cannot be determined by reflecting solely on the meaning of its constituents.

technocracy – a form of governance, based on the rule of (technical) experts.

testimonial injustice – see EPISTEMIC INJUSTICE.

testimony – Testimony as a source of knowledge is closely associated with the SPEECH ACT of assertion. It may be characterized as the assertion, by a speaker (or author), of a spoken (or written) sentence, which is offered as a ground for belief to the hearer (or reader). This is captured by saying that testimonial knowledge is knowledge on the basis of the say-so of others. Definitions of testimony vary across different contexts and between philosophical theories. For example, in the legal domain (admissible) testimony is often described as a form of evidence, whereas some philosophical theories propose different definitions, depending on whether one adopts the perspective of the speaker or the hearer. (See also SPEECH ACT; HEARSAY.)

testimony-based belief – Following Pritchard (2004), a testimony-based belief may be defined as any belief which a hearer reasonably and directly forms in response to what he reasonably takes to be testimony and which is essentially brought about and sustained by testimony. (See also TESTIMONY.)

TIBE – shorthand for *testimonial inference to the best explanation*. Whereas Lipton (2007) argues that a hearer is justified in accepting a piece of testimony only if the best explanation of its utterance entails the truth of the claim in question, Gelfert (2010b) argues for a dual role of inference to the best explanation: on the one hand, default acceptance is justified when there is sufficient abductive evidence for the reliability of our testimonial practices; on the other hand, a specific testimonial claim should be rejected when the best explanation of its assertion renders the claim improbable or unreliable. (See ABDUCTION; INFERENCE TO THE BEST EXPLANATION.)

transcendental argument – A transcendental argument takes some manifest aspect, X, of reality as given and then articulates the conditions $Y, Z, \ldots$ that necessarily have to be in place for X to be possible. Given that X is the case, it follows that $Y, Z, \ldots$ must likewise be the case.

transmission view of testimony – On the transmission view, testimony can at best transmit knowledge, justification or warrant from the speaker to the hearer, but cannot generate such epistemic properties *ex nihilo*. (See JUSTIFICATION; WARRANT.)

tripartite definition of knowledge – According to the tripartite definition of knowledge, an epistemic subject S knows that p if and only if: 1.) p is true, 2.) S believes that p, and 3.) S is justified in believing that p. Each of the three conditions is individually necessary. However, as *Gettier cases* show, they are not jointly sufficient: an epistemic subject may satisfy all three conditions, and yet fail to know that p. For example, I may look at my watch and form the true belief that it is 9:30 a.m. since this is what the hands seem to indicate, yet unbeknownst to me, my (normally reliable) watch stopped at 9:30 p.m. the night before. Although my belief is true and justified, it does not constitute knowledge. (See also EXTERNALISM; INTERNALISM; RELIABILISM; JUSTIFICATION.)

trust – At the interpersonal level, trust differs from (mere) reliance in that, when we trust, we willingly depend on the good will of the trusted; trust is not merely predictive in character, but has a moral component. At the psychological level, trust may be thought of as an *affective* attitude that shapes the emotional relationship between the truster and the trusted. In the case of *social* or *public trust*, we trust others not on the basis of emotional (or other interpersonal) bonds, but on the basis of their specific social roles and functions; this applies to individuals as well as to institutions.

trustworthiness – often used interchangeably with CREDIBILITY. In a narrower sense, trustworthiness contributes to (but does not exhaust) credibility, since the latter also requires relevant competence, knowledge or expertise on the part of the speaker. In LOCAL REDUCTIONISM, judgements of a speaker S's trustworthiness play an important inferential role, since they are thought to enable the hearer to bridge 'the logical and epistemic gap between "S

asserted that *p''* and "*p'''*' (Fricker 1994: 129).

truth-to-testimony conditional – see COVERAGE.

urban legend, urban myth – An apocryphal, highly stylized story, usually with a surprising or shocking twist, which is presented as true, either in informal conversation or via (typically local) news sources, and which has been adapted to local circumstances to increase its plausibility and newsworthiness. (See also RUMOUR; PATHOLOGY OF TESTIMONY.)

virtues, epistemic – An epistemic virtue is a character trait (or other quality of an individual or group) that is conducive to the acquisition of true beliefs, avoidance of false beliefs or the promotion of other epistemic values. Examples include intelligence, accuracy, sincerity, perspicacity, freedom from bias, open-mindedness, intellectual courage, and curiosity, among others.

warrant – Sometimes used as an umbrella term for (internalist) JUSTIFICATION and (externalist) ENTITLEMENT, in order to indicate that both aim at a more fundamental epistemic good, the (fallible) pursuit of truth. Somewhat confusingly, the term 'warrant' is occasionally used in other areas – for example, in the epistemology of religion – to refer to that property of true beliefs that makes them knowledge. (See also ENTITLEMENT; JUSTIFICATION.)

witness – Sometimes used interchangeably with 'testifier', 'interlocutor' or 'speaker'. In the narrower sense of *eyewitness*, anyone who can give a first-hand account of an event, experience or occurrence. In the legal context, anyone who is asked to testify, either on a matter he witnessed first-hand or on a subject matter of which he has relevant specialist knowledge (*expert witness*). (See also EXPERTISE; TESTIMONY.)

Bibliography

Adler, J. E. (1994), 'Testimony, trust, knowing', *The Journal of Philosophy*, 91, (5), 264–75.
— (2002), *Belief's Own Ethics*. Cambridge, MA: MIT Press.
— (2012), 'Epistemological problems of testimony', in E. Z. Zalta (ed.), *The Stanford Encyclopedia of Philosophy* (Spring 2013 edition). Available online at <http://plato.stanford.edu/archives/spr2013/entries/testimony-episprob/>, accessed 1 October 2013.
Allport, G. W. and Postman, L. (1947), *The Psychology of Rumour*. New York: Henry Holt.
12 Angry Men (1957), Screenplay by R. Rose, dir. S. Lumet, prod. H. Fonda and R. Rose. United Artists. Film.
Aquinas, Th. (1946), *The Trinity and The Unicity of the Intellect* (Super Boethium De Trinitate, c. 1261; transl. Rose E. Brennan). St Louis: Herder Book Co.
Aristotle (1991), *On Rhetoric: A Theory of Civic Discourse* (transl. George A. Kennedy). New York: Oxford University Press.
Asch, S. E. (1956), 'Studies of independence and conformity: a minority of one against a unanimous majority', *Psychological Monographs*, 70, (9), 1–70.
Audi, R. (1997), 'The place of testimony in the fabric of knowledge and justification', *American Philosophical Quarterly*, 34, (4), 405–22.
— (2002), 'The sources of knowledge', in P. K. Moser (ed.), *The Oxford Handbook of Epistemology*. New York: Oxford University Press, pp. 71–94.
— (2006), 'Testimony, credulity, and veracity', in J. Lackey and E. Sosa (eds), *The Epistemology of Testimony*. Oxford: Oxford University Press, pp. 25–49.
— (2011), *Epistemology: A Contemporary Introduction to the Theory of Knowledge* (3rd edition). New York: Routledge.
Ayim, M. (1994), 'Knowledge through the grapevine: gossip as inquiry', in R. F. Goodman and Aaron Ben-Ze'ev (eds), *Good Gossip*. Lawrence: University Press of Kansas, pp. 85–99.
Baier, A. (1986), 'Trust and antitrust', *Ethics*, 96, (2), 231–60.
Bailey, A. and O'Brien, D. (2006), *Hume's Enquiry Concerning Human Understanding (Reader's Guide)*. London: Continuum.
Barnes, J. (1980), 'Socrates and the jury', *Proceedings of the Aristotelian Society*, 54 (Suppl.), 193–206.
Bergmann, J. R. (1993), *Discreet Indiscretions: The Social Organization of Gossip*. New York: Aldine de Gruyter.
Bernecker, S. (2011), 'Memory knowledge', in S. Bernecker and D. Pritchard (eds), *The Routledge Companion to Epistemology*. New York: Routledge, pp. 326–34.
Blais, M. J. (1987), 'Epistemic tit for tat', *The Journal of Philosophy*, 84, (7), 363–75.

Bohman, J. ed. (2012), *Epistemic Injustice*. Special Issue, *Social Epistemology*, 26, (2), 145–261.
Bok, S. (1999), *Lying: Moral Choice in Public and Private Life* (3rd edition). New York: Vintage.
BonJour, L. (2010), *Epistemology: Classic Problems and Contemporary Responses* (2nd edition). Lanham: Rowman & Littlefield.
Bovens, L. and Hartmann, S. (2004), *Bayesian Epistemology*. New York: Oxford University Press.
Brandom, R. (2000), *Articulating Reasons: An Introduction to Inferentialism*. Cambridge, MA: Harvard University Press.
Brewer, S. (1998), 'Scientific expert testimony and intellectual due process', *The Yale Law Journal*, 107, (6), 1535–681.
Buenting, J. (2006), 'Re-thinking the duplication of speaker/hearer belief in the epistemology of testimony', *Episteme: A Journal of Social Epistemology*, 2, (2), 129–34.
Burge, T. (1993), 'Content preservation', *The Philosophical Review*, 102, (4), 457–88.
— (1998), 'Computer proof, a priori knowledge, and other minds', *Philosophical Perspectives*, 12, 1–37.
Caplow, T. (1947), 'Rumors in war', *Social Forces*, 25, (3), 298–302.
Carter, J. A. and Jarvis, B. (2012), 'Against swamping', *Analysis*, 72, (4), 690–9.
Cavell, S. (1979), *The Claim of Reason*. New York: Oxford University Press.
Chisholm, R. (1966), *Theory of Knowledge* (1st edition). Englewood Cliffs: Prentice-Hall.
— (1989), *Theory of Knowledge* (3rd edition). Englewood Cliffs: Prentice-Hall.
Christensen, D. (2007), 'Epistemology of disagreement: the good news', *The Philosophical Review*, 116, (2), 187–217.
Clifford, W. K. (1879), *Lectures and Essays* (vol. 2; ed. Leslie Stephen and Frederick Pollock). London: Macmillan.
Coady, C. A. J. (1989), 'Reid on testimony', in M. Dalgarno and E. Matthews (eds), *The Philosophy of Thomas Reid*. Dordrecht: Kluwer, pp. 225–46.
— (1992), *Testimony. A Philosophical Study*. Oxford: Oxford University Press.
— (2006), 'Pathologies of testimony', in J. Lackey and E. Sosa (eds), *The Epistemology of Testimony*. Oxford: Oxford University Press, pp. 253–71.
Coady, D. (2006), 'Rumour has it', *International Journal of Applied Philosophy*, 20, (1), 41–53.
— (2012), *What to Believe Now: Applying Epistemology to Contemporary Issues*. Chichester: Wiley-Blackwell.
Code, L. (1994), 'Gossip, or: in praise of chaos', in R. F. Goodman and Aaron Ben-Ze'ev (eds), *Good Gossip*. Lawrence: University Press of Kansas, pp. 100–5.
— (1996), 'Commentary on "loopholes, gaps, and what is held fast"', *Philosophy, Psychiatry, & Psychology*, 3, (4), 255–60.
Coleman, J. S. (1988), 'Social capital in the creation of human capital', *American Journal of Sociology*, 94 (Suppl.), S95–S120.
Collins, L. (1994), 'Gossip: a feminist defense', in R. F. Goodman and Aaron Ben-Ze'ev (eds), *Good Gossip*. Lawrence: University Press of Kansas, pp. 106–16.
Craig, E. (1986), 'The practical explication of knowledge', *Proceedings of the Aristotelian Society (New Series)*, 87, 211–26.

— (1990), *Knowledge and the State of Nature: An Essay in Conceptual Synthesis*. Oxford: Oxford University Press.
Daubert v. Merrell Dow Pharmaceuticals, 509 U.S. 579. Supreme Court of the United States, 1993.
Davidson, D. (1986), 'A coherence theory of truth and knowledge', in E. Lepore (ed.), *Truth and Interpretation: Perspectives on the Philosophy of Donald Davidson*. Oxford: Blackwell, pp. 307–19.
de Sousa, R. (1994), 'In praise of gossip: indiscretion as a saintly virtue', in R. F. Goodman and Aaron Ben-Ze'ev (eds), *Good Gossip*. Lawrence: University Press of Kansas, pp. 25–33.
Dentith, M. (2013), 'Have you heard? The rumor as reliable', in G. Dalziel (ed.), *Rumor and Communication in Asia in the Internet Age*. London: Routledge, pp. 46–60.
DiFonzo, N. and Bordia, P. (2006), 'Rumor in organizational contexts', in D. A. Hantula (ed.), *Advances in Social & Organizational Psychology: A Tribute to Ralph Rosnow*. London: Routledge, pp. 249–74.
Douven, I. and Cuypers, S. E. (2009), 'Fricker on testimonial justification', *Studies in History and Philosophy of Science*, 40, (1), 36–44.
Dummett, M. (1993), *The Seas of Language*. Oxford: Oxford University Press.
Dundes, A. (1965), *The Study of Folklore*. Englewood Cliffs: Prentice-Hall.
Ebert, R. (1998), 'It's the end of the world: "Armageddon" fails to miss any clichés', *Chicago Sun-Times*, 1 July 1998, p. 45.
Elga, A. (2007), 'Reflection and disagreement', *Noûs*, 41, (3), 478–502.
Elgin, C. (2001), 'Word giving, word taking', in A. Byrne, R. Stalnaker and R. Wedgwood (eds), *Fact and Value: Essays on Ethics and Metaphysics for Judith Jarvis Thomson*. Cambridge, MA: MIT Press, pp. 97–116.
— (2002), 'Take it from me: the epistemological status of testimony', *Philosophy and Phenomenological Research*, 65, (2), 291–308.
— (2005), 'Critical study: Williams on truthfulness', *The Philosophical Quarterly*, 55, (219), 343–52.
Emler, N. (1994), 'Gossip, reputation, and social adaptation', in R. F. Goodman and Aaron Ben-Ze'ev (eds), *Good Gossip*. Lawrence: University Press of Kansas, pp. 117–38.
Fallis, D. (2008), 'Toward an epistemology of *Wikipedia*', *Journal of the American Society for Information Science and Technology*, 59, (10), 1662–74.
Faulkner, P. (2000a), 'Testimonial knowledge', *Acta Analytica*, 15, (24), 127–37.
— (2000b), 'The social character of testimonial knowledge', *The Journal of Philosophy*, 97, (11), 581–601.
— (2006), 'On dreaming and being lied to', *Episteme: A Journal of Social Epistemology*, 2, (3), 149–59.
— (2007), 'On telling and trusting', *Mind*, 116, (464), 875–902.
— (2011), *Knowledge on Trust*. Oxford: Oxford University Press.
Feldman, R. (2006), 'Epistemological puzzles about disagreement', in S. Hetherington (ed.), *Epistemology Futures*. Oxford: Oxford University Press, pp. 216–36.
Fine, G., Campion-Vincent, V. and Heath, C. (2005), *Rumor Mills: The Social Impact of Rumor and Legend*. New Brunswick: Transaction Publishers.
Foley, R. (2002), *Intellectual Trust in Oneself and Others*. Cambridge: Cambridge University Press.

Fricker, E. (1994), 'Against gullibility', in B. K. Matilal and A. Chakrabarti (eds), *Knowing from Words: Western and Indian Philosophical Analysis of Understanding and Testimony*. Dordrecht: Kluwer, pp. 125–61.
— (1995), 'Telling and trusting: reductionism and anti-reductionism in the epistemology of testimony' (Critical notice of Coady 1992), *Mind*, 104, (414), 393–411.
— (2004), 'Testimony: knowing through being told', in I. Niiniluoto, M. Sintonen and J. Woleński (eds), *Handbook of Epistemology*. Dordrecht: Kluwer, pp. 109–30.
— (2006), 'Testimony and epistemic autonomy', in J. Lackey and E. Sosa (eds), *The Epistemology of Testimony*. Oxford: Oxford University Press, pp. 225–50.
Fricker, M. (2007), *Epistemic Injustice: Power and the Ethics of Knowing*. Oxford: Oxford University Press.
— (2008), 'Scepticism and the genealogy of knowledge: situating epistemology in time', *Philosophical Papers*, 37, (1), 27–50.
Frisch, A. (2004), 'The ethics of testimony: a genealogical perspective', *Discourse*, 52, (1–2), 36–54.
Gambetta, D. ed. (1988), *Trust: Making and Breaking Cooperative Relations*. Oxford: Blackwell.
Gelfert, A. (2006), 'Kant on testimony', *British Journal for the History of Philosophy*, 14, (4), 627–52.
— (2009), 'Indefensible middle ground for local reductionism about testimony', *Ratio*, 22, (2), 170–90.
— (2010a), 'Hume on testimony revisited', *Logical Analysis and History of Philosophy*, 13, 60–75.
— (2010b), 'Reconsidering the role of inference to the best explanation in the epistemology of testimony', *Studies in History and Philosophy of Science*, 41, (4), 386–96.
— (2010c), 'Kant and the Enlightenment's contribution to social epistemology', *Episteme: A Journal of Social Epistemology*, 7, (1), 79–99.
— (2011a), 'Who is an epistemic peer?', *Logos & Episteme*, 2, (4), 507–14.
— (2011b), 'Expertise, argumentation, and the end of inquiry', *Argumentation*, 25, (3), 297–312.
— (2011c), 'Steps to an ecology of knowledge: continuity and change in the genealogy of knowledge', *Episteme: A Journal of Social Epistemology*, 8, (1), 67–82.
— (2013a), 'Coverage-reliability, epistemic dependence, and the problem of rumor-based belief', *Philosophia*, 41, (3), 763–86.
— (2013b), 'Communicability and the public misuse of communication: Kant on the pathologies of testimony', in S. Bacin, A. Ferrarin, C. La Rocca and M. Ruffing (eds), *Proceedings of the 11th International Kant Congress (Pisa, Italy, 2010)*. Berlin: de Gruyter, pp. 257–68.
— (2013c), 'Rumor, gossip, and conspiracy theories: pathologies of testimony and the principle of publicity', in G. Dalziel (ed.), *Rumor and Communication in Asia in the Internet Age*. London: Routledge, pp. 20–45.
Gerken, M. (2013), 'Internalism and externalism in the epistemology of testimony', *Philosophy and Phenomenological Research*, 87, (3), 532–57.
Gerken, M., Kallestrup, J., Kappel, K. and Pritchard, D. eds (2011), *Social Cognitive Ecology and Its Role in Social Epistemology*. Special Issue, *Episteme: A Journal of Social Epistemology*, 8, (1), 1–125.

Gettier, E. (1963), 'Is justified true belief knowledge?', *Analysis*, 23, (6), 121–3.
Geuss, R. (2002), 'Genealogy as critique', *European Journal of Philosophy*, 10, (2), 209–15.
Gluckman, M. (1963), 'Gossip and scandal', *Current Anthropology*, 4, (3), 307–16.
Goldberg, S. (2005), 'Testimonial knowledge through unsafe testimony', *Analysis*, 65, (4), 302–11.
— (2006), 'Testimony as evidence', *Philosophica*, 78, 29–51.
— (2009), 'The knowledge account of assertion and the nature of testimonial knowledge', in P. Greenough and D. Pritchard (eds), *Williamson on Knowledge*. Oxford: Oxford University Press, pp. 60–72.
— (2010), *Relying on Others: An Essay in Epistemology*. Oxford: Oxford University Press.
Goldberg, S. and Henderson, D. (2006), 'Monitoring and anti-reductionism in the epistemology of testimony', *Philosophy and Phenomenological Research*, 72, (3), 600–17.
Goldman, A. (1979), 'What is justified belief?', in G. Pappas (ed.), *Justification and Knowledge*. Dordrecht: Reidel, pp. 1–23.
— (2001), 'Experts: which ones should you trust?', *Philosophy and Phenomenological Research*, 63, (1), 85–110.
Goodman, R. F. and Ben-Ze'ev, A. eds (1994), *Good Gossip*. Lawrence: University Press of Kansas.
Goodwin, J. (2010), 'Trust in experts as a principal-agent problem', in C. Reed and C. W. Tindale (eds), *Dialectics, Dialogue, and Argumentation*. London: College Publications, pp. 133–43.
Govier, T. (1993a), 'Needing each other for knowledge: reflections on trust and testimony', in E. Krabbe, R. Dalitz and P. Smit (eds), *Empirical Logic and Public Debate: Essays in Honour of Else M. Barth*. Amsterdam: Rodopi, pp. 13–26.
— (1993b), 'An epistemology of trust', *International Journal of Moral and Social Studies*, 8, (2), 155–74.
Graham, P. (1997), 'What is testimony?', *The Philosophical Quarterly*, 47, (187), 227–32.
— (2006a), 'Liberal fundamentalism and its rivals', in J. Lackey and E. Sosa (eds), *The Epistemology of Testimony*. Oxford: Oxford University Press, pp. 93–115.
— (2006b), 'Can testimony generate knowledge?', *Philosophica*, 78, 105–27.
'Grapes of Wrath.' *Black Books* (Episode 3). Written by D. Moran and G. Linehan, dir. G. Linehan and N. Wood. Channel 4, London, 13 October 2000. Television.
Green, C. (2008), 'Epistemology of testimony', in J. Fieser and B. Dowden (eds), *The Internet Encyclopedia of Philosophy*. Available online at <http://www.iep.utm.edu/ep-testi/>, accessed 1 October 2013.
Grice, H. P. (1957), 'Meaning', *The Philosophical Review*, 66, (3), 377–88.
— (1969), 'Utterer's meaning and intentions', *The Philosophical Review*, 78, (2), 147–77.
Gross, S. R. (1991), 'Expert evidence', *Wisconsin Law Review*, 1991, (6), 1113–232.
Gutting, G. (1982), *Religious Belief and Religious Skepticism*. Notre Dame: Notre Dame University Press.

— (2009), *What Philosophers Know: Case Studies in Recent Analytic Philosophy*. Cambridge: Cambridge University Press.
Haddock, A., Millar, A. and Pritchard, D. (2009), *Epistemic Value*. Oxford: Oxford University Press.
Hardwig, J. (1985), 'Epistemic dependence', *The Journal of Philosophy*, 82, (7), 335–49.
— (1991), 'The role of trust in knowledge', *The Journal of Philosophy*, 88, (12), 693–708.
Harman, G. (1986), *Change in View*. Cambridge, MA: MIT Press.
Hetherington, S. (2005), 'Gettier problems', in J. Fieser and B. Dowden (eds), *The Internet Encyclopedia of Philosophy*. Available online at <http://www.iep.utm.edu/ep-testi/>, accessed 1 October 2013.
Hinchman, E. S. (2005), 'Telling as inviting to trust', *Philosophy and Phenomenological Research*, 70, (3), 562–87.
— (2012), 'Can trust itself ground a reason to believe the trusted?', *Abstracta*, Special Issue VI, 47–83.
Holton, R. (1994), 'Deciding to trust, coming to believe', *Australasian Journal of Philosophy*, 72, (1), 63–76.
Hume, D. (2007), *A Treatise of Human Nature* (Clarendon edition, ed. David F. Norton and Mary J. Norton). Oxford: Oxford University Press.
— (2008), *An Enquiry Concerning Human Understanding* (Oxford World's Classics, ed. Peter Millican). Oxford: Oxford University Press.
Insole, C. J. (2000), 'Seeing off the local threat to irreducible knowledge by testimony', *The Philosophical Quarterly*, 50, (198), 44–56.
Intraub, H. and Richardson, M. (1989), 'Wide-angle memories of close-up scenes', *Journal of Experimental Psychology: Learning, Memory and Cognition*, 15, (2), 179–87.
James, W. (1890), *The Principles of Psychology* (2 vols). New York: Henry Holt.
John, S. (2011), 'Expert testimony and epistemological free-riding: the MMR controversy', *The Philosophical Quarterly*, 61, (244), 496–517.
Jones, K. (1999), 'Second-hand moral knowledge', *The Journal of Philosophy*, 96, (2), 55–78.
Kant, I. (1900–), *Kant's gesammelte Schriften* (Academy edition = AA). Berlin: Verlag von Georg Reimer, Walter de Gruyter.
— (1993), 'Of a newly superior tone in philosophy', in P. Fenves (ed.), *Raising the Tone of Philosophy: Late Essays by Immanuel Kant, Transformative Critique by Jacques Derrida*. Baltimore: Johns Hopkins University Press, pp. 51–81.
— (1996), *The Metaphysics of Morals* (transl. and ed. Mary J. Gregor). Cambridge: Cambridge University Press.
— (1998), *Groundwork of the Metaphysics of Morals* (ed. Mary J. Gregor). Cambridge: Cambridge University Press.
— (2006), *Anthropology from a Pragmatic Point of View* (transl. and ed. Robert Louden). Cambridge: Cambridge University Press.
Kapferer, N. (1990), *Rumors: Uses, Interpretations, and Images* (transl. Bruce Fink). New Brunswick: Transaction Publishers.
Kappel, K. (2009), 'On saying that someone knows: themes from Craig', in A. Haddock, A. Millar and D. Pritchard (eds), *Social Epistemology*. Oxford: Oxford University Press, pp. 69–88.
Kauffeld, F. J. and Fields, J. E. (2003), 'The presumption of veracity in testimony and gossip', *Proceedings of the 2003 OSSA Conference*. Windsor: University

of Windsor. Available at <http://web2.uwindsor.ca/faculty/arts/philosophy/ILat25/edited_new_kauffeld&fields.doc>, accessed 1 October 2013.

Kelly, T. (2005), 'The epistemic significance of disagreement', *Oxford Studies in Epistemology*, 1, 167–96.

— (2008), 'Evidence: fundamental concepts and the phenomenal conception', *Philosophy Compass*, 3, (5), 933–55.

Kenyon, T. (2013), 'The informational richness of testimonial contexts', *The Philosophical Quarterly*, 63, (250), 58–80.

Keren, A. (2007), 'Epistemic authority, testimony, and the transmission of knowledge', *Episteme: A Journal of Social Epistemology*, 4, (3), 368–81.

— (2012), 'On the alleged perversity of the evidential view of testimony', *Analysis*, 72, (4), 700–7.

Kornblith, H. ed. (2001), *Epistemology: Internalism and Externalism*. Oxford: Blackwell.

Kusch, M. (2002a), 'Testimony in communitarian epistemology', *Studies in History and Philosophy of Science*, 33, (2), 335–54.

— (2002b), *Knowledge by Agreement*. Oxford: Oxford University Press.

— (2009), 'Testimony and the value of knowledge', in A. Haddock, A. Millar and D. Pritchard (eds), *Epistemic Value*. Oxford: Oxford University Press, pp. 60–94.

Kutrovátz, G. and Zemplén, G. A. eds (2011), *Rethinking Arguments from Experts*. Special Issue, *Argumentation*, 25, (3), 275–413.

Kvanvig, J. (2003), *The Value of Knowledge and the Pursuit of Understanding*. Cambridge: Cambridge University Press.

Lackey, J. (1999), 'Testimonial knowledge and transmission', *The Philosophical Quarterly*, 49, (197), 471–90.

— (2006a), 'The nature of testimony', *Pacific Philosophical Quarterly*, 87, (2), 177–97.

— (2006b), 'It takes two to tango: beyond reductionism and non-reductionism in the epistemology of testimony', in J. Lackey and E. Sosa (eds), *The Epistemology of Testimony*. Oxford: Oxford University Press, pp. 160–89.

— (2008), *Learning from Words: Testimony as a Source of Knowledge*. Oxford: Oxford University Press.

— (2011), 'Testimonial knowledge', in S. Bernecker and D. Pritchard (eds), *The Routledge Companion to Epistemology*. London: Routledge, pp. 316–25.

Lackey, J. and Sosa, E. eds (2006), *The Epistemology of Testimony*. Oxford: Oxford University Press.

Laub, D. (1995), 'Truth and testimony: the process and the struggle', in C. Caruth (ed.), *Trauma: Explorations in Memory*. Baltimore: Johns Hopkins University Press, pp. 61–75.

Lee, H. (1960), *To Kill a Mockingbird*. Philadelphia: J. B. Lippincott & Co.

Lehrer, K. and Smith, J.-C. (1985), 'Reid on testimony and perception', in D. Copp and J. J. MacIntosh (eds), *New Essays in Philosophy of Mind: Series II* (Canadian Journal of Philosophy Supplementary, vol. 11). Guelph: Canadian Association for Publishing in Philosophy, pp. 21–38.

Levi, I. (1983), *The Enterprise of Knowledge: An Essay on Knowledge, Credal Probability, and Chance*. Cambridge, MA: MIT Press.

Levi, P. (1959), *If This is a Man* (transl. Stuart Woolf). New York: The Orion Press.

— (1965), *The Truce* (transl. Stuart Woolf). London: The Bodley Head.

— (1989), *The Drowned and the Saved* (transl. Raymond Rosenthal). New York: Vintage.
Lewis, J. D. and Weigert, A. (1985), 'Trust as social reality', *Social Forces*, 63, (4), 967–85.
Lipton, P. (1998), 'The epistemology of testimony', *Studies in History and Philosophy of Science*, 29, (1), 1–31.
— (2007), 'Alien abduction', *Episteme: A Journal of Social Epistemology*, 4, (3), 238–51.
Locke, J. (1975), *An Essay Concerning Human Understanding* (The Clarendon Edition of the Works of John Locke, ed. Peter H. Nidditch). Oxford: Oxford University Press.
Luhmann, N. (1995), *Social Systems* (transl. J. Bednarz, with D. Baecker). Palo Alto: Stanford University Press.
Lyons, J. (1997), 'Testimony, induction and folk psychology', *Australasian Journal of Philosophy*, 75, (2), 163–77.
Mackie, J. L. (1969), 'The possibility of innate knowledge', *Proceedings of the Aristotelian Society*, 70, 245–57.
Mäkelä, P. and Townley, C. (2013), *Trust: Analytic and Applied Perspectives*. Amsterdam: Rodopi.
Malmgren, A. S. (2006), 'Is there a priori knowledge by testimony?', *The Philosophical Review*, 115, (2), 199–241.
Maltzahn, H. v. (2006), *Das Zeugnis anderer als Quelle des Wissens: Ein Beitrag zur sozialen Erkenntnistheorie*. Berlin: Logos-Verlag.
Martin, C. ed. (2009), *The Philosophy of Deception*. Oxford: Oxford University Press.
Martin, C. B. and Deutscher, M. (1966), 'Remembering', *The Philosophical Review*, 75, (2), 161–96.
Matheson, D. (2005), 'Conflicting experts and dialectical performance: adjudication heuristics for the layperson', *Argumentation*, 19, (2), 145–58.
Matilal, B. K. and Chakrabarti, A. eds (1994), *Knowing from Words*. Dordrecht: Kluwer.
McDowell, J. (1994), 'Knowledge by hearsay', in B. K. Matilal and A. Chakrabarti (eds), *Knowing from Words: Western and Indian Philosophical Analysis of Understanding and Testimony*. Dordrecht: Kluwer, pp. 195–224.
McMyler, B. (2011), *Testimony, Trust, and Authority*. New York: Oxford University Press.
Merten, K. (2009), 'Zur Theorie des Gerüchts', *Publizistik*, 54, (1), 15–42.
Meskin, A. (2004), 'Aesthetic testimony: what can we learn from others about beauty and art?', *Philosophy and Phenomenological Research*, 69, (1), 65–91.
Michaelian, K. (2008), 'Testimony as a natural kind', *Episteme: A Journal of Social Epistemology*, 5, (2), 180–202.
— (2011), 'Generative memory', *Philosophical Psychology*, 24, (3), 323–42.
Mill, J. S. (1989), *'On Liberty' and Other Writings* (ed. Stefan Collini). Cambridge: Cambridge University Press.
Miller, B. and Record, I. (2013), 'Justified belief in a digital age: on the epistemic implications of secret internet technologies', *Episteme: A Journal of Individual and Social Epistemology*, 10, (2), 117–34.
Miller, D. E. (2006), 'Rumor: an examination of some stereotypes', *Symbolic Interaction*, 28, (4), 505–19.

Mößner, N. (2011), 'Review of Jennifer Lackey: learning from words', *Erkenntnis*, 74, (1), 131–5.
Montaigne, M. de (1958), *The Complete Essays of Montaigne* (transl. D. M. Frame). Palo Alto: Stanford University Press.
Moran, R. (2005), 'Getting told and being believed', *Philosophers' Imprint*, 5, (5), 1–29.
Mullen, P. B. (1972), 'Modern legend and rumor theory', *Journal of the Folklore Institute*, 9, (2/3), 95–109.
Nickel, P. (2012), 'Trust and testimony', *Pacific Philosophical Quarterly*, 93, (3), 301–16.
Oliver, K. (2004), 'Witnessing and testimony', *Parallax*, 10, (1), 79–88.
Olmos, P. (2008), 'Situated practices of testimony: a rhetorical approach', *Theoria: Revista de Teoría, Historia y Fundamentos de la Ciencia*, 61, (1), 57–68.
O'Neill, O. (2002), *A Question of Trust*. Cambridge: Cambridge University Press.
Origgi, G. (2004), 'Is trust an epistemological notion?', *Episteme: A Journal of Social Epistemology*, 1, (1), 61–72.
Owens, D. (2006), 'Testimony and assertion', *Philosophical Studies*, 130, (1), 105–29.
Pappas, G. (2000), 'Epistemic deference', *Acta Analytica*, 15, (24), 113–26.
Patterson, D. (2012), 'Meaning, communication, and knowledge by testimony', in R. Schantz (ed.), *Prospects for Meaning*. Berlin: de Gruyter, pp. 449–77.
Pelling, C. (2013), 'Testimony, testimonial belief, and safety', *Philosophical Studies*, 164, (1), 205–17.
Plant, B. (2007), 'On testimony, sincerity and truth', *Paragraph*, 30, (1), 30–50.
Plath, S. (2000), *The Unabridged Journals of Sylvia Plath, 1950–1962* (ed. Karen V. Kukil). New York: Anchor Books.
Pollock, F. and Maitland, F. W. (1898), *The History of English Law Before the Time of Edward I* (vol. 2). Cambridge: Cambridge University Press.
Prasad, J. (1935), 'The psychology of rumour: a study relating to the great Indian earthquake of 1934', *British Journal of Psychology*, 26, (1), 1–15.
Price, H. H. (1969), *Belief*. London: Allen & Unwin.
Prinz, J. (2006), 'Beyond appearances: the content of sensation and perception', in T. S. Gendler and J. Hawthorne (eds), *Perceptual Experience*. Oxford: Oxford University Press, pp. 434–60.
Pritchard, D. (2004), 'The epistemology of testimony', *Philosophical Issues*, 14, 326–48.
— (2008), 'Sensitivity, safety, and anti-luck epistemology', in J. Greco (ed.), *The Oxford Handbook of Scepticism*. Oxford: Oxford University Press, pp. 437–55.
Reid, T. (1872), *The Works of Thomas Reid* (vol. 1; ed. William Hamilton). Edinburgh: Maclachlan and Stewart.
— (1983), *Inquiry and Essays* (ed. Ronald E. Beanblossom and Keith Lehrer). Indianapolis: Hackett.
Reynolds, S. L. (2002), 'Testimony, knowledge, and epistemic goals', *Philosophical Studies*, 110, (2), 139–61.
Rosnow, R. L. (1988), 'Rumor as communication: a contextualist approach', *Journal of Communication*, 38, (1), 12–28.
Rosnow, R. L. (1991), 'Inside rumor: a personal journey', *American Psychologist*, 46, (5), 484–96.

Rosnow, R. L. and Fine, G. (1976), *Rumor and Gossip: The Social Psychology of Hearsay*. New York: Elsevier.

Ross, A. (1986), 'Why do we believe what we are told?', *Ratio*, 28, (1), 69–88.

Ross, J. F. (1975), 'Testimonial evidence', in K. Lehrer (ed.), *Analysis and Metaphysics: Essays in Honor of R. M. Chisholm*. Dordrecht: Reidel, pp. 35–55.

Rudolph, E. E. (1973), 'Informal human communication systems in a large organization', *Journal of Applied Communication Research*, 1, (1), 7–23.

Russell, B. (1948), *Human Knowledge: Its Scope and Limits*. London: Allen & Unwin.

Schacter, D. L. and Addis, D. R. (2007), 'The cognitive neuroscience of constructive memory: remembering the past and imagining the future', *Philosophical Transactions of the Royal Society B*, 362, (1481), 773–86.

Schiffer, S. (2001), 'Communication: philosophical aspects', in N. J. Smelser and P. B. Baltes (eds), *The International Encyclopedia of the Social Sciences*. Amsterdam: Elsevier, pp. 2311–16.

— (2003), *The Things We Mean*. Oxford: Oxford University Press.

Scholz, O. R. (2004), 'Quellen der Erkenntnis – Metapher, Begriff und Sache', in Th. Rathmann and N. Wegmann (eds), *'Quelle': Zwischen Ursprung und Konstrukt. Ein Leitbegriff in der Diskussion* (= Supplementary volume of Zeitschrift für Deutsche Philologie). Berlin: Erich Schmidt Verlag, pp. 40–65.

— (2009), 'Experts: what they are and how we recognize them – A discussion of Alvin Goldman's views', *Grazer Philosophische Studien*, 79, (1), 187–205.

Selinger, E. and Crease, R. P. eds (2006), *The Philosophy of Expertise*. New York: Columbia University Press.

Shaftesbury (1999), *Characters of Men, Manners, Opinions, Times* (ed. Lawrence E. Klein). Cambridge: Cambridge University Press.

Shibutani, T. (1966), *Improvised News: A Sociological Study of Rumour*. Indianapolis: Bob Merrill.

Shieber, J. (2009), 'Locke on testimony: a reexamination', *History of Philosophy Quarterly*, 26, (1), 21–41.

Shoemaker, S. (1963), *Self-Knowledge and Self-Identity*. Ithaca: Cornell University Press.

Shogenji, T. (2006), 'A defense of reductionism about testimonial justification of beliefs', *Noûs*, 40, (2), 331–46.

Simmel, G. (2011), *Philosophy of Money* (transl. David Frisby, with Tom Bottomore). London: Routledge.

Singh, S. (1998), *Fermat's Enigma: The Epic Quest to Solve the World's Greatest Mathematical Problem*. New York: Anchor Books.

Smith, B. L. R. (1992), *The Advisers: Scientists in the Policy Process*. Washington: The Brookings Institution.

Sosa, E. (1991), 'Testimony and coherence', in id., *Knowledge in Perspective: Selected Essays in Epistemology*. Cambridge: Cambridge University Press, pp. 215–22.

Stevenson, L. (1993), 'Why believe what people say?', *Synthese*, 94, (3), 429–51.

Taylor, G. (1994), 'Gossip as moral talk', in R. F. Goodman and Aaron Ben-Ze'ev (eds), *Good Gossip*. Lawrence: University Press of Kansas, pp. 34–46.

Thagard, P. (2005), 'Testimony, credibility, and explanatory coherence', *Erkenntnis*, 63, (3), 295–316.
Tollefsen, D. B. (2009), 'Wikipedia and the epistemology of testimony', *Episteme: A Journal of Social Epistemology*, 6, (1), 8–24.
Tolstoy, L. (2008), *Anna Karenina* (transl. Louise Maude). Oxford: Oxford University Press.
Townley, C. (2011), *In Defense of Ignorance: Its Value for Knowers and Roles in Feminist and Social Epistemologies*. Lanham: Lexington Books.
Townley, C. and Garfield, J. L. (2013), 'Public trust', in P. Mäkelä and C. Townley (eds), *Trust: Analytic and Applied Perspectives*. Amsterdam: Rodopi, pp. 95–107.
Turner, S. (2001), 'What is the problem with experts?', *Social Studies of Science*, 31, (1), 123–49.
Turri, J. (2010), 'On the relationship between propositional and doxastic justification', *Philosophy and Phenomenological Research*, 80, (2), 312–26.
Van Woudenberg, R. (2013), 'Thomas Reid between externalism and internalism', *Journal of the History of Philosophy*, 51, (1), 75–92.
Vendler, Z. (1980), 'Telling the facts', in J. R. Searle, F. Kiefer and M. Bierswisch (eds), *Speech Act Theory and Pragmatics*. Dordrecht: Reidel, pp. 273–90.
Walton, D. (1997), *Appeal to Expert Opinion: Arguments from Authority*. University Park: Pennsylvania State University Press.
— (2007), *Witness Testimony Evidence: Argumentation and the Law*. Cambridge: Cambridge University Press.
Webb, M. O. (1993), 'Why I know about as much as you: a reply to Hardwig', *The Journal of Philosophy*, 90, (5), 260–70.
Weinberg, S. B. and Eich, R. K. (1978), 'Fighting fire with fire: establishment of a rumor control center', *Communication Quarterly*, 26, (3), 26–31.
Weiner, M. (2003), 'Accepting testimony', *The Philosophical Quarterly*, 53, (211), 256–64.
Welbourne, M. (1981), 'The community of knowledge', *The Philosophical Quarterly*, 31, (125), 302–14.
— (1986), *The Community of Knowledge* (Scots Philosophical Monographs, vol. 9). Aberdeen: Aberdeen University Press.
— (1994), 'Testimony, knowledge and belief', in B. K. Matilal and A. Chakrabarti (eds), *Knowing from Words: Western and Indian Philosophical Analysis of Understanding and Testimony*. Dordrecht: Kluwer, pp. 297–313.
— (2001), *Knowledge*. London: Acumen.
Wells, G. L. and Bradfield, A. L. (1998), '"Good, you identified the suspect": feedback to eyewitnesses distorts their reports of the witnessing experience', *Journal of Applied Psychology*, 83, (3), 360–76.
Werning, M. (2009), 'The evolutionary and social preference for knowledge: how to solve Meno's problem within reliabilism', in G. Schurz and M. Werning (eds), *Reliable Knowledge and Social Epistemology* (Grazer Philosophische Studien, vol. 79). Amsterdam: Rodopi, pp. 137–56.
Williams, B. (1972), 'Knowledge and reasons', in G. H. von Wright (ed.), *Problems in the Theory of Knowledge*. The Hague: Martinus Nijhoff, pp. 1–11.
— (2002), *Truth and Truthfulness: An Essay in Genealogy*. Princeton: Princeton University Press.

Williamson, T. (1997), 'Knowledge as evidence', *Mind*, 106, (424), 717–41.
— (2000), *Knowledge and Its Limits*. Oxford: Oxford University Press.
Wittgenstein, L. (1969), *On Certainty* (transl. G. E. M. Anscombe and D. Paul; ed. G. E. M. Anscombe and G. H. von Wright). Oxford: Blackwell.
Wolff, R. P. (1970), *In Defense of Anarchism*. New York: Harper.

Index

a posteriori 227
a priori 10, 57, 73–4, 75, 119–20, 122, 140, 227
abduction 137–9, 141, 142, 174–5, 176, 227
Acceptance Principle 73–6, 100–1, 107, 130–1, 227
　Acceptance Principle, weakness of 75–6
accountability 177
accuracy 14, 17, 51, 66, 131, 141–2, 150, 183, 189, 198, 206–7, 220, 234
　accuracy as a norm 51, 198, 220, 234
　accuracy of content 150, 183, 206–7, 208
　accuracy of representation 66, 131, 189 *see also* epistemic norms; epistemic values
Accuracy 220–1 *see also* Sincerity
Adler, J. 89, 90, 102, 137
Allport, G. 196–8, 200
analytic 227 *see also* synthetic
anti-reductionism 95, 97, 99–101, 102, 107–10, 128, 227
　see also Acceptance Principle; assurance view; interpretationism; transcendental argument
anti-rumour campaigns 207
Aquinas, Th. 7
artefacts 27
artfulness 130
Asch, S. 61
assertion 16, 80–1, 91–2, 96, 100–1, 102, 107–9, 110–12, 137, 139–40, 147–8, 187, 221, 232, 233
assurance view of testimony 171–4, 227 *see also* Moran. R
attributability 28–9

Audi, R. 56, 57, 70, 148, 150–1
authenticity 17
autonomy 8, 50, 114, 118, 213
　see also epistemic autonomy
background
　knowledge *see* knowledge, background
bad faith 92
Baier, A. 164–5, 169, 174
Barnes, J. 7
basic law of rumours 197
Bayes's theorem 83, 227
　see also evidence, probabilistic models of
Bayesian epistemology 82–4
being evident 79–81
　see also Chisholm, R.
belief
　background beliefs 90, 118, 131, 133–4, 141
　belief duplication 40
　belief, evaluating 52, 85–6
　belief expression 161
　belief, false 9, 42–3, 46, 60, 80–1, 84, 85, 126, 135, 148–9, 152, 156, 165, 194, 234
　belief, grounds for 48, 87, 89, 112–13, 115, 125–6, 128, 180
　belief formation 12–13, 27, 45, 50, 52, 59–61, 64–5, 70–1, 77, 85–6, 96, 100–1, 104, 113, 125, 126, 131, 132, 134–5, 145, 151–2, 155–7, 168, 172, 230, 231–2
　belief revision 42, 82–3
　belief system 42–3, 46, 64, 82–3, 97, 107–8, 117–18, 135, 136, 137, 139, 223
　see also coherentism

belief, true 9, 22, 42, 45, 46–7, 52, 56, 60, 81, 102, 126, 149, 151–2, 165, 215, 216, 220, 221–3, 233, 234
  corpus of beliefs 42
  degrees of belief 57, 82–3
  rumour-based belief 199
  testimony-based belief 12–13, 30, 56, 77, 99, 102, 232–3
belief expansion 43–5, 46–8, 135
  inferential belief expansion 43
  routine belief expansion 43–5
Bergmann, J. 198–9, 201
Berlin 8, 39
Bernecker, S. 56
bias 185
Bihar earthquake 196
Blais, M. J. 166–7
Bok, S. 163
BonJour, L. 88
boundary extension 71
Brewer, S. 191
Buenting, J. 161
Burge, T. 72, 73–5, 100, 101, 131, 147, 153, 227, 228

Caplow, T. 207
cases/counterexamples
  case, consistent liar 151
  case, creationist teacher 149–51, 152–3, 154
  case, diary 29, 31, 35
  case, dinner bill 25–6
  case, eavesdropper 170–1
  case, eclipse 26
  case, Fermat 22–3
  case, H and twin-H 133–4
  case, King of Siam 21
  case, milk carton 156–7
  case, phone bill 21, 48, 67
  case, planted handkerchief 84, 91
  case, rain gutters 49, 140–1
  case, Taronga Park Zoo lion 29–30, 106
Cavell, S. 51, 92
censorship 206
chain of transmission. see rumour, transmission of; transmission model of testimony

Chakrabarti, A. 2, 37
children 110, 169
Chisholm, R. 79–80
Clifford, W. K. 86, 229
  see also evidentialism
Coady, C. A. J. 2, 21, 29, 32–3, 48, 61, 63, 67–8, 78, 83, 88, 106–8, 113, 120–1, 194–5, 231
Coady, D. 198, 207
Code, L. 56, 193
coherence 63–4, 82–3, 88, 134–5, 141–2 see also Bayes's theorem
coherentism 117–18, 134–5, 136, 227
cohesion 63
Collins, L. 204
commonability 40–1, 91, 158
commonsense constraint 102, 117, 145
communitarian views of knowledge 40–2, 158–60
community of knowledge 158
competence 24, 32–3, 40, 74, 94, 166, 182
complexity, reduction of 175
concept acquisition 61
conceptual analysis 45–6, 198, 216–17, 218
conditional probability 81–3
  see also Bayes's theorem; prior probability
conformity experiments 61
conspiracy theories 213
constancy assumption 226
  see also knowledge, genealogical approach
content preservation 72–4, 131
context of testimonial exchanges 30, 48, 75, 78, 90, 139, 181
contingent 16, 21, 140, 157, 208, 218, 227–8 see also necessary
contradiction 44
corpus of beliefs. see belief, corpus of
correction by others 118
coverage-reliability 42, 208–9, 228 see also epistemic coverage; truth-to-testimony conditional
Craig, E. 56, 217, 218–20

INDEX

credibility 19, 34, 77, 83, 103, 105, 109–10, 131–2, 134–5, 189, 200, 228
   assessing credibility 28, 103, 112–13, 132, 134–5, 184, 187–8
   credibility deficit 210
      see also epistemic injustice
      see also trustworthiness
credulism 101, 118, 125 see also anti-reductionism; Reid, T.
critique 216
culture 42, 116–17
curiosity 20, 41, 43, 199, 234
Cuypers, S. 118, 141

Daubert v. Merrell Dow Pharmaceuticals, Inc. 191
Davidson, D. 107–8
deception 9–10, 57, 111, 150, 152, 165, 169–70
   see also lying; speech acts, manipulative
deduction 64–5, 73, 228
   see also induction
defamation 212–13
default pathway 134–6 see also dual-pathway model
defeater 61, 228
   doxastic defeater 151–2
definition of testimony 30–6, 232
   broad view 31–2
   disjunctive view 36
   moderate view 33–5
   narrow view 32–3
Dentith, M. 207–8
dependence-responsiveness 171
Descartes, R. 9–10
desiderata (of theories of testimony) 49–50
Deutscher, M. 70
developmental phase 110, 113, 115–17, 118–19, 230–1
dialectical superiority 183, 187–9, 228
disagreement 9, 25–6, 190
disjunctive view 36
Douven, I. 118, 141
doxastic voluntarism 168, 228

dualism 128–30, 133
   weakness of dualism 129–30
      see also Lackey, J.; testimony, hybrid theories of
dual-pathway model 134–6
   see also testimony, hybrid theories of; Thagard, P.
Dummett, M. 67, 69–70, 153

Ebert, R. 23
education 140, 142
Elgin, C. 31, 134, 221
Emler, N. 204
empiricism 10–11, 56–7, 65, 70, 228
entitlement 52, 73–4, 86, 131, 170, 228, 234
episteme 57
epistemology
   epistemic agent 10, 42, 85, 98–9, 222–4, 231, 232
   epistemic asymmetry 170–1, 174, 181–2, 219
   epistemic authority 15, 33, 179, 181–2, 189–90
   epistemic autonomy 114, 115, 118
   epistemic coordination problem 224
   epistemic deference 190–1
   epistemic dependence 11–12, 13, 87–8, 179–81, 183–4, 208–9, 228 see also coverage-reliability
   epistemic environment 45, 108, 112–13, 122, 125–7, 133–4, 140, 148, 155–7, 175, 208–9, 228
   epistemic injustice 83, 193, 209–11, 212, 228
   epistemic interdependence 166–7, 222–4
   epistemic norms 203
   epistemic peer 25–6, 171, 184, 228–9
   epistemic practices 41–2, 225
   epistemic responsibility 23, 67, 68, 86, 111, 128, 191, 193–4, 224, 230
   epistemic risk 43, 155
   epistemic routines 208, 232
   epistemic suspicion 194
   epistemic values 234

epistemic virtues 25, 234
epistemology of acceptance 75
epistemology of perception 59
feminist epistemology 204
epistemophilia 193
error avoidance 43, 46–9, 135
   see also belief expansion
esoteric 26, 186–7
evidence 43, 48, 49, 51–2, 64, 67, 79–84, 85–6, 170, 180, 184–5
   'evidence of the senses' 79
   evidence, probabilistic models of 81–3 see also Bayes's theorem
   legal evidence 77–9, 87
   misleading evidence 78, 84, 91
   paucity of evidence objection 87–90
   potential evidence 33
   scientific evidence 87
   and testimony 87–8, 91–2, 170
evidentialism 85–6, 89–90, 92, 229
exoteric 186–7
expansion strategies. see belief expansion
expectation 165
experience 9–11, 19–20, 23, 24, 52, 56–60, 61–5, 79, 88–9, 102, 105, 119–22, 126, 135, 228, 234
expertise 179–81, 184, 186–7, 190, 229 see also witness, expert
   appeals to expert opinion 181, 189–91
   expert disagreement 184–5, 190 see also assessing expertise
   expert/expert problem 184
   expert status 182, 184–5, 187
   expert testimony 180–4, 185, 189–91
   expertise, assessing 181, 182, 185–9 see also dialectical superiority
externalism 84–5, 98–9, 125–7, 131–4, 138, 139, 149, 228, 229
   reliabilist externalism 126
eyewitness 14–15, 58, 76, 196

fallibilism 44, 100, 229
falsehood 150
Faulkner, P. 73, 74, 100, 130–4

Federal Rules of Evidence (U.S.) 14, 191
Fields, J. 16, 181
filtering 206
folk psychology 89, 137, 229
folkloristics 200
Foley, R. 178
foundationalism 9–10, 55–7, 60, 99–100, 102–4, 229
Fricker, E. 20, 31, 47, 48, 61, 67–8, 101, 110–16, 153
Fricker, M. 68, 193, 210–11, 228
fundamentalism 99–101 see also anti-reductionism

Garfield, J. 177
Gelfert, A. 121–2, 140–2, 199, 212–13, 233
genealogy 216–18, 220, 223–4, 229
genocide 17
Gerken, M. 99, 133–4
gestures 27
Gettier case 45–6, 216, 229, 233
Gettier, E. 45, 216
Geuss, R. 216
global error, possibility of 108
global reductionism 30, 104–7
Gluckman, M. 203
Goldberg, S. 123, 155–7, 208–9, 228
Goldman, A. 181, 183, 184–8, 190
good faith 90–1, 92
good informant 219–20, 222–4
Goodwin, J. 188
gossip 28, 194–5, 201–5, 209–10, 212–13, 229–30, 231
   celebrity gossip 34, 201, 202
   as distinct from rumour 201–2
   gossip, defence of 203–5
   gossip, definition of 229–30
   gossip, Kantian perspective on 203, 212
   gossip, negative aspects of 205, 212
   gossip, traditional view of 202–3
Govier, T. 40, 45, 164, 165, 166, 174–5
Graham, P. 34–6, 64, 147–8, 153
Green, C. 76
Grice, H. P. 172
Gricean mechanism 172

grooming analogy. see gossip, defence of
gullibility 48, 110–12, 113–14, 142

Hardwig, J. 11–12, 97, 166–7, 180, 182, 183, 185, 187
hearer testimony 33–6
hearsay 14, 28, 56, 78, 198–9, 201–2, 230 see also rumour
Henderson, D. 123
hermeneutical injustice 230
  see also epistemic injustice
hermeneutical resources 211
Hinchman, E. 165, 170–1, 177
history 140, 142
holism about social phenomena 175
Holocaust 17
Holton, R. 169
humans
  humans as finite social beings 7–8, 51, 97–8, 222, 224
  human nature 62–3, 67, 100–1, 111, 121–2
  human sociality 39–40, 51
Hume, D. 65, 70, 85–6, 119–22, 135
hypocrisy 203–5
hypothesis 81–4, 109, 185, 218, 227, 230

idiolect 109
Indian philosophy 5, 37
indicator-properties 219–20, 222
individualism
  epistemic individualism 158–9, 180, 187
  methodological individualism 175
  reductionist individualism 109
induction 62–5, 87, 102, 105–6, 120–1, 164–5, 175, 227, 230, 231
  see also deduction
inference 64–8, 77, 96, 105, 110, 112, 135, 137–8, 140–2, 188, 230
inferentialism 67–8, 113, 117–18, 136, 230 see also justification, testimonial; reductionism, local
infrastructure 164
inquiry-stopper 224
Insole, C. 101, 109, 110, 116
intelligibility 49, 73–6, 97, 100–1, 108–9, 130, 211, 233

intention 29, 32, 34–6, 137, 232
  speaker intention 111, 137, 170, 172–3
internalism 79–80, 84–5, 98–9, 112–13, 114, 125–7, 131, 148–9, 230, 234
internet 202, 225
interpretationism 107–8
invitation to trust view of testimony 169–71
  criticisms 170–1

James, W. 68
John, S. 184
Jones, K. 23
journalism 140
judgement 47, 51, 85, 113–15, 132, 185, 188, 190
jury 14–15
justification 57, 59–60, 61, 66–8, 70, 72–3, 74, 77, 79–80, 84–6, 96, 102–3, 131, 230, 233
justification, doxastic 154
justification, hybrid theories of 127–8 see also externalism; internalism; testimony, hybrid theories of
justification, propositional 154–5
justification, source of 57, 59–60, 66–8, 99–101, 104–5, 122
justification, testimonial 95–100, 102–3, 105, 136, 145, 147
  see also anti-reductionism; reductionism; testimony, hybrid theories of
justification, transmission of 72–3, 148
justification, unitary accounts of 128, 138
  see also reductionism, global; reductionism, local
justified true belief. see knowledge, tripartite definition of

Kant, I. 7, 11, 24, 51, 64, 102, 195, 203, 212–13
Kappel, K. 224
Kauffeld, F. 16, 181
Kenyon, T. 89–90

INDEX

knowledge
  background knowledge 49, 83, 88, 89–90, 91–2, 105, 110, 111, 122, 137–40, 146, 150, 171, 175–6, 188, 230–1
  knowledge as separate from belief 40–1
    see also commonability
  knowledge, community of 158–9, 227
  knowledge, concept of 215, 216, 218–20
  knowledge, definition of 80
    see also knowledge, tripartite definition of
  knowledge, evolutionary perspective on 223–4
  knowledge gaps 147–8, 153
    see also case, creationist teacher; transmission model of testimony
  knowledge, genealogical approach to the concept of 218–21, 222–4
  knowledge, general social 174
  knowledge, hierarchy of 56–7, 60
  knowledge, practical explication of 218
  knowledge, sources of 10, 13, 17, 41, 55–8, 91, 99–100, 131, 204, 205, 228
  knowledge, transmission of 72–3, 98, 239 *see also* transmission model of testimony
  knowledge, tripartite definition of 45–6
  knowledge, value of 215, 221–4
    see also knowledge, genealogical approach; Swamping Problem
'knowledge game' 167
'knowledge gaps' 148, 153
Kusch, M. 68, 159–60, 218, 219, 221
Kvanvig, J. 222

La Rochefoucauld, F. de 205
Lackey, J. 31, 35, 36, 128–9, 136, 147, 149–52, 153, 154, 157, 170–1
language 27, 61–3, 203, 217–18
  language, acquisition of 60–1
Laub, D. 17–18

laws of nature 120
layman 180, 183, 190
Levi, I. 42–5
Levi, P. 17
Lipton, P. 72, 120, 136–8, 140–1, 233
local reductionism 48, 67–8, 110–13
  local reductionism, criticisms of 113–19
Locke, J. 18–19, 21, 57
'losing face' 42
Luhmann, N. 175–6
lying 31–3, 66–7, 89, 101, 130, 151, 194, 203 *see also* deception; speech acts, manipulative
Lyons, J. 89

Macbeth 31–2
Mackie, J. L. 31, 105
Maltzahn, H. v. 117
Matheson, D. 188–9
Matilal, B. K. 2, 37
mature phase 110, 113, 115–17
  see also: developmental phase; reductionism, local
McDowell, J. 49, 68, 97, 209
McMyler, B. 173
meaning, nonnatural 172
  see also Gricean mechanism
mental states 84, 89, 125–6, 229
merit, aesthetic 24
Merten, K. 201
meta-experts 185
Michaelian, K. 71–2
Mill, J. S. 205
Miller, B. 226
miracles
  miracles, Hume's critique of 119–21
  miraculous testimony 16–17, 119–20
monitoring 43, 48, 67–8, 111, 113–15, 188
  monitoring, criticism of the idea of 113–15 *see also* silent monitoring
Montaigne, M. de 195
moon illusion 66
moral suspicion 194–5, 202, 209
Moran, R. 84, 91, 171–4, 233
Mößner, N. 129

memory 55-6, 57, 68-74, 86, 96, 121, 228, 231
   memory, constructive character of 71-2
   memory, declarative 69
   memory, explicit and implicit 69
   memory, historical 18
   memory images 69
   memory, preservative character of 70-1, 73-4
   memory, procedural 69
   memory, short-term and long-term 69
   memory, substantive 73
   memory, theories of 69-70
   and testimony 51-2, 72-3, 99
mockery 212
Müller-Lyer illusion 60
mundane asking and telling 40-2

necessary 231 *see also* contingent
Nickel, P. 171
non-reductionism
   see anti-reductionism
norms of testimony 223
novice/expert problem 182, 184-5, 188 *see also* expertise, assessing; expert/expert problem; novice/2-expert problem
novice/2-expert problem 184, 185-9 *see also* expertise, assessing; expert/expert problem; novice/expert problem
null setting 89-90

objectivization 220
Oliver, K. 18
Olmos, P. 90
ominiscient interpreter/being 107
O'Neill, O. 166, 178
optical illusions 60, 66
oral history 17
Origgi, G. 165, 167
overhearing testimony 174
   see also cases, eavesdropper
Owens, D. 161

pathologies of testimony 193-6, 212-13
   Kantian perspective 212-13
   taxonomy of 195, 212
paucity objection 88-90

perception 19, 55-6, 58-62, 64, 65-7, 131, 228, 231, 232
   perception, acquired 62
   perception, complex 62
   perception, original 62
   perception, role of testimony in 61-2
   perceptual beliefs 13, 43, 51-2, 59-60, 61, 62, 66, 79-80, 96, 99, 130, 155
   and testimony 60-3, 68, 74, 99-100, 130
performatives. *see* speech acts, performative
perjury 31, 79
persuading others 213
perversity argument 90-2
phenomenology of accepting/rejecting testimony 67-8, 92
physicalism 103-4
Plant, B. 50
Plath, S. 29, 31
positional advantage 20-1, 181-2, 219
possibility of local reduction thesis 110-11
   see also reductionism, local
Postman, L. 196-8, 200
Prasad, J. 196
prediction 26, 187
prejudice 83, 115, 210
   prejudice, identity-based 210
presumptive right (PR) thesis 101, 231
principle of assent 131-3
   see also trust theory of testimony
principle of charity 107-8, 231
principle of credulity 63, 101, 126
principle of veracity 63, 101, 126
Prinz, J. 59
prior probability 81-3 *see also* Bayes's theorem; conditional probability
Prisoner's Dilemma 167
Pritchard, D. 13, 125, 232-3
probability, probabilistic theories 81-3, 87
protoknowledge 219-20, 222-3
   protoknowledge, desiderata of 219
pseudoscience 213
psychoanalysis 17

racism 23
radio 138
rational choice theory 166-7

rational rejection 46–50, 95, 112, 115, 118, 127–8, 134, 136, 138, 140–1
 see also trusted acceptance
rationalism 9–10, 11, 62, 64–5, 231
reason 10, 11, 18–19, 24, 55, 56, 62, 64–5, 72, 74, 118, 213, 216
 see also inference
reasonableness 80
reasons for belief 85
rebuttal 29, 186, 188
recognition 17
Record, I. 226
reductionism 95, 101–4, 229, 230–1
 reduction base 103, 105, 115–17
 reductionism, global 30, 104–7
 reductionism, Humean 119–22
 reductionism, local 48, 67–8, 110–13, 113–19
 reductionism, physical 103–4
 reductionist thesis (RT) 120–1
reference class problem 29–30, 106, 121–2, 129, 231
reflection triggers 135, 141
reflective pathway 134–6
 see also dual-pathway model
Reid, T. 61–3, 66–7, 75, 100–1, 118, 120, 122, 126
reliabilism 86, 128–9, 149, 152–3, 157, 170–1, 173
 process reliabilism 60, 126, 171
reliance 164–5, 177 *see also* trust
remembering-that, remembering-how 69
representations, synchronous 223
reputation management 29
Reynolds, S. 222–3
ridicule 212
right of complaint 173–4
Ross, A. 92
Ross, J. 52, 80–1, 146, 148–9
rumour 28–9, 56, 194–5, 196–202, 205–10, 212–13, 231, 232
 rumour-based belief 199
 rumour, basic law of 197
 rumour, definition of 28–9, 196–9, 232
 rumour, reliability of 196–9, 205–8, 209

rumour, social function of 197–8
rumour, transmission of 196–8, 205–8
Russell, B. 31–2, 50, 70, 102

safety 155, 232 *see also* sensitivity; testimony, safe
scepticism 9–10, 48, 62
Schiffer, S. 137
Scholz, O. R. 56, 187
science
 science as an institution 140
 science, social organization of 139
 scientific knowledge 139, 166
scientia 57
search engines 225
second-personal accounts of testimony 171–4, 176
seeing-as, seeing-that, simple seeing 59
sense data 10–11, 65–6, 79, 84–5, 126, 232
sensemaking 17, 197–8
sensitivity 232 *see also* safety
sexism 204
sexual harassment 211
Shaftesbury, Earl of 19
Shibutani, T. 197–8, 200, 206
Shoemaker, S. 51–2
Shogenji, T. 109
signs, natural and artificial 62–3
silent monitoring 156–7, 206
Simmel, G. 163, 176
sincerity 51, 68, 88, 111, 169, 220–1, 228, 234
Sincerity 220–1 *see also* Accuracy
slander 212
small talk 194
social capital 175
social cooperation 175
social facts 8, 15
social institutions 139, 159
social network 201, 208
'social operations of the mind' 63, 225
social status 159
sociotechnical systems 164
Sosa, E. 31, 72

INDEX

sources
  notion of 'source' 57
  source monitoring 71
  source, rational 74
  sources, authoritative 28, 179
  sources, expert 97, 179
  sources, official/unofficial 28
  sources, 'on-board'/'off-board' 56
  stating one's source 41
  sui generis source of justification 100
de Sousa, R. 204–5
speaker testimony 33–6
'specious present' 68
speech acts 32, 51, 108, 159–60, 170, 172, 195, 209, 211, 212–13, 232
  see also telling, speech act of
  speech acts, manipulative 84, 91, 173, 213 *see also* deception; lying
  speech acts, performative 159–60
State of Nature 217–21, 232
Stevenson, L. 98, 102, 105, 108–10
sub-personal monitoring 112–15
  see also epistemic injustice; reductionism, local
sui generis 63, 95, 100, 104–5, 227, 229
Swamping Problem 215, 221–3
synthetic 232 *see also* analytic

Taylor, G. 202–3, 212
technocracy 180, 181, 232
technological mediation 27–8, 224–5
television 138
telling, speech act of 172
testimonial dependence 52–3
  see also epistemic dependence
testimonial exchanges 25, 39–40, 51–2, 90, 126, 134
  see also contexts of testimonial exchanges
testimonial inference to the best explanation (TIBE) 136–42, 233
  broad view of TIBE 136–8
  hybrid account of TIBE 140–2
    see also Gelfert, A.
  narrow view of TIBE 137
  problems of the unitary account 138–40

unitary account of TIBE 136–8
  see also Lipton, P; testimony, hybrid theories of
testimonial injustice 213, 232
  see also epistemic injustice
testimony
  h-testimony. *see* hearer testimony
  s-testimony. *see* speaker testimony
  testimony, aesthetic 21–2, 23–4
  testimony, anonymous 28
  testimony as bearing witness 16–18
  testimony-based belief 12–13, 30, 56, 77, 96–9, 102, 232–3
  testimony, computer-generated 27–8
  testimony, constative 159–60
  testimony, distinctiveness of 101, 130
  testimony, expert 180–4, 185, 189–91 *see also* expert disagreement; expertise
  testimony, formal 14–16, 181
  testimony, forms of 13, 14–18, 19–21, 27–8
  testimony, generativity of 148–52, 155–7, 158–60
  testimony of groups 27
  testimony, hybrid theories of 127–8
    see also dualism; dual-pathway model; testimonial inference to the best explanation; trust theory of testimony
  testimony, importance of 50–3
    see also epistemic dependence; testimonial dependence
  testimony, informal 181 *see also* rumour; testimony, formal
  testimony, institutional 13, 26–7, 186, 199, 230
  testimony, intentional/unintentional 29, 34
  testimony, kinds of 19–30
  testimony, legal 14–16, 18, 29, 32, 77–9, 87
  testimony, management of 15, 127–8, 136, 139 *see also* rational rejection; trusted acceptance

testimony, mathematical 21–4, 75, 102
testimony, miraculous 16–17, 119–20
testimony, moral 22–3, 102
testimony, mundane 20, 231
testimony, nature of 30–6, 56, 63–4, 67, 72–3, 78–9, 87–90, 100, 232 *see also* definition of testimony; evidence view of testimony
testimony, origins of 13–18
testimony, phenomenology of 67–8, 92
testimony, reliability of 14, 24, 140, 141–2, 176
testimony, religious 16–18
testimony, safe 155–7
testimony, scientific 138–9, 141–2, 166, 167, 176
testimony, supernatural 24, 102
testimony, unsafe. *see* safe testimony
Thagard, P. 134–6, 138, 141
think tanks 183
TIBE. *see* testimonial inference to the best explanation
'tit for tat' strategy 167
Tolstoy, L. 194
Townley, C. 177, 193
transcendental argument 108–10
transmission model of testimony 145–8, 153
 challenges to the strong interpretation 148–52
 defense of transmission model 153–5
 strong interpretation 146–7
 weak interpretation 146, 147–8, 153
transparency 177
trauma 17
tripartite analysis of knowledge 45–6
trust 8, 11, 18–19, 45, 47, 49, 90–1, 110, 111, 122, 163–6, 168–70, 173–4, 179, 208, 221, 233 *see also* trustworthiness
 cultivating trust 168–9, 176–7
 deciding to trust 168–71

trust, epistemic 90–1, 165, 169–71
trust in ethics 165–6
trust in science 166–7
trust, institutional 174–7
trust, public; *see* trust, institutional
trust, social function of 166, 175–6
trust theory of testimony 130–4
 problems of the trust theory 133–4
 see also Faulkner, P.; testimony, hybrid theories of
trust-based accounts of testimony. *see* assurance view of testimony; invitation to trust view of testimony
trusted acceptance 20, 46–8, 49–50, 67, 95, 107, 113, 115, 119, 127–8, 134, 136, 138, 141–2, 194 *see also* rational rejection
trustworthiness 67, 98, 100, 103, 110–13, 118, 130, 140, 157, 165–7, 168–9, 174, 177, 190, 198, 206, 221, 233–4
truth 10, 18–19, 22–4, 47, 65, 72, 84–6, 107–8, 112–13, 118, 128–9, 131, 135, 136–40, 151, 170–1, 193–4, 197, 219, 221–2
truthfulness 14, 51, 92, 166, 220
truth-to-testimony conditional 42, 209, 228, 234 *see also* coverage-reliability; epistemic coverage
Turner, S. 180

urban legend/urban myth 194, 195, 199–201, 213, 231, 234
 urban legend as rumour 199–201
utterances 27, 29, 31–2, 49, 67, 100, 107–9, 111, 113, 130, 134–5, 136–41, 159, 172–3, 232, 233

value of knowledge. *see* knowledge, value of
virtues, intellectual 189
 see also epistemology, epistemic virtues

Walton, D. 189–90
warrant 31, 72–5, 90, 111–12, 118, 120, 131–4, 153, 170, 234
  warrant, extended 73, 132–3, 153
  warrant, transmission of 132–4
    see also entitlement; justification
Weiner, M. 123
Welbourne, M. 40–1, 65, 91, 146–7, 158, 233
Werning, M. 233
wh-clauses 40

Wikipedia 28
Williams, B. 20, 22, 218–21, 223
Williamson, T. 84, 155
wishful thinking 86
witness 14–15, 16–18, 33, 77, 78–9, 83, 87, 234
  witness, expert 15, 182–4, 234
  witness, inner 17
  witnesses, independent 186
Wittgenstein, L. 52
Wolff, R. P. 23
world-picture 52